COUPLE ATTACHMENTS

COUPLE ATTACHMENTS

Theoretical and Clinical Studies

edited by

Molly Ludlam and Viveka Nyberg

KARNAC

First published in 2007 by
Karnac Books Ltd
118 Finchley Road, London NW3 5HT

British Library Cataloguing in Publication Data

A C.I.P. for this book is available from the British Library

ISBN 978 1 85575 452 2

Edited, designed and produced by The Studio Publishing Services Ltd
www.publishingservicesuk.co.uk
e-mail: studio@publishingservicesuk.co.uk

Printed in Great Britain

10 9 8 7 6 5 4 3 2 1

www.karnacbooks.com

ACKNOWLEDGEMENTS

We acknowledge the inspiration and enterprise of SCPP (The Society of Couple Psychoanalytic Psychotherapists)[1] and SIHR (The Scottish Institute of Human Relations)[2] in convening their joint conference on "Exploring Psychoanalytic Understanding of Power and Attachment in Therapy with Couples" in September 2005, and are grateful to them for inviting us to undertake the editorship of this book as an extension of the work of that event.

The book's contributors pay particular tribute to the couples who have informed their work and have taken all possible steps to protect the confidentiality of those whose relationships are described.

We are grateful to both to the Picasso Succession for permission to reproduce Picasso's "Le Couple" as our front cover illustration and to The Fondation Bemberg, Toulouse, for its permission and support in allowing us to use that drawing and the painting of "Le Couple" by Vuillard as illustrations.

We are indebted to the collaborative spirit of our fellow contributors, and also to Douglas Haldane, Christel Buss-Twachtmann, Brett Kahr and Monica Lanman for their encouragement, and to Francesca Calvocoressi and Jill Walker for their external observations

x

and suggestions. Belinda Thomson has generously shared her enthusiasm and expertise on Vuillard, and Laure Mitchell very helpfully assisted in communications with the Fondation Bemberg. We are grateful to Anna-Helga Horrox and Katarina Horrox for their consistent optimism.

We should also like to thank Christopher Ludlam and Alan Horrox for their generous support in dealing with our daily preoccupations during the editing process.

Notes

1. The Society of Couple Psychoanalytic Psychotherapists, established in 1993, promotes and provides education and training for couple psychoanalytic psychotherapists. It aims to maintain and raise standards and to promote the understanding and practice of couple psychoanalytic psychotherapy.
2. The Scottish Institute of Human Relations, founded in 1971, provides educational programmes and services. Using the growing body of knowledge about personal growth, human relationships and institutional change, derived from psychoanalytic and systemic perspectives, it aims to help those working with people in their day-to-day lives.

Jenny Berg is a consultant child, adolescent and family psychiatrist who works in a group private practice providing psychoanalytic based therapies to children and adolescents, families, and couples. Together with her colleagues from this practice, she has co-authored a number of papers on working with families and couples. She is the Chairman of Training for the New South Wales Institute of Family Psychotherapy, and has focused on developing and implementing training and supervision modules in couples and family therapy. She is also involved in teaching and supervising psychoanalytically based assessment and treatment for trainee child psychiatrists in the public sector.

Barbara Bianchini is a psychoanalytic psychotherapist who works with individuals, couples, and groups. She is an Associate Member of the SCPP, a Full Member of the Italian Association of Group Psychotherapy (APG), an Individual Member of the Confederation of Italian Organizations for Analytical Research into Groups (COIRAG), and a Founding Member of the Clinical Psychology Centre for Couples and Families ARCIPELAGO ONLUS in Milan. She is also Honorary Counsellor of Milan Appeal Court (Minors and Family Section). She lives in Milan, working in private practice and as Consultant in the Family Therapy Centre of Milan Health Authority.

Noela Byrne is a social worker and an individual, couple, and family therapist. She is in a child and family private practice with the two co-authors of their chapter. She is an active member of the New South Wales Institute of Psychoanalytic Psychotherapy, and an Executive Member of the New South Wales Institute of Family Psychotherapy. She teaches for the New South Wales Institute of Psychiatry and the New South Wales Institute of Psychoanalytic Psychotherapy, as well as supervising and consulting privately in individual and family psychotherapy.

Christopher Clulow, PhD, is a past Director of the TCCR, London, where he continues to practise as a visiting lecturer and researcher. He also chaired the Commission on Family and Interpersonal Relations, an international group of family organizations. He has published extensively on marriage, partnerships, and couple psychotherapy, his most recent edited book being *Adult Attachment and Couple Psychotherapy. The Secure Base in Practice and Research* (2001). He is a Full Member of the SCPP and Therapies Editor of the international journal *Sexual and Relationship Therapy*.

Carolyn Pape Cowan, PhD, Adjunct Professor of Psychology, Emerita at the University of California, Berkeley, co-directs research and intervention studies of couples with young children. Her writing and consultation focuses on family transitions, father involvement, and preventive interventions for couples in families. Dr Cowan co-edited *Fatherhood Today: Men's Changing Role in the Family* (1988); *The Family Context of Parenting in Children's Adaptation to Elementary School* (2005); and co-authored *When Partners Become Parents: The Big Life Change for Couples* (2000).

Philip A. Cowan, PhD, Emeritus Professor of Psychology at the University of California, Berkeley, co-directs several research and preventive intervention studies of couples who are parents of young children. His books include *Piaget: With Feeling* (Holt, 1978); co-author of *When Partners Become Parents: The Big Life Change for*

Couples (Erlbaum, 2000); and co-editor of *Family Transitions* (Erlbaum, 1993) and *The Family Context of Parenting in Children's Adapta - tion to Elementary School* (2005).

Charles Enfield is immediate past President of the NSW Institute for Family Psychotherapy. He is a child and family psychiatrist and family psychotherapist. He is also Emeritus Consultant to the Westmead Children's Hospital in Sydney.

Sylvia Enfield is a member of the NSW Institute of Family Psychotherapy. She is an individual and family psychotherapist who works in private practice in Sydney.

James Fisher was previously on the staff of TCCR; he now works in South London in his private psychoanalytic practice with individuals and couples. In addition he is active in supervising, teaching, and writing. Currently he is working on a book entitled *Bion and Beyond: A Dialogue with the Early Writings of W. R. Bion.*

David Hewison, Dcple Psych Psych, is Reader in Couple Psychoanalytic Psychotherapy and a senior clinical staff member at the TCCR and a Full Member of the SCPP. He is also a Jungian analyst and a Professional Member of the Society of Analytical Psychology. He has a particular interest in links between Jungian and psychoanalytic thinking, in developing analytically-sensitive research, and in analytic perspectives on film. He teaches and lectures on these themes in the UK and elsewhere. He has a private practice of individual analysis, couple psychotherapy, and supervision in North London, UK.

Penny Jools is a clinical psychologist working in a child and family private practice in a rewarding clinical and creative collaboration with the co-authors of their chapter. She is currently President of the New South Wales Institute of Family Psychotherapy. Penny completed a PhD in Child Development at Macquarie University in 1981, followed by a Clinical Masters on intergenerational relationships in single parent families. She taught at Macquarie University from 1975 to 1983, where she co-edited an interdisciplinary volume *The Family in the Modern World*, published in 1983. The most recent focus of her thinking, writing, and teaching has been on the application of psychoanalytic ideas to couple and family work.

Anna Kandell is an individual and couple psychotherapist. She works in private practice with individuals and couples, as well as supervising and teaching. She also works at the RFSU Clinic (The Swedish Association for Sexuality Education) in Stockholm, where she has been involved in different research projects. She trained as a psychiatric nurse at the Cassel Hospital, Richmond, London 1976–1977. She is a member of the Swedish Society of Psychoanalytic Couple Psychotherapy.

Timothy Keogh is Vice President of the NSW Institute for Family Psychotherapy. He is a clinical and forensic psychologist and family psychotherapist who works in private practice in Sydney. He is currently a candidate with the Sydney Institute for Psychoanalysis.

Maria Kourt is a member of the NSW Institute of Family Psychotherapy and the NSW Institute of Psychoanalytic Psychotherapy. She is a clinical psychologist and an individual and family psychotherapist who works in private practice in Sydney.

Jody Leader, PhD, is a clinical instructor and supervisor, Department of Psychiatry (Psychology) at Harvard Medical School (Massachusetts Mental Health Center), an associate clinical staff psychologist at the Boston Institute for Psychotherapy, and a candidate in psychoanalytic training at the Massachusetts Institute for Psychoanalysis. She also maintains a private practice in Brookline, Massachusetts. She is a graduate of Boston University (PhD, Clinical Psychology) and the Psychoanalytic Couple and Family Institute of New England's Advanced Training Program in Couples and Family Therapy.

Molly Ludlam, MA, is a psychoanalytic psychotherapist with individuals, couples, and parents in private practice and with SIHR clinical teams. An Associate Member of SCPP, her interest in couple, family, and parent–child relationships stems from experience as a secondary schoolteacher and a social worker in an NHS Child and Family Mental Health Team. She is a former chair of the Council of

SIHR. Her recent publications are "The parental couple: issues for psychotherapeutic practice", in *Sexual and Relationship Therapy* (2005), and "Psychotherapy for the parents as a couple", in D. Scharff & J. Savege Scharff (2006).

Una McCluskey, PhD, is a registered psychotherapist in the UK and a Senior Research Fellow in the department of social policy and social work at the University of York. She has published numerous articles in the field of couples, family, and group psychotherapy. She has carried out extensive research in the field of interaction between adults in the context of helping relationships and has developed a practice of attachment therapy with individuals and groups based on this research. Her recent book is titled *To Be Met as a Person: The Dynamics of Attachment in Therapeutic Encounters* (2005, Karnac, London).

Fabio Monguzzi, psychologist and psychotherapist, works in private practice with individuals and couples in Milan, Italy. His clinical experience is in various public health services, working as a psychotherapist with couples, family, and parent–child relationships. An Associate Member of SCPP, he is author of several papers. His recent book is *La coppia come paziente* (2006, Franco Angeli, Milan).

Elspeth Morley is a Senior Training Member of the British Association of Psychotherapists and a Full Member of the SCPP. Her forty years of ongoing private practice with individuals and couples includes work with her husband, Dr Robert Morley, as co-therapist. She trains couple counsellors on the TCCR's Postgraduate Diploma in psychodynamic couple counselling. Her 1994 MA thesis was on "Using the focus of couple psychotherapy in work with the individual patient" and her published papers include: "The importance of sibling relationships in psychoanalytic therapy with couple"s (SCPP, 2005) and "The influence of sibling relationships on couple choice and development" (Karnac, 2006).

Viveka Nyberg is a Full Member of the SCPP and a Senior Member of the British Association of Psychotherapists. She is a visiting clinician/lecturer at TCCR and works as a couple psychotherapist in the Adult Department, Tavistock Clinic, and as a principal psychotherapist in the City and East London Mental Health Trust. Her published papers include "Shadows of the parental couple" (in Grier, 2005).

Adrian Perkel, MPsych, DPhil, is a clinical psychologist in full time private practice working with individual adults, couples, and supervisees in Cape Town. He was previously a senior lecturer in psychology at the University of the Western Cape, past Chairperson of the Cape Town Society for Psychoanalytic Psychotherapy (CTSPP), past editor of the journal *Psycho-analytic Psychotherapy in South Africa*, and holds current membership of the CTSPP, and the Association of Couple Psychoanalytic Psychotherapists (ACPP) based in Cape Town. He has worked extensively in the area of couple theory and interventions, and has published several papers on the theory of couples.

Gullvi Sandin is a clinical psychologist, an individual and couple psychotherapist, and a psychoanalyst (IPA). She works in private practice with individuals and couples, as well as supervising and teaching. She also works at the RFSU Clinic (The Swedish Association for Sexuality Education) in Stockholm, where she has been involved in different research projects. She initiated and organized the first long-term training in psychoanalytic couple psychotherapy in Sweden, which was run by a training department at Stockholm County Council in co-operation with TCCR, London. She is a member of the Swedish Psychoanalytic Society, the Swedish Society of Psychoanalytic Couple Psychotherapy, and she is an Honorary Member of the SCPP, London.

Jill Savege Scharff is Co-Director of the International Psychotherapy Institute, Chair of the International Institute for Psychoanalytic Training, Clinical Professor of Psychiatry at Georgetown University, and Teaching Analyst at Washington Center for Psychoanalysis. Jill's books include: *The Primer of Object Relations* (2nd edition), *Object Relations Individual Therapy; Tuning the Therapeutic Instrument: Affective Learning of Psychotherapy; Projective and Introjective Identi - fication and the Use of the Therapist's Self; Self Hatred in Psychoanalysis; The Legacy of Fairbairn and Sutherland;* and *The Psychodynamic Image: John D. Sutherland* (2007). Jill's private practice of adult and child psychoanalysis and couple and family therapy is in Chevy Chase, Maryland.

David E. Scharff, MD, is Co-director, International Psychotherapy Institute, 1st Vice President, International Association for Couple and Family Psychoanalysis, Clinical Professor of Psychiatry, Uniformed Services University of the Health Sciences and Georgetown University, Teaching Analyst, Washington Psychoanalytic Institute, former president, American Association of Sex Educators, Counselors and Therapists, and member, American and International Psychoanalytic Associations. His books include *The Sexual Relation - ship*; *Object Relations Family Therapy*; *Object Relations Couple Therapy*; *Refinding the Object and Reclaiming the Self*; *From Instinct to Self: Selected Papers of Ronald Fairbairn*; *The Psychoanalytic Century: Freud's Legacy for the Future*; and *New Paradigms for Treating Relationships*.

Rika van den Berg trained as a clinical psychologist at the University of Cape Town, South Africa. She supervised UCT Masters' students in clinical psychology in in-service training programmes in disadvantaged communities. Her orientation to psychoanalytic psychotherapy has been informed by the challenges presented in these work settings. Work experience includes workshops in gender and race issues to university staff and students. Publications in applying psychoanalytic thought in community psychology include "Providing a containing space for unbearable feelings" in *Reflective Practice: Psychodynamic Ideas in the Community*. Rika is currently the Editor of the journal *Psycho-analytic Psychotherapy in South Africa*.

Christopher Vincent, BPhil, is a couple and individual psychotherapist in private practice. He trained originally as a social worker before joining the TCCR, where he worked from 1977 to 2002. In this period he was involved in a number of research projects looking at experiences of couples going through divorce and separation. He also helped instigate projects applying attachment theory measures to couple interaction. From 2002–2006, he has worked as a consultant psychotherapist in the National Health Service, offering a couple psychotherapy service to couples where one or both partners has a psychiatric illness.

Philip A. Cowan and Carolyn Pape Cowan

If leaders of Western industrialized countries were warned of an impending epidemic that could seriously affect half the population of men, women, and children in their nations, it is reasonable to assume that most would mount serious Public Health efforts to understand the problem and design interventions to treat those already affected and prevent further outbreaks. Yet, an epidemic of marital distress and instability has been spreading across modern societies for at least the past fifty years, with very few resources available to treat or prevent the resulting negative impact on family life. *Couple Attachments: Theoretical and Clinical Studies*, edited by Molly Ludlam and Viveka Nyberg, represents a distinguished contribution to the enterprise of understanding and working with troubled couples in increasingly sophisticated ways. It heralds the coming into maturity of the field of psychoanalytic couples therapy by integrating concepts from three important traditions: psychoanalytic therapy, attachment theory, and couples therapy.

Psychoanalytic therapy pays attention to object relationships from the past as they play out in the transference relationship between patient and therapist. Early relationships provide guidelines for understanding the projections that influence and often distort each partner's interpretations of the other's behaviour. Yet, psychoanalytic theory alone provides few guidelines about what to focus on and how to change the ongoing interaction between partners or between partners and therapists in the consulting room.

Attachment theory, created at the Tavistock Clinic between 1950 and 1970 by John Bowlby, and later elaborated by Mary Ainsworth, Mary Main, and others in the UK, USA, Israel, Germany, and elsewhere, brought *relationships* to centre stage in explaining both adaptive and maladaptive development. The central idea is that one primary source of anxiety that interferes with healthy functioning is the threat of separation and the loss of key intimate relationships, especially a child's relationship with a parent. In order to cope with actual or imagined relationship threats, children establish systematic behaviour patterns, and internal working models of these patterns, which shape their expectations about whether they are worthy of receiving love and can expect to be supported emotionally when they are vulnerable. These working models act as relationship templates that influence what happens when tension leads to distress and anxiety for one or both partners in intimate relationships. Although working models can endure for long periods of time, fortunately they are susceptible to modification, especially when therapists provide a safe environment in which partners can be helped to develop new insight into the source of their emotional reactions. In couples therapy, the hope is that the new understanding will ultimately lead to partners' ability to function as a secure base for each other.

What this volume shows clearly and elegantly, is how attachment theory creates "value added" by giving therapists and patients new ways to interpret the couple-defeating systems that partners develop collaboratively in attempts to alleviate the terror that a relationship they had built their hopes upon may be in imminent danger of collapse.

The work of the contributors to this volume is both exciting and daunting. It is not enough for therapists to say that they will now give attention to attachment issues in working with couples. In terms of attachment theory, "the couple" exists on a number of interrelated but distinguishable planes. First is each partner's representations of self and other—the "pictures in the mind" that are projections shaped by dynamic distortions of experienced reality.

Second is each person's representation of "the couple"—the working model that defines each partner's expectations about whether he or she is worthy of love and will receive love and support from this partner during anxious times. Third are therapists' own conscious and unconscious vulnerabilities with regard to couple relationships, based on their attachment experiences and their own models of ideal couple relationships. All of these are mental/emotional schemas residing within the individuals. The couples therapist is faced with the Herculean task of understanding how these schemas are expressed by each individual when the two partners are engaged in problem-solving, conflict resolution, care-giving, and the sexual aspect of their relationship, and how they are reflected in the transference and countertransference reactions that abound in the therapeutic encounter.

We applaud the editors' and authors' ability to bring together multiple perspectives on understanding how both internal and external perspectives on the couple relationship fit together in ways that are useful to therapists and to patients themselves. The carefully worked through examples come from the consulting room in individual, couple, group, and family treatment settings, and are enriched by examples from art, mythology, literature, and laboratory research. The authors provide perspectives about how psychoanalytic couples therapy, integrated with attachment theory and developed in the UK, applies to clinical work with couples in Italy, Sweden, South Africa, Australia, and the USA. Each chapter sheds light on understanding how strategies are formed for regulating emotion when relationships are threatened and how they can be modified or changed.

We write this preface from our perspective as couples therapists and researchers (Cowan, Cowan, & Heming, 2005) with an interest in attachment processes (Alexandrov, Cowan, & Cowan, 2005) and working in the United States where there has been an emphasis on "empirically validated treatments", most of which have focused on behavioural or cognitive–behavioural therapy for couples in distress (e.g., Baucom, Epstein, Rankin, & Burnett, 1996). Although this research literature shows some statistically significant differences in favour of behavioural and cognitive treatments for couples, it also reveals that a significant number of couples relapse in the year after treatment (Jacobson, Schmaling, & Holtzworth-Munroe, 1987).

More recent work with couples in the USA has begun to focus on the importance of each partner's inner life, with a special focus on attachment issues (Christensen et al., 2004; Gurman, 2002), and on the partners' attempts to regulate the emotions that threaten to disturb their equilibrium as a couple (Johnson, 2004). We believe that couples therapists in the international community have much to learn from the authors of this volume about how principles from psychoanalytic couples therapy, in combination with attachment principles, can enrich our understanding of the challenges for partners in intimate relationships at different points in their development as couples.

Couple Attachments: Theoretical and Clinical Studies represents a creative contribution to addressing the epidemic of family distress that follows from the inability of men and women to create long-lasting, satisfying relationships as couples. Just as couples therapists take seriously the need of partners to expand their frame in order to grow within their relationships, the authors here present material to encourage therapists to do the same.

References

Alexandrov, E. O., Cowan, P. A., & Cowan, C. P. (2005). Couple attachment and the quality of marital relationships: method and concept in the validation of the new couple attachment interview and coding system. *Attachment & Human Development, 7*(2): 123–152.

Baucom, D. H., Epstein, N., Rankin, L. A., & Burnett, C. K. (1996). Understanding and treating marital distress from a cognitive–behavioral orientation. In: K. S. Dobson & K. D. Craig (Eds.), *Advances in Cognitive-behavioral Therapy*, Vol. 2 (pp. 210–236). Thousand Oaks, CA: Sage.

Christensen, A., Atkins, D. C., Berns, S., Wheeler, J., Baucom, D. H., & Simpson, L. E. (2004). Traditional versus integrative behavioral couple therapy for significantly and chronically distressed married couples. *Journal of Consulting & Clinical Psychology, 72*(2): 176–191.

Cowan, C. P., Cowan, P. A., & Heming, G. (2005). Two variations of a preventive intervention for couples: effects on parents and children during the transition to elementary school. In: P. A. Cowan, C. P. Cowan, J. Ablow, V. K. Johnson, & J. Measelle (Eds.), *The Family Context of Parenting in Children's Adaptation to Elementary School* (pp. 277–312). Mahwah, NJ: Lawrence Erlbaum.

Gurman, A. S. (2002). Brief integrative marital therapy: a depth-behavioral approach. In: A. S. Gurman & N. S. Jacobson (Eds.), *Clinical Handbook of Couple Therapy* (3rd edn) (pp. 180–220). New York: Guilford.

Jacobson, N. S., Schmaling, K. B., & Holtzworth-Munroe, A. (1987). Component analysis of behavioral marital therapy: two-year follow-up and prediction of relapse. *Journal of Marital and Family Therapy, 13*: 187–195.

Johnson, S. (2004). *The Practice of Emotionally Focused Couple Therapy. Creating Connection* (2nd edn). New York: Brunner-Routledge.

Introduction

Molly Ludlam and Viveka Nyberg

The urge to pair is one of the most powerful of human drives. Indeed, from infancy, the longing to be part of a couple becomes, for many, associated with expectations of being an adult. In this collection of theoretical and clinical studies, the term "couple attachments" is used to encompass the many forms that adult couple relationships may take, alongside, and distinct from, other pairing relationships such as are made by friends, siblings, parents and children, and work colleagues. The attachment that cements couple relationships is a source of excitement and heartache, allure and frustration, and it has been widely explored and portrayed in artistic expression and in academic studies. This book offers the reader a selection of presentations that draw on artistic, academic, and clinical sources, from perspectives that are framed principally by psychoanalytic concepts and those of Attachment Theory.

No matter how desired they may be, couple attachments present challenges, as well as opportunities, to all who seek them. Some of the conflicts that underlie both the challenges and the opportunities are inherent in making such relationships. For example, while staying together may offer stability and security, in order to be sustained, the adult couple relationship must nevertheless be adaptive and itself incorporate development, so as to allow each of the partners to change and grow. And while coupling may offer joy and contentment, the mature couple relationship has also to find ways to accommodate frustration, disappointment, and loss.

Psychoanalytic thinking prompts us to perceive that, like all other relationships that are deeply desired, adult couple relationships exist in an inner world of phantasy, as well as being themselves responsive to the vicissitudes of external realities. The interaction between the inner, and less conscious, and the outer, and more conscious, worlds of feeling and thinking can give rise to tremendous anxiety and turbulence in the couple. There are often also disturbing echoes of the past in the present.

Psychotherapists who draw on psychoanalytic concepts and those who use the perspective of Attachment Theory share an interest in tracing patterns of relating that become established in childhood with such power that they recur repeatedly in adult attachments. While conflict may be inherent to coupling, albeit that it may presage growth, it is also recognized that the impact of unresolved couple conflict on family relationships is profound, with long-lasting and wide-reaching sequelae in present and future generations.

Couple relationships are often therefore founded on conscious and unconscious recognition of experience and understanding that is held in common, but also, importantly, couple relationships incorporate difference. It is not surprising, then, that couple psychotherapists, in their search to understand the complexities of couple relationships, should seek to learn from fellow practitioners who embrace similar, but different, perspectives. This is reflected particularly in the work and activities of members of the Society for Couple Psychoanalytic Psychotherapists (SCPP) and the Tavistock Centre for Couple Relationships (TCCR), in creating opportunities for meeting with, and learning from, colleagues both nationally and internationally. In 2005, SCPP collaborated with the Scottish Institute of Human Relations (SIHR) in hosting an international conference on couple psychotherapy, entitled "Power and Attachment". This book's chapters have evolved from presentations first made there. Accordingly, it might be said that that conference, and, following it, this book, pick up the "baton" extended by Christopher Clulow and co-contributors to *Adult Attachment and*

Couple Psychotherapy (Clulow, 2001) in promoting a dialogue between practitioners holding different theoretical perspectives on working therapeutically with couples, especially those based on Attachment and Object Relations theories.

Nevertheless, in spite of recognizing the importance of sharing thinking about our work with practitioners from across the world, there are also attendant anxieties about how easy it will be for us to find a common language. Do couple relationships take the same form and can they be considered in the same way the world over? How universally applicable are theoretical concepts and clinical approaches which have been developed for a particular age and community? What ethical considerations might arise in the practitioner's choice of theory or approach? This book raises questions of this kind and offers an opportunity to hear a number of voices and to join an international thinking community. As well as finding bridges between psychoanalytic and Attachment theories, our contributors present thinking from a range of different psychoanalytic theorists, notably Bion, Britton, Fairbairn, Freud, Kernberg, Klein, and Sutherland, and the analytical psychologist Jung, as well as thinking about where the new frontiers of theory might lie. Many authors draw on research into patterns of relating and attunement to substantiate their observations. Moreover, the reader is presented with a range of modalities of working with couples, by individual practitioners, conjoint therapists, and through the mediums of group and family therapy. All the contributors write as experienced psychotherapists with the aim of integrating theory with practice. We should add that, although the focus of this book is predominantly upon heterosexual couples, it is not the intention of contributors to ignore or exclude the concerns of same-sex couples. On the contrary, there is every reason to believe that the subject matter and themes explored in this book apply in equal measures to same-sex partnerships.

The book's sixteen chapters are grouped in four sections, addressing, respectively, internal and societal representations of the couple; developmental challenges encountered by the couple in the context of family life; the impact of power imbalances on couple relationships; and the importance of theory and research as resources for the couple psychotherapist. It is hoped that the contributing chapters can be seen, both separately and together, as offering new insights into attachment between couples, and as well-referenced teaching aids.

Part I, "The couple in the mind: shaping, perceiving, and presenting the couple identity", focuses on ways in which images, identities, and aspirations of the couple are formed and perceived by the couple, the therapist, the artist, the writer, and society at large. Molly Ludlam (UK) considers the "couple in the mind" as a psychodynamic image, and discusses its role in the shaping of "couple identity". Artists' illustrations are used to explore what frames our perceptions of couples, whether as partners or as couple psychotherapists. Using Shakespeare's play, *Macbeth*, James Fisher (UK) delineates his concept—that of the "shared proleptic imagination"—with which some couples communicate and which, in his chosen example, the Macbeths adopted with murderous consequences. Postulating that the couple psyche has a structure of its own, Adrian Perkel (South Africa) describes the impact of couple fusion and how forces of attraction contain the seeds of dissolution. This chapter also makes a bridge with the theme of Section Two in drawing a developmental sequence of a marriage, in this case of a very public couple, from their coming together, involving the mutual exchange of projections, to a distressing breakdown in confusion and de-fusion.

Part II, "The couple in the family: developmental and contextual perspectives", explores some of the developmental challenges that couples may encounter as part of family life, such as dealing with adolescent children, the childless older couple, and managing the impact of sibling relationships. Elspeth Morley (UK) and Jody Leader (USA), both explore an area that, until recently, has been much neglected in psychoanalytic thinking: the effect of family-of-origin on sibling relationships and, in particular, the way sibling relationships may impact on unconscious couple choice, as well as on couple interaction. Barbara Bianchini and Fabio Monguzzi (Italy) describe their experience of treating couples in a group therapy situation, where the couples' presenting difficulties were in parenting their adolescent children. Noela Byrne, Jenny Berg, and Penny Jools (Australia) explore the value of using an understanding of the attachment styles of the couple within an object relations framework.

Part III, "Couples in rivalry: power imbalance in couple relationships", investigates what can happen to the couple relationship when an emotional and psychic balance is altered, as, for example, by encompassing racial differences, through the impact of mental ill health, and the power relationship involved in prostitution. Rika van den Berg (South Africa) writes about her experience of working with a couple where issues of racial difference were an integral aspect of the work. The chapters by Chris Vincent (UK) and Viveka Nyberg (UK) explore how mental illness can impact on the couple relationship. Chris Vincent writes about his experience of working as a couple psychotherapist in a psychiatric unit and his observation of how "couple voids" can open up between couples where one or both partners suffer from psychiatric illness. Viveka Nyberg describes, in detail, working with a couple that shared an experience of having grown up with mothers who suffered from mental illness. Gullvi Sandin and Anna Kandell (Sweden) offer a Swedish perspective, outlining a study in which they worked as psychotherapists with men and women involved in the buying and the selling of sex.

Part IV, "The power of theory and research: the psychotherapist's aids to thinking about the couple", focuses on ways in which clinical practice can be underpinned by theory and research. David Hewison (UK) explores the myth of Oedipus, which has powerfully inspired theorizing about couple relationships. He compares it with the Indian myth of Ganesh, in thinking about how our theories are socially and culturally constructed and observed. David Scharff and Jill Savege Scharff (USA) make a case for using chaos theory as a new paradigm for understanding the dynamics of the development, maintenance, and therapy of the couple relationship, supporting their hypothesis with new findings from attachment theory, neuroscience, and trauma theory. Christopher Clulow (UK) considers how attachment theory might "add value" to couple psychotherapy. By linking the mirroring processes in child development with clinical material from a couple therapy session, he explores in detail ways in which an Attachment perspective might help build an evidence base for clinical conviction. Una McCluskey's (UK) research into affect attunement in psychotherapy and her concept of "goal-corrected emphatic attunement" are used to support the use of Extended Attachment Theory in considering the implications of different motivational systems for therapeutic work with couples. Finally, Timothy Keogh, Maria Kourt, Charles

Enfield, and Sylvia Enfield (Australia) describe how bridging work that identifies attachment styles with use of object relations theories was significant in working with a couple in a family context where there was an extensive history of childhood sexual abuse among siblings, as well as in the parental background.

Couple psychotherapy is currently undergoing a renaissance within the field of psychotherapy. Until recently, couple psychoanalytic psychotherapy in particular was considered as a hybrid profession, lacking the status of a discipline in its own right. Increasingly, however, it has come to be regarded as a distinct field of applied psychoanalysis, operating in parallel with mainstream psychoanalytic psychotherapy. As practitioners, we are all preoccupied with trying to understand the fabric of the couple relationship, the intricate web of psychic fantasies, shared unconscious anxieties, and external realities that bind a couple together. An integral part of the couple psychotherapist's work is to understand and work with the inherent tensions between a couple's needs for attachment and relatedness on the one hand and the couple's fears and anxieties about intimacy and emotional connectedness on the other. In coming together to present our thinking, our values, and our commitment to keeping couple relationships in mind, we hope to encourage debate and further exploration amongst colleagues.

Reference

Clulow, C. (Ed.) (2001). *Adult Attachment and Couple Psychotherapy*. London: Brunner-Routledge.

PART I

THE COUPLE IN THE MIND: SHAPING, PERCEIVING, AND PRESENTING THE COUPLE IDENTITY

CHAPTER ONE

Our attachment to "the couple in the mind"

Molly Ludlam

> "The way in which Vuillard's figures gradually emerge from the shadows, their presence uncertain, ambiguous amid the overlapping shapes and muffled tonalities of their surroundings may be attributable to those experimental productions at the Théâtre d'Art in which the actors were often only partially visible to the audience"
>
> (Thomson, 1988, p. 84)

Introduction

The focus of this exploration is the couple as an internal object, or "the couple in the mind", taking as its premise that human beings commonly hold a life-long bond or attachment to an internal couple. This dynamic inner object may assume a variety of forms, symbolizing both togetherness and conflict. Its presence helps to shape the individual's relationships with couples and the making of couple relationships in adult life, be they heterosexual or homosexual, married or unmarried. This chapter explores how might we envisage this internal couple through our mind's eye, and, given the requisite artistic skill, how it might be drawn. Perhaps artistic representations of couple relationships can offer insight and illumination to couple psychotherapists.

I shall attempt thereby to delineate a "psychodynamic image of the couple", drawing inspiration from Sutherland's case for envisioning a "The psychodynamic image of man" (1979). Such an image would reflect both an outer and an inner life, along with the emotional forces that move continually between them, as well as between the past and the present. I shall consider the development of a sense of couple identity and the relatedness of such an identity with an internal couple object; and further, the relatedness of the couple in the couple's mind with the concept of a couple ego, as Kernberg proposes (1995), with its own superego and ego ideal. Sutherland's concept of a psychodynamic image may help couples and couple psychotherapists to appreciate more fully the impact felt when the couple ego ideal is lost or irrevocably changed. This exploration then further considers the attachments to mental images of the couple that are carried by couple therapists, and how notions of what a loving couple should look like might distort the way in which we, as therapists, perceive couples who are seeking help.

To address these questions, I shall present different perceptions of the couple. One kind is pictorially represented in the visual arts, here in pictures by Vuillard and Picasso; another is the perception formed at a first meeting in the consulting room, which becomes the basis for an initial assessment, and, in turn, a clinical formulation. Such perceptions may be summed up as the "couple fit". I hope to show that in all of these, there is arguably an interaction or dialogue between the impressions that are objectively realized and those that are subjectively evaluated and communicated. I am seeking through this to suggest that how we see ourselves, as individuals and in our couple relationships, is mediated by how we see, and are seen, by others. I presume in this that the way in which people perceive themselves in their most intimate relationships has a powerful impact on their sense of self-image and identity.

Picturing the object

Where might we start looking for the couple in the mind? Freud (1918b) famously hypothesized a "primal scene" of the parental couple engaged in intercourse, which, whether derived from memory or phantasy, remains as a life-long inner object on which all kinds of projections may be hung. From this, Klein (1929) conjured the child's paranoid–schizoid phantasy of a combined parental object whose perpetual embrace has the power malevolently to lock out their child. It seems an important task for the couple therapist to find ways of gaining access to this internal couple. As Freud and Klein show, the internal couple may be both emotionally experienced and intellectually configured. Thoughts about it are likely also to be evoked by pictures. From all the potential depictions of couples, I have chosen two, by Picasso and Vuillard, which intrigue me. They are juxtaposed in my mind because they hang in the same gallery, the Fondation Bemberg in Toulouse.

This book's front cover picture offers us a starting point. Picasso's "The Couple, 1967" portrays a mythological pairing. It invites us to consider what a picture can convey to us and what we might read into the overtly symbolic, or, for that matter, the enigmatic. On the surface Picasso's couple appear archetypal, confident in their sexuality and creativity. Looking closer, the picture is full of ambiguity. This might be a post-coital or "after the primal scene" image. From her darkened right nipple and the abdominal *linea negra* we see that the woman is fertile; she is either pregnant, or has recently given birth, although her left breast is relatively "virginal". The man is blowing his trumpet, but his penis is both erect and flaccid. He has a man's girth, but a boy's head and shoulders. We do not know whether this couple represent Cupid and Psyche, or Goddess and faun, or Mother and Son, or, indeed, a mature woman with her young lover. We might wonder if it portrays an engagement or rather two people who are each self-absorbed. Looking again, I wonder if the boy-man might be permanently excluded from the woman's self-embrace, so caught up is she in her triumphant fecundity. The experience of seeking out and thinking again about this and other familiar pictures prompts thoughts about first impressions and how perceptions may change on re-seeing.

The second picture, which also appears differently to me on re-examination, is Vuillard's picture "The Couple". I am as intrigued by what other people see in it as by what it suggests to me about the couple's relationship. This is a relatively small picture, only

"The Couple", by Vuillard, ca. 1890. Fondation Bemberg, Toulouse.

29 × 22 cm, and its cameo nature and sombre tones seem to invite closer scrutiny. Apparently, there is some debate about its date and title. At the Fondation Bemberg, it is known as "The Couple" and dated at "about 1890". The complete Vuillard catalogue, however, entitles it "The Reprimand" and dates it at 1894. This leaves us then to wonder who is being reprimanded, the man or the woman? Are they indeed a couple, and if so, in what sense?

If this picture is familiar to you, I wonder if your present impression differs in any way from your first? My experience of showing it to others bears out my own. Some see a woman's face in profile, while others, like the complete Vuillard catalogue, see her face as buried in her hands. For several years, I saw only her covered face, and, perhaps consequently, read desolation and shame into her posture. Then an outline of her face was pointed out to me and I can no longer reconstruct my first impression. In the blink of an eye, the picture can morph from a subtle exposé of anguish to an almost comic caricature of outrage. Art historians have suggested that

Vuillard, like Picasso, intentionally incorporated ambiguity. So we might question what to make of this couple's separate and contrasting stances. I read into them a deeply divided relationship, imagining the gulf between the couple being filled with repudiated anger and unspeakable shame. I have heard others interpret it as picturing the couple's disorganized attachment.

I hypothesize that most people, when invited to search through an internal "picture library", will come across their own couple images. Perhaps these pictures are external representations of an inner couple object. They may emanate from early or recent, professional or personal, experience, or be a familiar painting or photograph that at some time powerfully captured the imagination and later accrued projections, interpretations, and a whole kaleidoscope of personal meanings. To access a more closely veiled internal couple object, such as a "primal scene" as described by Freud, is, however, challenging. Sometimes it emerges in dreams, or we may catch sight of it when considering our motivation for practising psychotherapy. What is it that drives us metaphorically to knock on the bedroom door and/or to ask the warring couple to make peace? Whether we as couple therapists are prompted by guilt, envy, shame, or the need to lick the narcissistic wound of being excluded, there is something powerful about our attachment to the introjected couple that induces a compulsion repeatedly to enact the encounter by seeking out couples in our professional lives. Whether or not this has been explored analytically, personalized images which illustrate for us that symbolized union, be it contented or conflictual, form powerful reference points in early life and for our later understanding of theoretical concepts of relationships.

"O . . . to see ourselves as others see us . . ."

Let us turn now to the relationship between how we see ourselves and how others see us. Robbie Burns' cautionary tale (1798) about a close encounter of a lady with a louse, invites us to picture the poet sitting behind a finely dressed woman in church. Albeit that in his eyes she is a lady, he watches with awful fascination as a louse crawls over her bonnet. Borrowing heavily from Adam Smith's text (1759), he concludes:

O wad some Pow'r the giftie gie us
To see oursels as ithers see us!
It wad frae monie a blunder free us
An' foolish notion:
What airs in dress an' gait wad lea'e us,
An' ev'n Devotion!

In meetings for therapy, couples invite us to see them as they see themselves, what Rosenthall (2005) calls their "shared 'couple picture'", and to compare and, perhaps, to reconcile, their impression of themselves with the one that we might form of them. If the psychotherapy goes well, we may be able to explore with them our perception of them as a couple. Our observations may be new to them or may confirm thoughts they already have, but it is possible that our impression of their relationship can help to shed fresh light on their painfully conflicting perceptions of their identities as partners and as a couple.

It is, of course, no small task for the therapist to be receptive, empathic, containing and imaginative, while at the same time retaining the ability to think in the face of a crisis, and to think separate thoughts that are challenging, even disturbing. It can feel like being destructive and creative in the same moment. It is especially challenging for the therapist who is working alone and who therefore has to hold a personal meta-position, or "third position" as Britton describes it (1989). This entails seeing oneself seeing the couple.

This requirement re-emphasizes the importance of couple psychotherapists being acquainted with their own internal couple object. We need to know how that object frames the way in which we perceive couples professionally, by interposing itself between us and the couple seeking help. How attached are we to the model offered by such an inner object? As Burns observed, we are not always what we seem, or would have others think us to be. The finest dressed folk may also have lice, or thinly disguised weaknesses, or shameful secrets. We might ask whether the couple in our minds has "airs" and is pretentious, or whether it is defensively idealized. And what narcissistic cloak might have been put around it? This leads couple psychotherapists to question how much our view of other couples is coloured by the transference born of our relationship with our own internal couple. Do we believe we know what is best for the couples we meet?

Further reflections on perception, image, and identity

We may wonder what it is we see when looking at a picture of a couple. The urge to pair is so deeply and powerfully embedded in the human psyche that we have imbued the idea of "the couple" with a mystique, making it more than the sum of its parts. In socio-logical terms, it has been invested as an institution with status and authority, safeguarded with legal protection and with societal privi-lege. Getting married is not only a rite of passage, but, in most societies, a wedding is also a very public statement. Additionally, a vast economy is attendant on this and on the need for the image that the couple and their families want to project. As evidence, we need only to look at popular gossip magazines.

Fairbairn (1941) has helped us to consider the urge to pair and attachment to pairing in the human psyche with his proposition that, from the first, human beings are object or relationship-seeking, since he saw the infant's search for relatedness as innate. We might envisage this innate reaching out as a search for a coupling, a dyad that will ensure the continued provision of nurture and relatedness; food for the body, mind, and perhaps even the soul. We might further propose that, if seeking for relatedness is innate, the desire to replicate this in a coupling is thus embedded in the mind. Kernberg (1995), alternatively, sees this as a later introjection, equat-ing the longing to become a couple with a wish to fulfil deep uncon-scious needs for a loving identification with our parents. As we grow and weaning occurs, we are challenged to come to terms with a rival couple, our parents, and from this oedipal struggle we may or may not emerge with a sense of ease about being separate from, and even excluded by, the parental couple.

All of this has a profound effect on the developing mental picture we assemble, as we grow up, of what a couple should be, or of the couple that we would like to be part of, as well as form-ing a norm of how couples are, warts and conflicts and all, and of the kind of couple we can expect to have to settle for. When I am thinking about this kind of norm or reference point for the partners in a relationship, it seems important to establish whether their predominant internal model of the couple is that of an adult couple, or whether it is a couple comprising a parent and child, and, furthermore, an indissoluble, never-to-be-parted parent–child couple. Indeed, if we follow Jung (1925) in conceptualizing marriage as a medium in which individuals seek psychological development, it becomes significant to discover whether the model that the respective partners are seeking is one that they share and whether each is ready to make the necessary personal development that attaining it might require. Attachment to an inner couple object, after all, leaves us with an unconscious propensity to form relationships that recreate significant early conflictual relationships. While a part of us hopes to resolve the conflict through recreating it, another part fears loss of the relationship that contained it.

What makes a couple a couple?

Couples who seek a therapist's help may therefore do so for a variety of motives, and perhaps one is to seek an outsider's view with which to confirm or clarify their view of themselves. Implicitly they often seem to be asking, "Are we a couple?" Perhaps two people need the confirmation of a third that they are indeed a couple, as Phillips (1996) observes, "Coupledom is a sustained resistance to the intrusion of third parties . . . Two's company, but three's a couple" (p. 94). Apart from forming a defensive alliance however, what is it that makes two people a couple? Surely coupling is not just in the eye of the beholder? When we say that two people are relating, or not relating, as a couple, it might be helpful to define what precisely we are observing.

Describing the characteristics of an individual's sense of wholeness and responsible autonomy, Sutherland (1979), instanced the importance "of feeling 'somebody' and being 'a somebody' to others" (p. 268). It is tempting to think that, as he often spoke of a universal need to be "somebody's somebody", he might have characterized a couple as two people who feel the same degree of self-confidence in each knowing that they are the other's somebody.

Morgan (2001) describes the dynamic process when two people develop "'a couple state of mind', alongside but integrated with, the awareness of being fundamentally separate and different from the other" (p. 18). Although not easily achieved, once found, this state of mind enables couples to find a crucial "third position from which to view themselves [as a couple] in the relationship" (*ibid.*, p. 23). When that third position is lacking, a couple therapist may be sought to take it up. Further, the potential of even one initial consultation can be greatly enhanced if the therapist adopts a "creative couple state of mind" (Morgan and Ruszczynski, 1998), because the couple will experience such an approach as the most containing (Morgan, 2001).

How does containment work in such an encounter? The couple's impression of themselves is received and metabolized by the therapist. Following this, the therapist's own impression is developed, ideally creatively informed by understanding and experience, and in turn offered back to the couple. We might thus imagine a creative space being nurtured between the initial impression the therapist receives of the couple and the potential growth that the therapist enables the couple to envisage in their relationship. And we could hypothesize that a creative gift of this kind, respecting as it must the partners' "wholeness and responsible autonomy", would constitute the very antithesis of any conscious, or unconscious, narcissistic desire on the part of the therapist to replicate in clients a personal image of the ideal couple.

The psychotherapist's view at assessment

Given that experience tells us that nothing bodes so well as a good beginning, how can therapists make the most of a first meeting? Assessment is necessarily crucial at this stage. Attachment theorists have thought a great deal about what might be learned from replicating the "Strange Situation Test", as devised by Ainsworth, Blehar, Waters, and Wall (1978), to assess what that might tell us about couple attachment patterns (Clulow, 2001b). Working outside a clinic setting however, other ways of enabling couples consciously and unconsciously to describe themselves and their difficulties are probably more feasible.

My usual practice is to invite couples to write to me before the first consultation, letting me know briefly how they see the difficulty they want to address and what they hope will be the outcome of our meeting. I leave it to them to decide whether to write jointly or separately. Their response gives me an opportunity to form an initial mental impression and to sketch a hypothesis, and it gives them an opportunity to define their difficulty and to frame their expectations. While I do not ask them to describe their marriage, or their sense of identity as a couple, their descriptions of themselves reveal a great deal, not just what is said, or how it is said, but also in what is not said.

I am interested in whether they write as a couple, whether collaboratively and creatively, or perhaps out of terror at the thought of separating. Do they write separately, acknowledging difference in healthy acceptance of autonomy, or because they hope to engage me in a one-to-one understanding, rather than to begin a three-way conversation? Sometimes writing the account forms a useful starting point for the therapeutic process; sometimes it expresses the divide that cannot be bridged, with statements written that cannot be shared between them. Sometimes only one party writes on an individual basis; the other, usually the more reluctant participant in the referral, expresses tacit ambivalence and reservation about commitment.

These accounts, whether joint or separate, often give important clues as to their sense of couple identity. The identity as a couple might, however, have become merely a social construct and maintained at the expense of one partner's individual identity, often, but not always, that of the wife. In such instances she has become the "Company Wife" or the "Navy Wife", or she is married to a man who is married to the job, such as the "Vicar's wife". These apparent gender stereotypes are really accommodations of power imbalance that are also apparent in same-sex relationships. The couple's couple identity survives and grows, but only if the partners' individual identities have also been allowed to grow. We can note current societal pressures on very public marriages for the less prominent spouse to defer to the marriage and so eclipse his or her own identity; some notable royal consorts or prime minister's wives, however, manage to stay just one step ahead of that.

In the assessment process, which in truth can last throughout the treatment, the therapist builds up a picture of impressions and images, based on the couple's narratives, the experience of witnessing their interaction, and on powerful countertransference feelings. The creative third comes into play if all the while the therapist can call on theoretical and experiential resources as aids to thinking. These allow reference to a spectrum of well-identified patterns of relating, such as that of couples' "shared phantasies" (Pincus, 1960), and of "unconscious complementariness", the unwittingly found defensive fit, which underpins marital relationships both positively and negatively (Dicks, 1967). Based on these observations, further models have been developed, characterized as "Babes in the wood", "Cat and Dog", and "Net and Sword", (Mattinson & Sinclair, 1969). Latterly, theorists have also identified how attachment styles, secure, preoccupied, disorganized, as first described by Bowlby in relationships between children and their care-givers, are replicated, albeit in complex forms, in adult dependent relationships (Clulow, 2001a; Fisher & Crandell, 1997).

The underlying assumption in all of this is that by focusing on the dynamics created by the couple, whether consciously or unconsciously, and whether to the benefit or handicap of their relationship, the couple psychotherapist is enabled to relate to the couple relationship as an entity, rather than to the two individuals to whom it belongs. As the patient is thus the couple relationship, therapeutic work becomes extremely difficult once it appears that the relationship itself has been irretrievably lost.

The consequences of loss

It seems as if some couples seek a social label of "Mr and Mrs" to wrap around themselves. Although in a crisis that wrapping may have become very thin and barely cover up the divergence in the lives they now lead, the prospect of losing it constitutes such a devastating social demise, that it is considered as almost unthinkable. Loss of partnership does not come alone. With it come loss of status, identity, and family. Sometimes both partners lose their home. Certainly both experience loss of love and or companionship, and probably a loss of pride and of face. Children of parents who have lived through such losses understandably often choose never to make an initial commitment or risk truly investing themselves.

In pre-consultation accounts I receive, couples say repeatedly, sometimes resentfully or as if bewildered, "We are not the couple we were. We have lost something wonderful and magical, and cannot think how it happened." My freely associated image then is often of Adam and Eve, expelled from Eden and wandering in a wilderness of confusion, shame, and mutual recrimination for the loss of grace. It seems important to manage this not knowing by reconstructing the partners' narratives of how they have come from their first meeting and wooing to be in crisis and meeting with me. I also wonder about how the couple they now see themselves to be compares with the *idea* of the couple relationship they once held and have now lost. In other words, how might the couple they now describe compare with the couple in their minds?

The romanticized picture of a couple's early relationship in its "first wedded bliss", seems to be a reflection of the idealization that happens on falling in love. So was the inner couple, now lost, like the Garden of Eden, idealized and romanticized? If it was, it seems likely that, at some point, there would be a loss, an expulsion from the garden, or, at the very least, a letting go and a moving on from the heady state of being in love. Being besotted or blinded by love might be likened, mentally, to a closed system. As a self-limiting condition, it must either atrophy or evolve as it is exposed to reality.

Dicks however, quoting Fairbairn's (1943) thinking, recognizes the challenge posed: "Reality-testing that follows the honeymoon may activate the return of the repressed" (Dicks, 1967, p. 71), because it breaches idealizations to allow the re-emergence of ghosts of past relationships from partners' respective inner worlds to haunt their present couple relationship. Building on the concept which sees idealization as a defence against hate, Dicks vividly describes the strategy of "collusive marriage", in which idealiza-tion, as a shared defence, serves to create a joint "false self" for the couple, so that, unconsciously, they can place a veneer over a very precarious inner world.

Once outside the Garden of Eden's walls, therefore, there are at least two onward paths. On one, the loss of idealization may presage growth. On the other, the couple may be waylaid by the unwelcome return of the repressed. A further defence then employed against the profound loss at finding themselves so trans-posed is to convert the loss into rage to be projected on to one another. It then appears to each of them as if it is the *other* who has stolen the dream and denied them happiness.

A process of mourning, together and separately, is necessary. But, if that is too painful, anger and resentment often block shared grieving and the opportunity to take the crucial "third position" is lost. The couple's sense of being a creative couple may have been damaged already, perhaps through infertility or through the death or handicap of a child. Perhaps they have lost a necessary balance in mutual dependency, because of one partner's chronic illness.

An object relations view

A long family tree of object relations thinkers guides our exploration into the inner world of the couple. Kernberg dedicated *Love Relations* (1995) to Sutherland, because Sutherland had first introduced him to the work of Dicks and *his* application of Fairbairn's object relations' ideas to marital conflict. Kernberg's interest was aroused by his interest in relationships of his borderline patients with their respective partners. Albeit that his perspective is shaped primarily by individual psychotherapy, Kernberg describes the couple relationship as a dynamic entity in its own right, what we might call a couple ego, which "activates both partners' conscious and unconscious superego functions, resulting in the couple's acquiring, over time a superego system of its own in addition to its constituent ones" (1995, p. 97). He argues that the maturity of the superego of each partner will determine the impact of their shared superego system on the couple relationship. The primitive—and therefore inordinately powerful—superego functions of one partner may take over the relationship, imposing, as in the case of sado-masochistic relationships, "a symbolic reign of terror" on both. He develops the idea that, paradoxically, while a mature superego takes care of the self and the partner and nurtures committed love, nevertheless ever-present residual oedipal conflicts may inhibit expression of sexual desire and tenderness for the same object. Thus, the superego can work to promote life-long sexual fulfilment, "or that very agency may destroy it".

Kernberg envisages the ego ideal as a substructure of the superego. Thus, on falling in love, idealization of the beloved mirrors projected aspects of the lover's ego ideal. And, because that projection happens along with attachment to this projected ideal, the beloved seems to embody or bring to life in the external world something ideal for which internally there has been a deep longing.

Love Relations nevertheless seems to offer hope, because mature, healthy patterns of relating are set alongside primitive, pathological ones. The mature superego in each partner frees them to care for one another and the mature couple superego acts to express concern and protection for the relationship, so that aggression is not acted on. Additionally, there is potential for parts of both partners' ego ideals to collaborate in creating a "joint structure of values". Provided that the mature superego of one or both partners is able to withstand attacks of the other or attacks from the environment, this is developmentally helpful.

There may indeed be times of stress for anyone, or any couple, irrespective of the maturity and resilience of their superego, when they are vulnerable, and in need of support to regain their balance. It is, perhaps, the recognition of the very normality of this, together with the recognition of a capacity for maturity in the couple, that is offered by the therapist who has a "*creative* couple state of mind".

If we can conceptualize the creation of a couple ego ideal, whether that works negatively as a defence, or positively to inspire the couple, it may help to understand more about the possible consequences of its loss. To do this, however, it is important to hold in mind the feelings of contempt and shame. These two very disturbing, hard-to-hold-on-to feelings, which are so corrosive of relationships, seem to be significantly linked together and linked with loss.

Gottman (Gottman and Silver, 1999) has developed an interesting process to identify the constructive and destructive elements in relationships. His close analysis of interactions between couples involves leaving couples alone to discuss an aspect of their relationship. Viewing their exchange "forensically", he hopes to isolate a "distinctive pattern" or "the marital DNA" that comes to the surface in any meaningful couple interaction. At the very least, this process challenges us to think about assessment and the key issues that we should identify and can successfully address with a couple.

Gottman and Silver identify "Four Horsemen", which decide the apocalyptic fate of an intimate relationship, are criticism, defensiveness, stonewalling, and, most destructive of all, contempt. They predict that if a couple's exchanges reveal contempt, even unwittingly, and this is not attended to, ultimately their relationship will break down.

What is it that fuels contempt to make it such a lethal weapon? We might conjecture that it stems from a loss of respect, but wonder how it can arise, especially between couples who once professed love. Contempt serves to punish and belittle. In the desire to humiliate, is shame being projected? Mollon (2002) suggests that contempt and devaluation of the other may be a defence against shame, envy, and jealousy. Rycroft's psychoanalytic dictionary notes that Freud (1896) saw shame as stemming from a fear of ridicule; that Piers (1953) sees it as the reaction to failure to live up to one's ego ideal; whereas Lynd (1958) closely connects it with identity and insight. Shame is

> provoked by experiences which call into question our preconceptions about ourselves and compel us to see ourselves through the eyes of others and to recognise the discrepancy between their perception of us and our own over simplified and egotistical perception of ourselves. [cited in Rycroft, 1968, p. 153]

The painful losses associated with the loss of love may thus be compounded by shame. This helps to explain why the loss of the ego ideal, when there is no psychological container to metabolize and work through the loss, is so devastating. Shame itself provides a profound deterrent to further exploration of pain, and therefore to seeking help. Of those couples who choose separation or divorce, we know that a relatively small proportion seek therapeutic help and at a point when it might be useful to them.

Returning to both Vuillard's and Picasso's images of the couple, we might now see greater significance in the reprimand, or in the woman's apparent indifference to her would-be partner's desire and attempts to serenade. I wonder if others also see depictions of shame, or at the very least, some humiliation aroused by rejection or uncertainty of standing in the other's eyes? Our projections on to pictures can, of course, be considered either as distortions of the artist's original message, or as part of a creative "dialogue" that the artist has inspired through his use of ambiguity.

The painter's perspective

It may be useful at this point also to consider the perspective of the painter and to wonder what it was that might have inspired him. I have idiosyncratically chosen two very different artists whose work is exhibited in the same gallery.

Picasso's pen and ink couple was executed in 1967 at the age of eighty-five, almost at the end of his life (1881–1973). In this latter period he re-explored a number of themes significant in his earlier career, including erotic encounters and mythological settings. In his personal life, this phenomenal lover of women had, in 1961, married his second wife, then aged thirty-five, almost at the same time as his eldest son had also married again. The Picasso household was full of children and grandchildren. Perhaps "The Couple, 1967" expresses Picasso's sense of frequent rejuvenation in his conquest of women; there is certainly vigour in the quest. The mythological references may also serve to denote this as a symbolic couple, who safely dwell in a dream world that is perpetually pregnant with hopeful longings.

By contrast, the younger Vuillard comes from another era, albeit also from premature middle age. His "The Couple" is an early work. Born and brought up in a Parisian family of modest means, his father an army officer and his mother, intriguingly, a corset maker, Vuillard is best known for his paintings of domestic interiors, which, as Thomson (1991) notes, "conventionally symbolised the enclosed domain of women", and reflected the frugal circumstances of the petite bourgeoisie. He shared his life (1868–1940) with his extended family, his grandmother, widowed mother, elder sister and brother, and eventually with his mother alone until her death in 1928. Although he had several close women friends, he never married.

His friend, the painter Ker-Xavier Roussel, encouraged him to become an artist rather than follow his father into the army. In 1889 he joined a small dissident group of art students, known as the Nabis, one of whose principles states:

The artist should forget the object he was seeking to represent and concentrate instead on the idea and emotion of that object and the means by which to set down its equivalent. [Thomson, 1991, p. 10]

Vuillard exemplified this in his journal in 1890:

A woman's head has just produced in me a certain emotion. I must make use of that emotion alone and I must not try to remember the nose or the ear—they were of no importance. [*ibid.*]

It is fascinating to reflect that Vuillard was developing as a painter as Freud was developing theories of psychoanalysis. Moreover, it is interesting to compare the painter with the psychotherapist. They both observe and describe what they see; both seek a particular relationship with those they observe. Painters are often also deeply affected by the emotions they sense, as Thomson notes:

As a realist imbued with the aspirations of Symbolism . . . Vuillard . . . had a rare ability to evoke the atmosphere of an interior, to get beyond the superficial and penetrate the mysterious core of reality. In portraits his great gift was to catch the mood of his models during their most private unguarded moments. [Thomson, 1988, p. 7]

Another Vuillard painting of a couple depicts sadness that almost takes my breath away. Painted in December 1896, "Married Life" shows how deeply affected Vuillard could be by his subjects. The scene is a living room dimly lit in the gathering gloom of a winter evening. In the foreground a woman sits stiffly, staring vacantly at a table on which stand drained teacups. Leaning by the window at the far back of the room her husband, hands in pockets, looks on helplessly. Between them a child's high-chair stands empty and unused. The bright colours in the painting have a superficial quality. The story behind this picture is that Vuillard had introduced his best friend, Ker-Xavier Roussel, to his sister Marie. They married, but were unhappy together. Marie had a miscarriage. Roussel openly had an affair. After reconciliation, they decided to have another child, who, to everyone's delight, was born in August 1896. Tragically, in November he died. Vuillard's picture of desolate grief was painted a month later. The emptiness and helplessness it shows will be familiar to many couple therapists.

Conclusion

How do we hold on to the potential for a creative couple state of mind, in the presence of such desolation, shame, and often cruelty? We know the importance of empathy, and, like the painter, that we must not become overwhelmed. A grounding in theory offers ways of symbolizing and of conceptualizing, and this helps us to hold on to the authority of our experience. We can also draw on the growing body of research. Kernberg (1995) asserts "there are no 'objective' rules about what values should determine a couple's relationship, particularly their way of dealing with conflicts" (p. 96). This, however, runs counter to a current popular desire, expressed in a somewhat manic craving for manuals and experts to prescribe on the management of relationships.

In the presence, too, of our own powerful defences embodied in an internal couple ideal, how free is the psychotherapist to let it go and to allow the couple to create their own image and *modus vivendi*? It is not easy to follow Bion's maxim to be free of all desire. We might question whether we really suspend all judgement, as if we deny our own transference, and that therapists might also have a view about what a couple should be; about what is normal and acceptable and what makes a relationship work; whether we, and this couple, have "what it takes". As our superego and internal couple ideal are involved in these judgements, we crucially need self-examination and self-awareness the better to see ourselves as others see us. I am reminded that a vital part of the process of working through, for both the therapist and the couple, is that of seeing and re-seeing the image.

References

Ainsworth, M. D. S., Blehar, M. C., Waters, E., & Wall, S. (1978). *Patterns of Attachment: A Psychological Study of the Strange Situation*. Hillsdale, NJ: Lawrence Erlbaum.

Britton, R. (1989). The missing link: parental sexuality in the Oedipus complex. In: J. Steiner (Ed.), *The Oedipus Complex Today: Clinical Implications* (pp. 83–101). London: Karnac.

Clulow, C. (Ed.) (2001a). *Adult Attachment and Couple Psychotherapy*. London: Brunner-Routledge.

Clulow, C. (2001b). Attachment theory and the therapeutic frame. In: C. Clulow (Ed.), *Adult Attachment and Couple Psychotherapy*. London: Brunner-Routledge.

Dicks, H. V. (1967). *Marital Tensions, Clinical Studies towards a Psycho - logical Theory of Interaction*. London: Karnac, 1993.

Fairbairn, W. R. D. (1941). A revised psychopathology of the psychoses and psychoneuroses. In: *Psychoanalytic Studies of the Personality*. London: Routledge and Kegan Paul, 1952.

Fisher, J. V., & Crandall, L. (1997). Complex attachment: patterns of relating in the couple. *Sexual and Marital Therapy*, 2(3): 211–223.

Freud, S. (1918b). From the history of an infantile neurosis. *S.E.*, 17: 7–122. London: Hogarth.

Gottman, J. M., & Silver, N. (1999). *The Seven Principles for Making Marriage Work*. New York: Three Rivers Press.

Jung, C. G.(1925). *Marriage as a Psychological Relationship in the Deve - lopment of Personality, C.W., 17*. London: Routledge and Kegan Paul.

Kernberg, O. F. (1995). *Love Relations*. New Haven and London: Yale University Press.

Klein, M. (1929). Infantile anxiety-situations reflected in a work of art and in the creative impulse. *International Journal of Psychoanalysis, 10*: 436–443.

Mattinson, J., & Sinclair, I. (1979). *Mate and Stalemate: Working with Marital Problems in a Social Services Department*. Oxford: Blackwell.

Mollon, P. (2002). *Shame and Jealousy*. London: Karnac.

Morgan, M., & Ruszczynski, S. (1998). The creative couple. Unpublished paper presented at the Tavistock Marital Studies Institute 50th Anniversary Conference.

Morgan, M. (2001). First contacts: the therapist's "couple state of mind" as a factor in the containment of couples seen for consultations. In: F. Grier (Ed.), *Brief Encounters with Couples: Some Analytical Perspec - tives* (pp. 17–32). London: Karnac.

Phillips, A. (1996). *Monogamy*. Faber and Faber.

Pincus, L. (1960). *Marriage: Studies in Conflict and Emotional Growth*. London: The Institute of Marital Studies.

Rosenthall, J. (2005). Oedipus gets married: an invetigation of a couple's shared oedipal drama. In: F. Grier (Ed.), *Oedipus and the Couple* (pp. 181–200). London: Karnac.

Rycroft, C. (1968). *A Critical Dictionary of Psychoanalysis*. London: Nelson.

Smith, A. (1759). *The Theory of Moral Sentiments*. Cambridge University Press, 2002.

Sutherland, J. (1979). The psychodynamic image of man. In: J. Scharff (Ed.), *The Autonomous Self* (pp. 268–282). Northvale, NJ: Aronson, 1994.

Thomson, B. (1988). *"Vuillard"*. Oxford: Phaidon.

Thomson, B. (1991). *Edouard Vuillard: Intimiste de la Belle Epoque*. Catalogue for National Vuillard Exhibition. London: The South Bank Centre.

CHAPTER TWO

The marriage of the Macbeths*

James V. Fisher

Introduction

I n this chapter I develop a reading of the marriage of the
Macbeths, in parallel with my clinical experience in couple
psychoanalytic psychotherapy, of a particular dynamic in
couple relationships, that of the "shared proleptic imagination". I
shall seek to elucidate this concept here first by using Bion's distinction between a "Work Group" and a "Basic Assumption" state of
mind, and then by illustrating this dynamic in the relationship of
the Macbeths and in a clinical vignette. The primary aim is to
explore these couple dynamics with the help of Shakespeare's char-
acters, although it may also be interesting to see how this view of a
couple's relationship affects the reader's view of the play as a
whole. My reading of Shakespeare's *Macbeth* parallels a unique and
insightful interpretation of the play by the RSC now available on
DVD (Doran, 2001), the viewing of which, in conjunction with the

* A longer version of this paper was published in 2006 in the *Journal of the
British Association of Psychotherapists*, 44(1): 19–35.

chapter, would aid the reader in seeing the play in terms of the couple relationship.

Shakespeare's pictures of the dynamics of human experience are almost always intriguing, including, of course, the ways he imagines marriage and couple relationships, that of the Macbeths most particularly. Among the many interpretations of their marriage, Harold Bloom's (1999) must stand as one of the more unusual. He writes:

> The sublimity of Macbeth and Lady Macbeth is overwhelming: they are persuasive and valuable personalities, profoundly in love with each other. Indeed with surpassing irony Shakespeare presents them as the happiest married couple in all his work. [Bloom, 1999, p. 518]

It is true that the troubles these two people encounter seem, at first glance, to have to do with what is external to their marriage and not within it. However, even if we see the description "happy" as ironic, I find Bloom's characterization idiosyncratic at best. If we shift our focus from "happiness" to intimacy, what comes to my mind are the astute observations by Stephen Greenblatt in his marvellous *Will in the World*. In it, he discusses what we know of Shakespeare's own marriage, interspersed with detailed examinations of the poet's various attempts to portray intimate relationships (Greenblatt, 2004, pp. 118–149).

What kind of intimacy does Shakespeare think husbands and wives can expect? Taking all of his plays together, Greenblatt concludes that Shakespeare's answer is: very little (!) and that Shakespeare found it "difficult to portray or even imagine fully achieved marital intimacy" (*ibid.*, p. 128), except in the marriages of two of his least appealing couples.

There are two significant exceptions to Shakespeare's unwillingness or inability to imagine a married couple in a relationship of sustained intimacy, but they are unnervingly strange: Gertrude and Claudius in *Hamlet* and the Macbeths. These marriages are powerful in their distinct ways, but they are also upsetting, even terrifying, in their glimpses of genuine intimacy (*ibid.*, p. 137).

Greenblatt focuses the matter for us nicely when he observes that it is startling "the extent to which they inhabit each other's minds" (*ibid.*, p. 139). Freud, in reflecting on the Macbeths, suggests

that, psychologically, the husband and wife represent two comple-
mentary aspects of the same person (Freud, 1916d, pp. 323–324).

I should like to explore this dimension of the relationship of the
Macbeths, this idea of an intimacy that Greenblatt characterizes as
two people "inhabiting each other's minds", in terms of the notion
of the proleptic imagination, a concept I explored previously in relation to the Macbeths (Fisher, 2000a). The term "proleptic" I take
from the now out-of-fashion study of rhetoric. There it indicates
taking something in the future as already having happened. It is
appropriate in that sense in reference to the Macbeths, as I shall
show. I also want to use it in a broader sense to include taking
anything imagined, pictured, perceived, assumed, or believed as
true. No reality testing is required or tolerated.

In that earlier paper I looked at proleptic imagination in each of
the Macbeths individually, but I did not see it as a genuinely couple
phenomenon, no doubt because I had not yet become aware of it in
my consulting room (Fisher, 2000a). I propose now to illustrate this
couple phenomenon as it appears in the Macbeths' marriage and in
my consulting room, as a possible way of thinking about some
pernicious, but all-too-common, couple dynamics that can affect
not only marital couples, but also the analytic couple. My focus
here is on the marital couple, although the implications for the
analytic couple can be seen in the dynamics between the analyst
and the marital couple.

Work Group and Basic Assumption Group states of mind

Because the notion of the proleptic imagination, let alone that of a
shared proleptic imagination, is not in general use, and doubtless
because currently I am working on Bion, I shall appropriate two
well-known terms from Bion's early work as a way of introducing
these ideas. These are the Work Group mentality and the Basic
Assumption mentality (Bion, 1952).

Before I explain my use of those terms, I should mention the
concept that comes to mind when Greenblatt speaks of "two people
inhabiting each other's minds": that of projective identification.

The dynamics of projective identification are doubtless at work
in *Macbeth*. But to use that concept here, we need to keep in mind

the distinction between a projective identification that aims at evacuation of something into the other, and a different, but related process that, in effect, says, "You're one too", or "You and I are both . . . (whatever it is)". The shared proleptic imagination, a kind of shared unconscious phantasy which I have in mind, is not an evacuation of something into the other, but an unconscious certainty, sometimes conscious, that both share exactly the same emotional state of mind.

My attraction to using Bion's early group terms for two different kinds of unconsciously shared states of mind is perhaps apparent. I realize there is risk of implying that I view the couple as a group, but I have to assume the understanding that there is a fundamental difference between the intimacy of the two and that of three or more. I will use these two terms simply to have a way to introduce two very different shared emotional states of mind, as well as two very different modes of sharing emotional experience.

By a Work Group state of mind I mean to designate a shared emotional orientation to any shared interest; for example, watching a play, raising children, trying to have a serious conversation, or a frivolous one, going for a walk, making love, or whatever. The main point, as Bion emphasizes, is that it is a "realistic" state of mind, or one that is open to reality testing. I should emphasize that, by reality-testing, I have in mind judgements about both what we call "internal" reality, the reality of one's own emotional experience, as well as what we experience as external reality. Action that is based on such judgements has, in principle, been open to review, and similarly the sharing in a "Work Group" or "realistic" state of mind must always be subject to review, a choice, to some degree, whether to continue or to withdraw.

In contrast, there is what Bion calls a Basic Assumption state of mind, in which a particular cluster of emotions dominates and there is *no possibility of not sharing* in that state of mind. The mode of linking here Bion calls "valency", the capacity of individuals, unconsciously and instantaneously, to hold "each other in involuntary and inevitable emotional combination" (Bion, 1952, pp. 242, 246). Again projective identification may be a sub-category of this form of connection, but we need to keep in mind a broader sense of being drawn into a shared unconscious state of mind. My own preference is to designate this as a *shared proleptic imagination*.

It is important to note that a "Work Group" or "realistic" state of mind is not without emotion. To the contrary, this state of mind not only allows for an experience of the whole range of emotions, it is necessary to that emotional experience. It is centred on the emotion of curiosity, or what Bion later calls "K", the urge to know. This is explored further in "The emotional experience of K" (Fisher, 2006). Therefore, the primary distinction between the "Work Group" or "realistic" state of mind and that of the "Basic Assumption" is not the distinction between reason and emotion. It is the difference between being able to think *while* feeling, sometimes intense, emotion, and being swept along by emotion unthinkingly. The first uses the process of reality-testing in reference to internal and external reality, thinking one's emotional experience and making judgements on that basis of "thinking, seeing, feelingly" (Fisher, 2000b). The second is the experience of overwhelming, instantaneously shared emotions about which thinking is impossible, competing feelings are intolerable, and the urge to act on those un-thought emotions is virtually irresistible. For the couple it is a shared state of mind that resembles that of the mob.

The suicidal patient and her husband

I want now to flesh out these ideas by seeing how they help us to understand the marriage of the Macbeths as portrayed by Shakespeare.Let us begin by approaching the couple in the way we often encounter couple dynamics, especially in public mental health services, by observing first the "identified patient", Lady Macbeth, or, more precisely, to sit in on an observation of her (*Macbeth*, 5.1.1–5.1.76, 1951). Subsequently we will have an opportunity to observe the patient's husband and his mental state, as well as, interestingly, his discussion with the doctor about the condition of his wife.

As you read, watch, or recall this scene, I invite you to attend to this observation in a clinical state of mind, forgetting what you know about their background from the rest of the play, that is, in Bion's terms, to approach it without memory or desire. On the basis of these observations, what hypotheses might we form about (1) their current state of mind and (2) in what way their relationship is involved, either as a consequence or as a contributory factor? This "consultation" has been prompted by the gentlewoman, the "nurse", who is caring for the Queen, Lady Macbeth, calling in the doctor because of her patient's sleepwalking, although we are soon aware there is more to it than that.

In this disturbing scene I want to focus on two features; the presence and function of hallucinations and the couple dimension of what we have witnessed.

We are quickly aware that there is indeed more involved than just Lady Macbeth's sleepwalking that led the nurse to summon the doctor. Sleepwalking is, in a way, a form of hallucination in that the person is both in a dream-state and is taking intentional action in the physical world. I shall return to hallucination since it is critical to an understanding of the couple dynamics I am trying to describe. But the first question concerns the content and the significance of what Lady Macbeth is hallucinating. We note that it leads the doctor to be concerned about the possibility of her committing suicide. He orders her to be watched and any means of her harming herself to be removed. He also forms an opinion as to what might have led to her "suicidal" state of mind, although he lets slip that he has been influenced by rumours, "foul whisp'rings". It all makes him think he ought to refer his patient to a "higher authority":

> Foul whisp'rings are abroad. Unnatural deeds
> Do breed unnatural troubles: Infected minds
> To their deaf pillows will discharge their secrets.
> More needs she the divine than the physician. (5.1: 68–70)

The more interesting question for me has to do with the evidence on which one might base a judgement about whether this is indeed a suicidal state of mind and, if it is, what has led to it? The doctor, it seems to me, bases his judgement on Lady Macbeth's hallucinations, primarily her repeated "washing her hands" and what she says as she does so:

> Yet here's a spot. (5.1: 30)
> . . .
> What, will these hands ne'er be clean? (5.1: 41
> . . .
> Here's the smell of the blood still: all the
> perfumes of Arabia will not sweeten this little hand.
> Oh! oh! oh! (5.1.47–49)

. . .

> Yet who would have thought the old
> Man to have had so much blood in him? (5.1.37–38)

If this were a nightmare, we would see its images as a picture of an emotional experience of guilty fear or remorse, a dream-picture of an anxious desperation to expunge that emotional experience in the face of her inability to integrate it satisfactorily into her life. And in this hallucination, as in a dream, a nightmare, her actions are futile.

Why doesn't she inquire further, or seek a second opinion, about this strange phenomenon of the stain and smell of blood she cannot get rid of? Because she is asleep, and in dreams, even if we do inquire, being a dream-state, it would be as difficult to get a responsible answer as to get rid of the bloodstain. But she acts as if she were awake and conscious. What if she were fully awake and conscious and still did not, indeed refused, to question the experience? Because she knows, she is certain what she sees and what she smells. That is what we call hallucination. We can define it as a proleptic dream state of mind, a dream state experienced as reality and marked by unquestioning certainty.

My second observation concerns the couple aspect of what we have observed. I have previously written about "couple dreams" (Fisher, 1999). But these so-called "couple dreams" happen while our couples are awake and conscious. I hope through this chapter to show how important hallucinations are for understanding some of the most difficult dynamics in the intimate couple relationship, and most particularly *shared couple hallucinations* or a shared proleptic imagination. As a phenomenon in couples they are a most insidious form of shared unconscious phantasy, a shared unconscious phantasy that is acted on as if it were a fact.

In the scene we have observed we could ask whose hands Lady Macbeth is talking about. Clearly, when she asks, "will these hands ne'er be clean?", she seems to be looking at and thinking about her own hands. But notice she also says:

> Wash your hands, put on your night-gown;
> look not so pale. I tell you yet again, Banquo's
> buried: he cannot come out on's grave. (5.1: 58–60)

It is evident that most of Lady Macbeth's comments sound like a part of a conversation, an urgent, desperate dialogue; but with

whom? In her repeated sleepwalking dream, or hallucinated dialogue, she seems to be struggling to integrate something that drives
her to the edge of madness. To whom is she saying, "Wash your
hands", and why does she mention Banquo and reassure her inter-
locutor that he is buried and cannot come out of his grave? What is
it, what is the emotional experience that this woman cannot integrate *in* her mind and *into* her life?

And what about her husband? What is the current state of the
other half of this couple?

What do we see when we observe Macbeth for ourselves as he
questions the doctor regarding the condition of his wife (5.3: 1–62
and 5.5: 1–28)? The doctor hedges, not mentioning that he is anxious
about her possible suicidal state of mind. To Macbeth he simply says
it's just her "thick-coming fancies" that keep her from sleep. Macbeth's retort might make us wonder, given what we have seen. It is
difficult not to hear him speaking about himself as well as his wife:

> Cure her of that:
> Canst thou not minister to a mind diseas'd,
> Pluck from the memory a rooted sorrow,
> Raze out the written troubles of the brain,
> And with some sweet oblivious antidote
> Cleanse the stuff'd bosom of that perilous stuff
> Which weighs upon the heart. (5.3: 39–45)

Not "give sorrow words"! Not acknowledge the reality of conflicting emotions! But "pluck out", wipe out of existence these troubles,
these conflicts, with sweet, oblivion-making medicine. Macbeth
finds no sweet antidote to give him some peaceful oblivion,
although perhaps he seeks it in this scene in his attempted schizoid
razing of his capacity for emotional experience. He appears to
disdain that "sweet oblivious antidote" his wife has chosen,
although his final duel with Macduff may be his version of it. There
may be some temporary satisfaction in his cynicism, and in his
disparagement of his emotional experience, his strutting and fret-
ting his hour on the stage. He is a template for many of those we
see in therapy. But cynicism offers him no peaceful oblivion:

> Life's but a walking shadow; a poor player,
> That struts and frets his hour upon the stage,

And is heard no more: it is a tale
Told by an idiot, full of sound and fury,
Signifying nothing. (5.5: 17–28)

Destroy or damage the capacity for emotional experience and you damage or destroy the meaning in life, and, paradoxically, find yourself in an increasingly despairing emptiness. But how did these two people come to this sorry state? And what, if anything, has their relationship had to do with what has happened?

The shared unconscious proleptic imagination

In order to think about those questions let's look at some of what has happened between wife and husband. Soon after Macbeth's famous victory in the service of King Duncan, which earned him the new title of Thane of Cawdor, Lady Macbeth reads a letter from her husband from the battlefield. He barely mentions the victory, but excitedly tells her of an experience so strange he must share it with her immediately. Prophecies from some strange women, "Weïrd Sisters", that seem straightaway to become true: a new title and wealth already his, and a pronouncement that he will be king. Without hesitating or stopping to ponder on it all, he sends an urgent message to his "dearest partner of greatness" so that the picture in his mind might be their shared picture of the greatness that is promised.

Why then, do we imagine, does Lady Macbeth immediately think about her husband's weaknesses, or what she assumes are weaknesses, as, for example, his reluctance to act when it conflicts with his sense of honour, or that he is "too full of the milk of human kindness"! She is convinced it is just his timidity and he needs her to stir him into action. Otherwise, she fears, he will miss the destiny he covets, the kingship with which fate and supernatural powers have already crowned him (1.5: 1–73).

It is not just that Lady Macbeth enters into what she takes to be the spirit of the letter, it is almost as if she were there ahead of her husband, already thinking about the problem of his "character weaknesses", at least as she perceives them. Perhaps she is right. It is not a matter of misperception that I want to call attention to here when I suggest that Lady Macbeth *misreads* her husband. It is not that she is wrong about Macbeth's character flaws, perhaps his "fear", or his being "too full o' the milk of human kindness" to do what he must do if he is to succeed.

No, the misreading, I am suggesting, lies in two errors. One was to take his obvious excitement, and perhaps *his* proleptic state of mind, his picturing the words of the "Weïrd Sisters" almost as if an accomplished fact, as the *totality* of his emotions and potential emotions. The other error was to take his letter picturing the two of them in royal splendour, as if he were stating a fact and not primarily communicating his emotional state. Perhaps it struck such a resonant chord with Lady Macbeth and her own imaginings of glory and power that it became a reality for her as soon as her husband painted for her a picture of it, her proleptic imagination.

Clinical example

I want to illustrate my observations by describing briefly a similar dynamic in a couple I met for psychotherapy. She was struggling with her ambivalence, having left the marital home, but also having initiated the couple therapy. He was mystified, unable to cope with her leaving and suspicious of her motives in suggesting therapy. I want to focus only on a critical moment well into a very intense process when she announced that she did not want to be with him and wanted to end the therapy in the next month or two. Taking her at her word, he was despairing, especially given that he thought they were making progress and had even managed some of their most satisfying intimate moments ever. He responded that it was just what he had suspected, that she intended this all along and had just been going through the motions. He then repeated his theory that there was something in her that made her want to spoil anything good between them, especially when it was going well, since she could never decide what she really wants. Her reaction was to look at me upset and wanting to know why he was attacking her. For her it confirmed just why the marriage is impossible.

I have learned the hard way with this and other couples how difficult it is not to respond to such comments that are couched as decisions as if they were, in fact, decisions. Communication of emotional experience does not always come with the preface, for example, "I feel as if I never want to see you again." In fact it seldom does, especially when strong feelings have been suppressed, but it is extraordinarily challenging to remain in a state of mind to hear them as communications of emotional experience. At cooler moments, the woman in this couple has often explained to me that she makes "decisions", that she "decides" she is going to do this or that, all the time, but only knows it is a real decision when she gets to the point of acting on it.

I try to talk with them about what she has said as an emotional communication of how she feels at this point about the therapy and the marriage. But, in this atmosphere and in this marriage, is there really any possibility for her to articulate such intolerable feelings: intolerable for him, because it feels like a decision to him, and intolerable for her, because it feels like a decision to her? In a sense this can be seen as an example of the ambivalence the couple has been talking *about* so much. Of course, it does not quite feel like that, for them or for me. Ambivalence appears most often not as a thoughtful state of mind, but serially, as singular states of mind. Especially where there is an intense internal conflict, each side of that conflict is experienced as absolutely and only what one is feeling when feeling it. An invitation, whether to partner or patient, to remember and consider returning to the opposing emotional state of mind can be experienced as an attempt to deny the reality of what is being felt. Who then holds on to the ambivalence?

I want to make a further observation about technique, which is implied in the work with this couple. Nowadays, in psychotherapy with couples and individuals, one of the commonly held key therapeutic goals lies in the withdrawal of projections and owning what is one's own. I would stress Bion's discovery in analysis of psychotic patients that projective identification is an evacuation, a projection of unwanted or intolerable feelings *and* potentially a primitive form of communication (Bion, 1957, 1958). We are accustomed to the idea that one major therapeutic leverage in analysis lies in the analyst's capacity to take in those "projections", not being overwhelmed or defined by them, in order to experience them as a mode of communication. The same dynamic operates in couple therapy and in couple relationships. At some points in a relationship it is not the withdrawal of projections that is important;

indeed, they are misperceived as projections, or as only projections. To insist on their withdrawal would be to reject them as a communication. The critical capacity, on the part of the analyst, and ultimately each partner in an intimate relationship, is to be able to experience them as communications. That, I suggest, is the fulcrum of the dynamic of intimacy.

With this couple we were skating close to the edge where emotional experience becomes action, where what is being imaged is taken *proleptically* as already a reality. How long can we survive at the edge? Long enough for the two of them to think through together such intense emotional experiences?

It is similar with the Macbeths, I am suggesting. The difference lies in the emotional experiences of each couple and the actions to which they might lead. For both couples the question is; do emotions, particularly intense emotions, sweep away the possibility of thinking? Can there be a shared Work Group thinking rather than a shared Basic Assumption flight to action? The Macbeths unthinkingly swept along towards assassination. Lady Macbeth is thinking, but only about *how*, not whether, to do the deed. Or the couple described above unthinkingly swept along to final separation. Both have the quality of the actions of a Basic Assumption mob.

Of course the couple I describe, or the Macbeths, might reasonably proceed to those actions thinkingly, but only if they can "think feelingly"; that is, think while in that emotional state. The difference would be that the choice then would not result in madness or a schizoid state that in effect destroys the emotional conflict. The fact that in the end the Macbeths display both madness and schizoid meaninglessness suggests to me that it is action flowing from a shared proleptic imagination, action taken not so much on the basis of thought-through emotion, as action flowing from and thus part of a Basic Assumption state of mind.

The couple and ambivalence: Macbeth's equivocation

With both couples I have described, there is evidence, I think, of a profound ambivalence hidden beneath the intensity of the passions of the moment. If the conflicting feelings could be really, that is experientially, acknowledged, it would disrupt the flight into a shared Basic Assumption mentality. The story of the Macbeths allows us a poignant insight into tragedy of an inability to recognize and acknowledge the more hidden emotions that can constitute an ambivalence felt to be intolerable. In this play we get a particularly vivid picture of Macbeth's ambivalence and his internal torment that goes with it. What follows is my evidence that Lady Macbeth has unthinkingly misread her husband, something she later begins to recognize, but struggles against acknowledging because she senses it will drive her into madness (1.7: 1–83).

Macbeth's state of mind clearly was affected by his wife's greeting that his letters have transported her beyond "this ignorant present". She feels now the future in the instant. She takes him as having decided, but weak, unable to take action. His, perhaps surprising, initial response is to say to her, "We will speak further". In this scene we hear him, on his own away from her, thinking about what he does feel.

This moment is the heart of the story for me. I have a special affection for it because this is the kind of thing I have seen beneath the mask of so many schizoid men in couple therapy. This does not pertain only to men of course, but I find men in particular susceptible to the myth of the emotionally literate woman who all-too-often uses a fluent psychological vocabulary to distract herself and her partner from her emotional experience. The man, as we may discover, is full, often over-full, of feeling, usually seriously conflicting emotions, so full he cannot imagine experiencing them. Indeed, he would think that it would be mad to do so.

In Macbeth's agonizing in his private moments, I suggest that we hear him thinking *realistically*. That is, he is imaginatively reality testing, thinking about how it will be if he, or they, follow the course that is beginning to feel inevitable. Imagining what might happen and what it might be like, based on our experience, is one of the most important ways we have of reality testing, sometimes the only way.

When Macbeth thinks about his relationship to Duncan, as his kinsman, his host, and his subject, he discovers emotions in himself that make assassination feel impossible. In some of Shakespeare's most poignant lines, Macbeth imagines the murder of a good man:

> his virtues
> Will plead like angels, trumpet-tongu'd, against
> The deep damnation of his taking-off;
> And Pity, like a naked new-born babe,
> Striding the blast, or heaven's cherubin, hors'd
> Upon the sightless couriers of the air,
> Shall blow the horrid deed in every eye,
> That tears shall drown the wind. (1.7: 18–25)

This is the same man who later despairs:

> [Life] is a tale
> Told by an idiot, full of sound and fury,
> Signifying nothing. (5.5: 17–28)

How do we understand this apparent contradiction? Some have said that Macbeth was an evil man, some that he was emotionally coerced by a wicked, evil woman. It is no doubt plausible to see them both as epitomizing evil. I suggest that we can see some all-too-common couple dynamics here. We saw her in that earlier scene where, caught up in her conviction that this was what her husband wanted, she seeks to empty herself of her femininity and any of her own conflicting feelings. In their place she invites the spirits to "unsex" her so that she can give her husband what she thinks he needs to achieve his aspirations, and hers. She is willing to sacrifice all for the passion of his ambition, of their ambition. But why, we might wonder, does it focus in such a disturbing image of a woman's attack on her maternal feelings?

> I have given suck, and know
> How tender 'tis to love the babe that milks me:
> I would, while it was smiling in my face,
> Have pluck'd my nipple from his boneless gums,
> And dash'd the brains out, had I so sworn
> As you have done to this. (1.7: 54–59)

Macbeth hears this not as a rejection of herself as mother, but, to the contrary, as the possibility of the conception of the children, the *male* children, this couple do not have:

> Bring forth men-children only!
> For thy undaunted mettle should compose
> Nothing but males. (1.7: 73–75)

Greenblatt describes him as "weirdly aroused by this fantasy" (Greenblatt, 2004, p. 139). Is it weird, or is this the form their shared proleptic imagination takes? Macbeth joins his wife in what looks like an unconscious phantasy in which the murder of King Duncan is somehow equivalent to this couple bringing forth male children to secure the crown, their crown, in an unbroken line into the future. When she invites the spirits to "unsex" her so that no feminine weakness can mate with her husband's anticipated hesitation, she becomes in his mind the mother of soldiers who, like their mother, would show no hesitation, weakness, or ambivalence. With this shared single-minded potency, she says, "What cannot you and I perform . . ."! Can they bring forth male children?

Against this dream, this hallucination, there is the growing realization that it is Banquo's heirs, as the "Weïrd Sisters" had said, who threaten to inherit the kingdom. Macbeth's nightmarish murderous attempts to prevent this prove futile. Lady Macbeth is convinced more and more that in this waking nightmare, all thinking about their emotional experience must go. She can see where it will lead: "it will make us mad" (2.2: 32–33).

In the last scene to which I want to call attention, the "nightmare dinner party", we observe Lady Macbeth beginning to comprehend how desperate and disturbed her husband is. And she, too, has begun to realize their plight:

> Nought's had, all's spent
> Where our desire is got without content:
> 'Tis safer to be that which we destroy,
> Than by destruction dwell in doubtful joy. (3.2: 4–7)

Still she seems able to cope with disappointment, and chides her husband again for too much thinking. After the murder of Duncan she had tried to calm her husband, telling him to wash his hands: "a little water clears us of this deed!" Now she says:

> Things without all remedy
> Should be without regard: what's done is done. (3.2: 11–12)

But Macbeth knows how close he is to madness:

> O! full of scorpions is my mind, dear wife!
> Thou know'st that Banquo, and his Fleance, lives. (3.2: 36–37)

Is this when she begins to realize something of the reality of their shared unconscious phantasy, the imagining that the murder of Duncan was the bringing forth of male children? Is her husband being driven mad, not just because of their insecurity, but also because of his realization that there will be no children, no heirs?

> Upon my head they plac'd a fruitless crown,
> And put a barren sceptre in my gripe,
>
> . . .
>
> No son of mine succeeding. (3.2: 4–7)

It is at this point that Macbeth takes action *independent of his wife* in an attempt to master the emotions that are tormenting him. She asks desperately: "What's to be done?" He responds, with apparent affection,

> Be innocent of the knowledge, dearest chuck
> Till thou applaud the deed. (3.2: 36–37)

What she will soon discover is that Macbeth has organized killers to murder Banquo and his son. When Banquo dies but his son escapes, Macbeth is distraught. His wife will make one last attempt to keep him from falling into madness.

The nightmare dinner party

How bizarrely appropriate that we see something close to the denouement of the couple nightmare in the scene we could describe as "the nightmare dinner party". Here we see portrayed this couple's final attempt to sustain some sense of normalcy (3.4: 31–143). Why is it finally unsustainable? I suggest Macbeth's acting independently has broken the spell of their shared Basic Assumption state of mind. In her husband's hallucinations Lady Macbeth begins to see, but cannot yet bear fully to acknowledge to herself, that this means he, at some fundamental level, has been acting against some of his own important feelings. That is, there has been a profound internal conflict in Macbeth which means that her proleptic imagination, which became their shared imagination, only related to an aspect of what her husband felt. In some basic way she has misread him.

This dawning awareness drives her to the edge of madness because she, too, at some fundamental level is profoundly ambivalent about what has happened. Macbeth seems completely unaware of this. As she struggles to avoid acknowledgement of that reality at the end of the dinner party, we can almost hear her nursery sing-song voice in her sleepwalking madness: "The Thane of Fife had a wife: where is she now?" (5.1: 40). The Thane of Fife, Macduff, also had children. Where are they now?

And Macbeth? As his wife slips irretrievably towards her own hallucinations, in which she tries to recreate the single-mindedness of their shared dream of potency, he takes the opposite route, destroying his capacity for emotional awareness so there is nothing left to think about. In the end, as with his wife, action precedes, even precludes, thinking:

> Strange things I have in head, that will to hand,
> Which must be acted, ere they may be scann'd. (3.2.4–7)

If they were scanned, then it would be impossible to experience life as a tale told by an idiot, signifying nothing, as if one felt nothing. Macbeth sees no way back to thinking what he is feeling, as he says to his wife at the end of this scene,

> I am in blood
> Stepp'd in so far, that, should I wade no more,
> Returning were as tedious as go'er. (3.4: 135–137)

And yet this is also the man who, when at the end of the play he encounters Macduff, cries:

> But get thee back, my soul is too much charg'd
> With blood of thine already. (5.8: 5–6)

Again Macbeth is on the verge of thinking what he is feeling. But from the moment their shared imagination became a shared hallucinatory nightmare, everything Macbeth had done, and continues to do until, but not including, that final duel with Macduff, is shaped by being caught up in the couple nightmare. Macbeth's continuing desperate murders were a futile attempt to establish the certainty of their power, a potency they have unconsciously imagined as absolute, the power of the Basic Assumption mentality.

Having invited you into this story, the disturbing reality is that, no matter how painful to watch, for the Macbeths there is nothing we can say or do that will illumine their way back from these destructive couple dynamics—perhaps not even as an uninvited guest at this nightmare dinner party.

Postscript

Some have expressed concern that this chapter written for clinicians ends on such a despairing note. But the burden of paper is that unless we as therapists, as well as the couples who come to us, can take in fully the stories they tell, individually and together, as images of their emotional experience, it will be impossible for the clinical encounter to be a seeing, a thinking feelingly with them. And, in a corresponding way, each partner must be able to take in fully the other's story as a communication of emotional experience. This ability to think feelingly with each other is the basis of being genuinely heard by the other.

References

Bion, W. R. (1952). Group dynamics: a review. *International Journal of Psychoanalysis*, 33(2): 235–247 [reprinted in *Experiences in Groups*, London: Tavistock, 1961].

Bion, W. R. (1957). Differentiation of the psychotic from the non-psychotic personalities. Reprinted in *Second Thoughts* (pp. 43–64). London: Karnac, 1967.

Bion, W. R. (1958). On arrogance. Reprinted in *Second Thoughts* (pp. 86–92). London: Karnac, 1967.

Bloom, H. (1999). *Shakespeare: the Invention of the Human*. London: Fourth Estate.

Doran, G. (2001). DVD version of the Royal Shakespeare Company performance of *Macbeth*.

Fisher, J. V. (1999). *The Uninvited Guest: Emerging from Narcissism to Marriage*. London: Karnac.

Fisher, J. V. (2000a). The Macbeths and the proleptic evasion of mourning. Unpublished paper presented at the Tavistock Centre for Couple Relationships, November 2000.

Fisher, J. V. (2000b). A father's abdication: Lear's retreat from "aesthetic conflict". *International Journal of Psychoanalysis*. *81*(5): 963–982.

Fisher, J. V. (2006). The emotional experience of K. *International Journal of Psychoanalysis*, *87*(5): 1221–1237. Presented at the UCL "Wilfred Bion Today" conference, London, June 2005.

Freud, S. (1916d). Some character-types met with in psycho-analytic work. *S.E.*, *14*: 309–334. London: Hogarth.

Greenblatt, S. (2004). *Will in the World*. London: Jonathan Cape.

Shakespeare, W. (1951). *Macbeth*. In: K. Muir (Ed.) The Complete Works (3rd Arden edn). Walton-on-Thames: Thomas Nelson and Sons Ltd, 1997.

CHAPTER THREE

Fusion, diffusion, de-fusion, confusion: exploring the anatomy of the couple psyche*

Adrian Perkel

Introduction

"It is as hard to pair a couple as it is to split the Sea of Reeds"

(Babylonian Talmud)

T his ancient saying (cited in Goldwurm, 1993) offers a point of departure for this chapter about the struggle that many couple relationships encounter, and always have, in order to survive. Adult couple relationships are hard to sustain and marriages frequently end in break-up and divorce. This chapter explores the way couple relationships evolve and develop through recurring phases of fusion, diffusion, and de-fusion. As a leit-motif throughout the chapter runs an account of the marriage between Nelson and Winnie Mandela, an iconic coupling of the so-called "Mother and Father of the South African Nation". The fate of their

---

* This is a substantially revised and expanded version of the paper "Fusion, diffusion, defusion, confusion: exploring the anatomy of the marital psyche", published in 2005 in *Psycho-analytic Psychotherapy in South Africa*, 13(2): 60–77.

marriage illustrates how "fusion" is fraught with difficulties. The question for couple psychotherapists is "Why?", and in this chapter I address this question through a psychoanalytic exploration of the couple psyche.

A couple is a living entity and it follows a developmental cycle. In the beginning, two individuals fuse together psychically to form a positive merger. This fusion leads to an exchange of mental contents, a process whereby psychic boundaries are loosened and become diffuse. With time, this exchange invariably becomes problematic and a renewal of individuation occurs, a de-fusion, but not all the exchanged elements are withdrawn or reclaimed. Instead, confusion and conflict can manifest, with its inherent drive towards dissolution. These trends are explored with a view to understanding the anatomy of the couple psyche.

Fusion

When Nelson Rolihlahla Mandela, the most famous political prisoner in the world, walked out of prison, the world caught its first glimpse of this symbol of freedom. The Nobel Peace Prize, honorary doctorates, statues, concerts, and T-shirts—all offerings to an icon representing the triumph of good over evil. Hand in hand was his loyal wife Winnie Mandela, known as the "Mother of the Nation". Also a symbol of righteous struggle, she had been legally banished for years to an arid dorp in Brandfort, a virtual prisoner in an alien place. Yet, through decades of loneliness she stood firm by her husband until the magical day of his release. *Twenty-seven years!* It was like a great and tragic fairytale in which most South Africans took pride. Two great icons of morality in one beautiful moment of history. So what went wrong?

I begin this exploration by describing a significant pattern in intimate relationships. The basis of the initial attraction appears to contain the self-same qualities and dynamics that later become the source of tension and breakdown. Attraction and repulsion, fusion and de-fusion appear to emerge from the same unconscious source. This "make–break" dimension is so consistent as to be of great theoretical interest to the character of psychological mating. A patient told me, "I was attracted to his reliability and consistency. But now I am so frustrated. He is so unadventurous, so controlled! He *bores* me!" What couples need in each other initially, they tend to fight over later.

Back in the 1950s, Mandela's tale was just beginning. When Nelson first saw Winnie at a nearby bus stop, he wrote:

> I noticed out of the corner of my eye a lovely young woman wait-ing for a bus. I was struck by her beauty, and I turned my head to get a better look at her . . . She had recently completed her studies at the Jan Hofmeyer School of Social Work . . . and was working as the first black female social worker at Baragwaneth Hospital. I cannot say for certain if there is such a thing as love at first sight, but I do know that the moment I first glimpsed Winnie, I knew that I wanted to have her as my wife. [Mandela, 1994, p. 199]

Attraction and repulsion

Time has a tendency to build dissatisfaction in relationships and, as mentioned, the forces that initially compel the attraction become the self-same ones that lead to repulsion and its subsequent disso-lution. This is perhaps like the fine tension between the life and death instincts, which, as Freud (1920g) points out, spur develop-ment. In nature this tension is everywhere, between homeostasis and development that is spurred by external impingements. In 1920, Freud made a theoretical modification to the pleasure princi-ple, introducing the concept that, as in the organic world, psycho-logical instincts, and in particular the death instinct, seek stasis and quiescence and, when stimulated, a restoration of the resting state. He pointed out that instincts are

> therefore bound to give a deceptive appearance of being forces tending towards change and progress, whilst in fact they are merely seeking to repeat and reach an ancient goal by paths alike old and new. [Freud, 1920g, p. 38).

The repetition compulsion is central to this tendency and has important implications for psychotherapy. Development is fuel-led by conflict. In psychological life the opposing forces of two psyches enable a relationship, this abstract and fragile entity, to evolve towards higher development, and, as I shall discuss later, a restoration of intrapsychic equilibrium. The nuclei of attraction and repulsion derive from the same source, enabling the emergence of a new entity, while simultaneously prompting towards de-fusion.

Mandela was dazzled by Winnie and noted later, "I knew at once that I wanted to marry her—and I told her so. Her spirit, her passion, her youth, her courage, her *wilfulness*—I felt all these things the moment I first saw her" (Mandela, 1994, p. 200, my italics).

Mandela was himself, of course, very headstrong, and in his own words "stubborn". His birth name, Rolihlahla, means "pulling the branch of a tree"—but its colloquial meaning more accurately would be "troublemaker". Friends and relatives would in later years ascribe to his Xhosa birth name, as he put it, "the many storms I have caused and weathered" (*ibid.*, p. 3). This character was present in his relationship from the beginning. When Nelson was teased later that he never actually proposed to Winnie, he argued, "I asked her on our very first date and simply took it for granted from that day forward." But his stubborn side was well sublimated. Outwardly, he presented as a martyr, sacrificing life and limb for his people. "I never promised her gold and diamonds", he said, "and I was never able to give them to her" (*ibid.*, p. 201).

We are seeing here the birthing of an emergent entity in the Mandela relationship, rich in projections and an exchange of psychological elements. Apparently opposite in some ways, yet on closer examination, so similar, a new entity was forming.

The third psyche: the couple lacuna

I have often been struck by how the personality of a patient as expressed in an intimate relationship can be so opposite to its presentation outside that relationship. The dominant, decisive, executive comes home and transforms into a meek, submissive husband. I have also noticed in couple therapy how, when one person leaves the room to go to the lavatory, the other person becomes, instantly, quite different. This transformation can be marked and intriguing to witness.

A third entity that is generated when two people merge into a couple cannot be understood through understanding the individuals alone (Perkel, 1997). Just as the individual psyche emerges out of the brain, but can never be reduced to neurons, so, too, the marital psyche emerges irreducibly from the amalgam of the two contributing psyches. The chicken, once hatched, cannot be put back into the egg. This "third psyche" is enabled by the exchange of psychological and libidinal energies to move into a shared space. I call this space the "lacuna", meaning an entity that is given content by the two contributing psyches.

Freud's recognition that underlying somatic experiences in infant development provide the prototypes upon which defences and personality were built (mind emerges from somatic experience) (1905d), provides us with a means to understand how a couple emerges from simpler contributing components. A new level of analysis is required. Everywhere in nature, according to the physicist Davies (1995), there is a trend toward higher levels of complexity. New and more elaborate systems can "suddenly and spontaneously leap into more elaborate forms" (ibid., p. 198). Each layer of emergent complexity demands its own, relatively autonomous laws according to which it operates. A relationship represents such a quantum jump, as an emergent system with its own life, or as Grier (2005) put it, "the sum of a couple is more than the addition of its parts" (ibid., p. 5).

Many authors have tackled this complex notion of a "third" in psychoanalytic work from differing perspectives (Britton, 2004; Gerson, 2004; Green, 2004; Ogden, 2004). A common thread in thinkers in this area appears to be that "thirdness" is an emergent property out of dyadic two-ness, and one which amounts to more than its component parts. Ogden (1994) introduced the notion of the interplay between the subjective and the intersubjective in the analytic situation which gives rise to the "analytic third". Thinking about couples, however, introduces added complexities, particularly in relation to the exchange of mental contents. Green (2004), interestingly, talks of the "relational unconscious" that is both intrapsychically and intersubjectively influenced. He notes that therapists working with couples regularly make use of the notion of a shared unconscious, a third entity that transcends the subjectivities of the two participants. Ruszczynski (2004) also argues that a couple is made up of the two individuals in the partnership, with their relationship being a third element. "The relationship" may be said to have its own distinct identity, apart from the identities of the two individuals.

Overall, there is a clear trend in conceptualizing the couple psyche as a distinct emergent entity, one that enters the therapy room with its own character and defensive constellations.

Mutual exchanges

If this third entity is the focus of analysis and intervention with a couple, we need to understand what prompts this psychological mating to occur. It is common to hear in social circles surprise upon hearing of someone's new partner. "She's involved with *who?!* But they're so *different!*" The attraction of opposites is well known in both nature and mating. People vow to never repeat their parents' mistakes and invariably end up doing so. So often we hear someone in therapy recognize their parent in their partner, leaving them horrified that their determination to be opposite to their parent has led them precisely there. Discovering their own rejected internal objects in their partner can be too much to bear. This may lead couples towards de-fusion and emotional rejection for entirely mistaken reasons. In fact, I would argue that most couples seem to separate or divorce for, psychologically speaking, misguided reasons, an assertion I will attempt to justify below.

The determination to avoid previous disappointments is met by other psychic forces—the need for mastery over one's internal world and the compulsion to repeat the familiar. Instead of disappearing from psychic life, repressed experiences and affects continue to find ways to live, since no part of the psyche can be eradicated, not even by denial or repression. Perhaps similar to, but also different from, Klein's illuminating concept of projective identification, partners in the "relationship alloy" acquiesce to share each others projections in a mutual exchange, accepting as their own the other's projected parts. That is why there is never really a victim in a relationship and why one partner can never justly be held to blame. Psychoanalytic thinking prompts always to look for the unwanted part in the unconscious of the other.

Case example

The following example illustrates how a mutual mental exchange is created in which the overt and the covert do not coincide. When a male patient made an appointment for couple therapy and brought his girlfriend of over ten years, the problem was framed in their shared picture of the relationship. She wanted to get married, while he felt unable to take this step, but did not want to lose the relationship. It was easy to share in this view, given her vibrant energy and his high levels of anxiety. Couple therapy, however, began to reveal that his high anxiety and tendency to resist change was premised on early trauma of abandonment and a deficit in emotionally processing this. He had created a rigid and routine way of life to preserve a sense of constancy and lessen his anxiety. As a result, his resistance to marriage connected to an unconscious fear that she might refuse his proposal, and hence recreate his abandonment. She, on the other hand, had been traumatized by an early parental divorce and a determination never to repeat the pain of a broken marriage, so that unconsciously she was actually resistant to marriage, despite the overt display of wanting it more than anything.

This duality reflected the dynamic of her splitting off and handing to him her unresolved fears of marriage and of him, in turn, handing over his profound anxiety about abandonment. She carried and felt abandoned by his resistance to marriage, and he felt strangely contained by her repeated desire to have him. He felt less anxious about abandonment by carrying her independence and unconscious resistance to marriage. For both of them, unintegrated aspects of their psychic experience was placed into the other via the lacuna, enabling equilibrium to be restored. Now that they were in their early thirties, developmental pressures began to challenge this, and her contemplation of her biological clock began to exert an upward pressure on these repressed aspects. Only at this point did they present for therapy, which assisted them to take the step into marriage.

If either of these two had chosen individual therapy only, it is possible that another outcome would have occurred. It is often apparent that when a patient undergoes individual psychotherapy, that patient's couple relationship becomes threatened. Some individual therapists have been known to say, "She outgrew him", as repetitive patterns, driven by the repetition compulsion, are resolved. They may view dissolution of the couple as being more healthy and desirable. "They needed permission to end the relationship", might then be their interpretation of a successful therapeutic outcome. In my view, such an outcome is not always positive, and I will support this by referring to some basic elements of mating. The question arises: why do people mate at all? What motivates deep attachment?

The intolerability of loneliness: people as object-seeking

To almost all people the absence of relating with others for any length of time appears to be intolerable. Even those who are schizoid and seem to show a preference for being alone will seek people through distance contact, such as drinking coffee at an open-air café and imbibing the energy of others. Moreover, depression invariably haunts those who struggle on alone signalling a yearning for human contact, even when this yearning is ego-dystonic. We know that people deprived of human contact through solitary confinement often find this a form of torture more intolerable than physical abuse. Humans are irresistibly dependent on others; it is an utterly compelling drive. What, however, is the source and nature of this compulsion? We know that early physiological experiences form the template of the emerging infant's psyche, and that defences and personality interface with sensory experiences of the inner and outer world. The infant is an agent of interpretation and experience, being moulded by and, in turn, moulding experience. In the early stages of development, the mother–infant symbiosis involves an intimate exchange of projections. Mental contents and projections are not merely from the infant into the mother, they are also from the mother into the infant. The infant can also be a container for the mother and a repository for her unconscious "deposits". The split-off fragments of mother that are taken in by the infant, such as her anxieties and aggressions, fill the infant's rudimentary lacuna. From this internal world of rudimentary objects, the infant feeds psychologically.

We might say that human interchange of mental contents is so vital for mental survival, development, and sustenance, that its absence cannot be tolerated. Left alone, human beings, whether infant or adult, will pine, wither, and even die. This innate striving for bonding is structural, driven by the life instinct, Eros, which aims at combining into ever-larger unities and prolonging life (Freud, 1920g, 1930a). In the couple, it also involves a mutual exchange of mental contents that has specific individual experiential character. During times of struggle and threat, the need for bonding may become more overt. Adults do not become exempt from this mental requirement; the infantile drive towards attachment is as compelling in later life so long as the life instinct remains ascendant.

We may hypothesize that Mandela, in his loneliness, fed off Winnie as a psychic introject. During his period of terrible personal and political crisis in the early 1960s, Mandela was facing the death penalty. He wrote:

> Though I was on trial for treason, Winnie gave me cause for hope. I felt as though I had a new and second chance at life. My love for her gave me added strength for the struggles that lay ahead. [Mandela, 1994, p. 202]

Projections as object-seeking

If people inherently seek object-attachments, driven by the deepest life instincts (Freud, 1920g), their projections are also object-seeking. This may seem like odd usage of what is technically a mechanism of psychic defence, but projections seem to have the characteristic of constantly scanning for a container in which to be taken up. As Freud (1920g, 1930a) explained, projection, internal "unpleasure", or unwanted parts that are repressed, tend to be treated by the psyche as if they were acting not from the inside but from the outside, as if parts of the ego therefore do not belong to oneself and are instead ascribed to the external world. The psyche, hence, "rids" itself of these unwanted encapsulated objects and affects by projecting them outwardly, but, I argue, not with the final aim of ridding itself, but to find completeness. In the case example above, psychological completeness was only achieved through the couple's mutual exchange of split-off parts. Such projections do not necessarily go away by acquiring different partners. Hence, simply dissolving what seems like an intractable situation may not be ultimately helpful.

One can notice that projections are always in motion, seeking places to attach themselves. Unlike Klein's (1975) dyadic detoxifying functions of the mother, or Bion's (1962) two-way notion that includes an exchange of projections, the external world does not necessarily assist in processing or accepting them. But, as Wright (2001) has pointed out, the interactive nature of mother–infant communication, with an ever-present process of projection of inner contents, is linked to an innate need to bond with another, and so finding a recipient for projections remains compelling.

By way of a parallel, libido can exist without an external object—that is, it originates from within—yet "love strives after objects" (Freud, 1930a). Libidinal energy "yearns" constantly for external objects on which to cathect. So, too, with repressed mental contents; repressed parts of the psyche will find a place in which to continue living to restore internal equilibrium. This quality drives the compelling need for merger and fusion with an object in which parts of the self can be put. Gerson makes the point that

> the unconscious is not only the receptacle of repressed material driven underground to protect one from conflict-induced anxieties; it is also the holding area whose contents await birth at a receptive moment in the contingencies of evolving experience. [Gerson, 2004, p. 69]

This compensatory aim of inter-relatedness is vital to mental stability and to enabling relationships, but makes for difficult mating. It is the exchange of these "contents" that enables the lacuna to be formed, that third psychic entity between two people, creating an added layer of meaning "beyond the two poles" (Green, 2000, cited in Gerson, 2004.)

This interpsychic lacuna is therefore that mutually beneficial psychic space in which two psyches become zipped together, creating a third living entity with its own peculiar dynamic. The inherent striving for psychic completion seems to enable unconscious objects to continue living where they are unable to be integrated in the ego. It is, in other words, driven by a compulsion, not just for repetition, but also for compensation.

On the loneliness drive

This drive towards compensation might remain dormant, however, were it not assisted by a process that is very poorly visited in the literature: loneliness. Loneliness presents in therapy repeatedly as a major underlying emotional state. Klein considered loneliness to be an inevitable consequence of a lack of a full integration of aspects of the self, especially split-off parts that are defended against. Related to the protection of good from bad, or positive introjects from persecutory ones, parts of self are split off, repressed, contributing to the feeling, as she puts it, that "one is not in full possession of one's self, that it does not fully belong to oneself or, therefore, to anyone else. The lost parts are felt to be lonely" (Klein, 1963, p. 302).

These feelings of loneliness are compelling in their demand for remedy, since they reflect deep psychic dis-equilibrium that emerges over time. Accordingly, they can develop a powerful drive-like quality in nudging the individual towards integration. The emotional content of loneliness is powerful, and its purpose is to give life to parts of self that have been repressed.

The psyche is no different from any other system in nature in striving for equilibrium. It cannot "vaporize" any part of itself, even though, as Freud (1916d) pointed out, it can find compromise solutions to its conflicts, though, in excess, these will lead to some symptom. The psyche needs to maintain equilibrium from its point of view, and finding a recipient to "hold" disowned fragments enables a restoration of equilibrium. Freud's (1920g) repetition compulsion helps us understand the underlying psychological compulsion to restore this equilibrium and return to some form of resting or quiescent state.

Caught between the ego and repression, the psyche finds a compromise through projecting split parts into another, seeking to account for all pieces of the puzzle. The lacuna, which offers a structure for psychological exchange, enables a mutual handover of repressed fragments. This is akin to Freud's (1916d) compromise model, but in the interpersonal realm. If this striving to find a recipient is blocked, the unconscious awareness of incompletion can be disturbing, especially when the amount of instinctual energy or affect bound up with this repression is great. A profound sense of loneliness will result. The lacuna provides a mechanism of compensation, enabling a subjective restoration of feeling complete.

Loneliness, therefore, is both a by-product of a lack of psychic integrity and also drives towards corrective action. In pathological states, such as paranoia, this projection does not rely on a mutual reciprocity. It forces itself into random containers that are imagined to be part of a psychological relationship with the patient. In more normal states, when both the projective and incorporative aims are fulfilled, loneliness subsides in its fuller sense. Falling in love is the epitome of this (Perkel, 2001).

Duality and self-limitation

The deep sense of completion that comes from falling in love is later met by new challenges of its "souring". Making sense of both love and love's undoing is connected to understanding "duality". In the natural world there are dualities constantly at play, as there are in psychological life. How can something be two things at once, but never both at the same time?

A relationship demands that one be both "I" and "we" simultaneously, an expectation to be simultaneously both singular and plural. This theme of duality is everywhere, with converging and diverging forces constantly at play: life itself and death's tussle with it; masculine and feminine; side-effects of medication and resistance to therapeutic interpretation. Momentum in one direction quickly spawns forces pulling in the other. The universe is indescribably complex, yet systems at all levels operate within a narrow band close to their nature. We are unable to deviate far from our nature without incurring physical and psychological harm and disease.

Psychosexual energy, as Freud (1905d, 1930a) pointed out, has the characteristic of cathecting with erotogenic zones in the body and deriving symbolic, mental representations of them, which evolve into intellectual, emotional, and spiritual representations. Libido cathects with both the genital organization and the highs of attraction, but also with the anus and its contents, and hence the potential for disgust and repulsion. According to Freud (1905e), disgust becomes a means of affective expression in the sexual sphere because of this proximate association, the excremental being intimately and inseparably bound up with the sexual—since the position of the genitals, "inter urinas et faeces—remains the decisive and unchangeable factor" (Freud, 1912d, p. 189). It is, for example, hard to imagine touching, tasting, and hoarding faecal matter, and in general, excrement does not promote attraction, yet genitals do. It is striking that such divergent emotional responses can be evoked by two parts of the body so very closely allied to each other. Why would the biological apparatus that holds the factories of life and its tools for creation be also the apparatus for excretion? The highest spiritual and emotional potentiality, creating life, is married so directly with the basest of functions, excretion? Why would an intelligent town planner place an opera house next-door to the sewage works?

There is a fine line between one energy and another, and sometimes, as with the life and death instinct, pain and pleasure, love and hate, one is just a breath away from morphing into the other. Could we fairly say that there could not be the one without the other? It seems that the juxtaposition of opposites, like the contraction pains of labour, are as essential for life as they are painful. Placing opposites together prevents the absolute reification or denigration of either pole. It ensures a counterpoint that enables self-limiting balance to develop and helps us understand why couples both fuse and de-fuse around the same dynamics. The deep bonding and conflict that are part of the creation–dissolution cycle of relationships are really two sides of one coin. Relationships are therefore governed by a self-limiting principle. Duality seems to provide the mechanism by which this self-limitation is imposed. Systems are glued together by the tensions of opposites and for the human couple this is both the fuel for its creation but also the means of its dissolution. The life and the death instincts are, therefore, present in this emergent system.

Let us look at this paradox beginning to emerge in the early stages of the Mandela couple's development. Winnie has had a child, and the couple is now moving out of the first flushes of romantic symbiosis. He wrote:

As soon as Winnie was up and about, I undertook the task of teaching the new mother of the household how to drive. Driving, in those days, was a man's business; very few women, especially African women, were to be seen in the driver's seat. But Winnie was independent-minded and intent on learning ... Perhaps I am an impatient teacher or perhaps I had a headstrong pupil, but when I attempted to give Winnie lessons along a relatively flat and quiet Orlando road, we could not seem to shift gears without quarrelling.

Finally, after she had ignored one too many of my suggestions, I stormed out of the car and walked home . . . and she proceeded to drive around the township on her own for the next hour. [Mandela, 1994, pp. 212–213]

Here we see attachment with an emerging power struggle, one that came to play itself out in both the personal and public arenas. Even in these early days, Mandela was a symbol of moderation and compromise but Winnie's wilfulness and passion, which so attracted him initially, were beginning to rub against his own headstrong and uncompromising side. He, after all, was the adversarial lawyer who was later to initiate and lead violent armed struggle. Yet this was perhaps not fully acknowledged. Instead, his headstrong aggression may have been handed over to Winnie, who took on these projections and became noted for her stubborn, aloof character, and, later, her violent one. The social worker, and caring, maternal Winnie seemed to get lost as Nelson took ownership of and became associated with these "softer" traits.

Diffusion

The diffusing of mental contents and their projections gives rise to an emergent psychic structure, like combining hydrogen and oxygen to create water, a substance quite distinct from its components. Each person in a relationship brings a distinctive montage of internal psychological components, a heritage of life experience through infancy and subsequent development. This complex tapestry of unconscious material is contained in the psyche's vast unconscious reservoir. This tapestry is richly embroidered through the first years of life, especially through the oedipal stage, which Freud aptly termed in 1905, the "nuclear complex of the neuroses". Object choice is integral to this phase of experience, built on the pre-oedipal matrix. Through primary narcissism to secondary narcissism, through autoerotic to external object choice, the child's internal object world is being carved and much of this will be repressed. In this alchemical furnace, the "personality" of the adult relationship, the lacuna, is already being forged. This lacuna is made up of three primary elements: unconscious early emotional object-attachments and the "imagos" contained in these prototypes (Freud, 1921c, p. 138), instinct-driven libidinal energy which cathects with these objects and is repressed, and the need for compensation of these repressed parts through projection. Without this combination, it is possible that sexual union would be instinct-driven only and hence of a far more fleeting nature.

The wounds of early phases, particularly those that have been strongly repressed and bound up with unresolved affect, will require later compensation through an external object in adulthood (Perkel, 1995, 2001). This compensatory compulsion, infused as it is with libidinal and erotic energy, is the driving force behind intimate bonds. We know about the "repetition compulsion", that "extraordinarily strong upward drive in the shape of the 'compulsion to repeat' . . ." (Freud, 1923c, pp. 117–118), but there are also the compensatory aspects, the psyche's attempt to restore "wholeness" and equilibrium. Not only do we see here the emergence of a new layer of interpsychic dynamics with its own life and processes, but also the principle of self-limitation. In the compulsion to find compensation for internal imbalances, repressed aspects of the psyche are projected into the lacuna to be taken up and enabled. The lacuna provides a counterpoint in which energies that cannot remain dormant (as energies, by their nature, cannot), find a living space. In this exchange, the lacuna, with its quantum jump into a living system, brings balance back, at least temporarily, into the internal world. Self-limiting mechanisms in the internal world prevent too great a polarization of some qualities or defences at the expense of others. To restore homeostasis, the lacuna becomes the psyche's invaluable mechanism of balance, helping to restore equilibrium for parts of self that have become internally split off.

De-fusion

The couple lacuna has specific characteristics that are different from the psychological "third" in therapy. It is not premised on transference phenomena and a receptive container, nor are projections "contained" or necessarily metabolized. Rather, an enlivened, ongoing entity that is inseparable and involves an exchange better characterizes the nature of the couple lacuna.

This makes matters confusing, however, when compensatory aspects that are projected outwardly, taken up in this exchange, begin to irritate and a de-fusing occurs. This is driven partly by developmental pressures towards individuation and the tussle between the life and death instincts contained in this. Without attaching judgement to this, it is my view that the natural psychological tendency of the marital dyad is towards some form of dissolution, just as happens in the physical body. This is not to say that destruction is by any means the desirable or *inevitable* outcome, but that without everyday processing, the inherent pull of the marital relationship is towards a state of renewed psychological quiescence, or non-being.

Some may find this view pessimistic, although it does no more than acknowledge the universal existential paradox of all living beings, that the natural consequence of life is non-life, or organic quiescence. Once again, according to Freud (1920g), the concept of the repetition compulsion, driven by the death instinct, occupies a central place in this schema. He noted that at the organic level, too, there is a universal tendency in all living matter towards reinstating a state of non-being, "to return to the quiescence of the inorganic world" (p. 62), and "an urge inherent in organic life to restore an earlier state of things" (p. 36). Freud encapsulated this as "the aim of all life is death", and, looking back, "the inanimate was there before the animate" (p. 38). Unless ongoing metabolizing restores equilibrium, and keeps the life instinct ascendant, there is a premature drag to illness and death. Even when it is present, death is ultimately inevitable.

The implication of this is that the couple psyche has a *structural* compulsion to repeat towards some form of dissolution, certainly in the absence of continuous nourishment and metabolizing. Moreover, this couple third is not as stable as the individual psyche, which is housed biologically. Nevertheless, when a very ill couple does present for therapy in a state of apparent "quiescence", we still have to assume that their presence implies that a pulse beats in their relationship, however feeble that pulse might be. Therapy should not then aim to be its final euthanasia.

When a process of dissolution occurs, those aspects previously cited as a source of irritation in the partner may become re-introjected. The shifting of these mental contents can be confusing and throw couples into disarray. On the basis of homeostatic principles, we can suppose that when occupancy of specific spaces within the lacuna is withdrawn, a crisis of dis-equilibrium may be created, demanding restoration of balance. It is here that confusing struggles play themselves out. Since everyone has unresolved issues, a relationship can certainly prove therapeutic even though it is not itself couple therapy. The extent to which a free-flow of energy is available so as to enable growth will depend on whether the couple leans towards flexibility or rigidity. When couples do separate or divorce, it is usually because the exchange of split off inner parts that enabled the initial compensatory embrace, now places the partner in the (projected) enemy camp. And so, such a relationship's demise happens for the wrong reasons since there is no resolution.

It is now the 1990s and we have jumped ahead twenty-seven years. Nelson Mandela is free. But within two years of his release from prison, he delivers a press statement about his failing marriage:

> In view of the tensions that have arisen owing to differences between ourselves on a number of issues in recent months, we have mutually agreed that a separation would be best for each of us.

The great fairytale had come to a tragic end. Winnie had been charged with the kidnapping, assault, and murder of a fourteen-year-old boy. Over the years, her criminal credentials were to be increased with charges of fraud and other misdemeanours. Her status as the "Mother of the Nation" corroded dramatically and her image increasingly became associated with criminality and dark dealings.

Concluding comments

On the face of it, Nelson and Winnie Mandela started out as two martyrs of a difficult struggle, holding the moral high ground through decades of bitter political war and suffering immeasurable personal costs. It was notable, in the beginning of their relationship, that they both had strong-willed, headstrong, and stubborn temperaments. This was to create difficulties between them even before the "Long Walk to Freedom" was well under way.

Nelson came to represent a universal symbol of light, virtue, self-lessness, dignity, and heroism. Since his release, the world has continued to maintain him as a great icon, the famous "Prisoner 46664". The "Father of a Nation" has become the "Grandfather of a Nation". Winnie, however, has come to represent the opposite, the epitome of the sinister, not-to-be-trusted gangster, a symbol of darkness. The "Mother of the Nation" has become the "Wicked Witch". Such opposites have emerged from such apparent similarity! Could it be that in the personal realm of the Mandelas, as in the political one, Winnie came to be the recipient of unintegrated stubborn, headstrong, aggressive, projected deposits, freeing Nelson the freedom-fighter turned political statesman to maintain his stature as the "Virtuous One"? And that Winnie, the caring social worker, has handed over her sensitivity to be held by him? People find partners in whom to project their repressed feelings and characteristics. The attraction and the dissolution, the fusion and the de-fusion, are two sides of one coin.

Why nature has devolved such an important function as psychological reproduction to such a fragile entity as the couple lacuna remains unclear. For inherent to such an unstable phenomenon is the promise of difficulty and pain and the conduit for the transmission of psychopathology.

Again it may be noted that the thrust towards dissolution carries with it some higher or more general purpose, perhaps, like life itself. Indeed, the complexity of living does not guarantee stability or permanence in either the biological or the psychic aspects of life. Nevertheless, understanding the dynamics of life and helping to optimize them can certainly make the journey of living much less painful, and, one hopes, much more fulfilling.

References

Bion, W. R. (1962). *Learning from Experience*. London: Heinemann.

Britton, R. (2004). Subjectivity, objectivity, and triangular space. *Psychoanalytic Quarterly*, LXXIII(1): 47–61.

Davies, P. (1995). *The Cosmic Blueprint: Order and Complexity at the Edge of Chaos*. Harmondsworth: Penguin.

Freud, S. (1905e). *Fragment of an Analysis of a Case of Hysteria* ("Dora"). *S.E., 7*: 3–124. London: Hogarth.

Freud, S. (1905d). *Three Essays on the Theory of Sexuality. S.E., 7*: 125–245. London: Hogarth.

Freud, S. (1912d). On the universal tendency to debasement in the sphere of love. *S.E., 11*: 179–190. London: Hogarth.

Freud, S. (1916d). Some character-types met with in psycho-analytic work. *S.E., 14*: 323–324. London: Hogarth.

Freud, S. (1920g). *Beyond the Pleasure Principle. S.E., 18*: 7–64. London: Hogarth.

Freud, S. (1921c). *Group Psychology and the Analysis of the Ego. S.E., 18*: 67–143. London: Hogarth.

Freud, S. (1923c). *Remarks on the Theory and Practice of Dream Interpretation. S.E., 19*: 107–122. London: Hogarth.

Freud, S. (1930a). *Civilisation and its Discontents. S.E., 21*: 59–145. London: Hogarth.

Gerson, S. (2004). The relational unconscious: A core element of intersubjectivity, thirdness, and clinical process. *The Psychoanalytic Quarterly, LXXIII*(1): 63–98.

Goldwurm, E. (Ed.) (1993). *Talmud Bavli (Babylonian), Tractate Sotah.* Schottenstein Edition. New York: Artscroll.

Green, A. (2000). The intrapsychic and intersubjective in psychoanalysis. *Psychoanalytic Quarterly, 69*: 1–39.

Green, A. (2004). Thirdness and psychoanalytic concepts. *The Psycho - analytic Quarterly, LXXIII*(1): 99–135.

Grier, F. (Ed.) (2005). *Oedipus and the Couple.* London: Karnac.

Klein, M. (1963). On the sense of loneliness. In: M. Masud & R. Kahn (Eds.), *Envy and Gratitude and Other Works 1946–1963.* International Psychoanalytic Library. London: Hogarth, 1975.

Klein, M. (1975). *Love, Guilt, and Reparation and Other Works, 1921–1945.* New York: Delta.

Mandela, N. R. (1994). *Long Walk to Freedom.* Randburg, SA: Macdonald Purnell.

Ogden, T. H. (1994). The analytic third: working with intersubjective clinical facts. *International Journal of Psychoanalysis, 75*: 3–19.

Ogden, T. H. (2004). The analytic third: implications for psychoanalytic theory and technique. *The Psychoanalytic Quarterly, LXXIII*(1): 167–195.

Perkel, A. (1995). Troubled marriage: The psychosexual matrix and Oedipus revisited. *Psycho-analytic Psychotherapy in South Africa, 3*(1): 35–45.

Perkel, A. (1997). The interpsychic lacuna: speculations on the nature of the marital dyad. *Psycho-analytic Psychotherapy in South Africa, 5*(1): 40–53.

Perkel, A. (2001). Psychological mating: the compulsion to compensation. *Psycho-analytic Psychotherapy in South Africa, 9*(1): 46–58.

Ruszczynski, S. (2004). Reflective space in the intimate couple relationship: the "marital triangle". In: F. Grier (Ed.), *Oedipus and the Couple* (pp. 31–47). London: Karnac.

Wright, K. (2001). Bion and beyond: whither projective identification? The Enid Balint Memorial Lecture 2000, Tavistock Centre, 1 December 2000. *Society of Psychoanalytical Marital Psychotherapists, 8*: 8–16.

PART II

THE COUPLE IN THE FAMILY: DEVELOPMENTAL AND CONTEXTUAL PERSPECTIVES

CHAPTER FOUR

When siblings become couples

Elspeth Morley

Introduction

As we celebrate the 150th anniversary of Freud's birth, his themes of infantile sexuality and the oedipal–castration complex retain their place at the heart of psychoanalytic theory. The designations of pre- and post-oedipal phases serve only to emphasize this presumed centrality of the oedipal, even when its meaning is stretched to cover all movement from twos to threes. The psychoanalyst Juliet Mitchell, the most prominent advocate of comparable attention being given to the hitherto extraordinarily neglected sibling relationships, is not seeking to displace Oedipus as the signifier of the universal trauma of all "vertical" (i.e., inter-generational, parent–child) relationships. She asks only for a comparable place to be given in "lateral" (i.e., intra-generational, sibling) relationships to the equally universal trauma of the loss of sole status as "His/her Majesty the Baby" (Mitchell, 2003, 2006). Mitchell argues that this "strong" trauma is of a different order, but is as inescapable in the development of the human psyche in lateral relationships as the oedipal trauma must be in vertical relationships.

Mitchell clarifies that she is talking not of "weak", in the sense of variable and avoidable, trauma, but of what she defines as the "strong" trauma that is universally inescapable; it breaks through psychological barriers with an implosion which "is absolute for all time; it cannot be repressed or defended against" (Mitchell, 2006, p. 158). Furthermore, the strong trauma is man-made, like the law prohibiting incest, from which the strong trauma of the oedipal castration complex is the universally unavoidable consequence in vertical relationships (Mitchell, 2006). Her contention is that the same universally unavoidable strong trauma for the lateral relationship lies in the inevitability of the birth of a sibling, whether or not an *actual* birth, causing "weak" trauma, takes place before or after the birth of the child. So the only child, or the youngest, is subject to the same strong trauma as the oldest, because to develop into an autonomous capacity to relate to autonomous others, she or he has to recognize their separate existence. She or he must relinquish the phantasy of sole occupation of the lateral dimension, as surely as the phantasy of being in sole possession of the opposite-gender parent in the vertical dimension.

In this chapter I propose the opposite thesis: that neither the oedipal–castration complex of the vertical relationship, nor the acceptance of the existence of lateral others is necessarily universally traumatic in Mitchell's definition of strong trauma. I adhere to the view that the *only* universal strong trauma for all human experience is the fact of initial total helpless dependence on another for life itself; and that other is one who can detach herself, and is able to choose whether to sustain or abandon the totally dependent infant. So the only universal rite of passage for the development of all human relationships is the negotiation from total dependency, pre-birth and at birth, on the primary maternal attachment figure into an empowered autonomous existence. A choice can then be made whether to attach to, or detach from, equally autonomous others; and then whether to join, however fleetingly, with another, to create a child who will in its turn again be initially dependent for its existence on the choice of another. Factually, this choice may not be recognized, even by the mother. Emotionally, it is no more imperative for either gender to relinquish an original impotent/ omnipotent phantasy. This is the equivalent in Kleinian terms of maintaining a paranoid–schizoid position.

A lateral and vertical "staircase"

I have described (Morley, 2006) this alternative interdependence of the vertical with the lateral as analogous to a staircase, with each lateral tread being preceded and followed by a vertical riser. My contention has been that it is in the unconscious choices and development of couple relationships that this staircase of alternate vertical and lateral is theoretically and clinically at its crucial interface.

For the even-handed symmetry of the staircase, it could be expected that developments, or lack of them, on the lateral sibling treads should be just as worthy of psychoanalytical attention as the vertical parent–child risers. In fact, the massive volume of psychoanalytic theoretical and clinical research has focused on the study of the development of the infant from its first vertical couple with the mother. Attachment theory and neurological research has served, generally, to support and enrich psychoanalytic thought. It must indeed, then, be puzzling that we have failed hitherto, as Mitchell suggests, to develop as equally succinct a theory of unavoidable strong trauma on the lateral step as on the vertical riser. But if the *only* unavoidable human trauma is the development from the original total dependence on the mother, then the movement from one symbiotic attachment, at first inside and then outside the mother, is always going to be seen as a vertical parent–child development, whether the first trio to succeed the duo is through recognition of there being a (vertical) father or of a (lateral) sibling who is seen to occupy the third point of the triangle. So the lateral will always be subservient to the vertical. Only in twins, above all in identical twins, could a case be made for locating the original symbiosis in any other than that of infant–mother; and one twin is not in fact able to give or withhold life and nurture to the other; both start life just as totally dependent on the mother as the single-birth child needs to be.

There are, however, important differences in the way the first triad is likely to develop, or to be defended against, from the original mother–child couple, depending on whether this is via the vertical or the lateral route. Is the father the first to shatter the symbiotic mother–child duo, or is it the sibling? My contention, on which I want to focus throughout this paper, is that the route taken for this crucial development is dictated, *within the context of the*

mother's capacity to move from one-to-two-to-three, by the child's position in the family. It is the first-born child who is likely to be subject,
without dilution, to the mother's capacity to move up the
emotional staircase. Where was she in her own family of origin?
Was she able comfortably to fulfil a gender role without destructive
lateral or vertical competition? If she has indeed moved from the
primary unit of self–mother, was it via recognition of an older
sibling's relationship to the mother, or through an acceptance of a
parental couple, supposing there was one, which excluded her? Did
she set up a duo, in fact or phantasy, that only replaced the
mother–child duo by excluding her, on a lateral plane, with a
sibling or peer, or on a vertical plane with her father, stepfather,
grandparent, teacher or other adult? Or did she fail to relinquish the
primary unit at all? Aided and abetted by *her* mother, did she
manage to move into a lateral couple with a partner who became
the child's father by effectively supplanting a duo in her family of
origin rather than gaining a detached "third" position? Was the
partner she chose as co-parent someone who had the capacity to
move from one duo to another, and on to the next vertical riser,
using whatever *his* or *her* (in the case of a lesbian couple rearing a
child) position in the family dictated?

But let us presume that, unlike the mythical Oedipus, our first-
born is in the fortunate position of entering the world as the baby
part of a primary unit, of whom the mother has indeed managed the
emotional step of detachment from her own primary attachment
unit. For her lateral coupledom she has gone on to find a similarly
emotionally developed partner as co-parent. Both parents
stay alive, together, maintaining their coupledom, attached and
detached from the generation above and below. Then the first-born
should, all things being equal, be in the best place to deal with the
next onslaught if it occurs, of coping with the birth of a baby sibling.
This event will, in its turn, be generally more manageable if the new-
comer is a healthy easy baby, of the opposite gender, who stays alive
and gratifies the parents. This new sibling may even become a mutually enjoyable companion for the first-born. It is interesting to note
in this context that Freud's first displacing sibling was a boy who
died and that Freud seems never to have envisaged that a sibling
relationship could be experienced as mutually pleasurable. This will
then ease the process of further development for the first-born on to

the lateral step of siblings and peers, and then a partner who will themselves be managing their own attachment–detachment progression on the emotional vertical–lateral staircase with its secure couple junctions, ready to produce the next generation.

What an idyllic, though perhaps unlikely scenario! But maybe not so unlikely an idyll for the later-born, whose world from the start already contains a lateral other. The older sibling is, stereotypically, far more likely than the father to be the hands-on available third, ready at the maternal knee to interrupt the seamless primary unit of mother and new baby.

The later-born, of course, has the same journey to travel as the first-born, encountering the same potential obstacles to its progress from primary attachment to detachment. But she or he has what can so frequently be judged to be an advantage in having an older sibling to take the brunt of the tumultuous feeling that generally accompanies the mother's first experience of parenting. The first-born may have encountered any of the common vicissitudes of the helpless infant's initial dependence on the giants, particularly the giantess, of the world she or he has been born into. If the mother, or later the father, seeks to turn a child into an extension of herself, fulfilling the idealized phantasies of how life might have been for her "if only . . .", then the first-born is the one most likely to carry the strongest undiluted focus of this maternal–paternal repetitive compulsion. If the parental couple has not matured, individually or together, in the capacity to manage their own move from their original primary units, through their fused duo, into the triangular space that a child should be able to impose on them, then it is the first-born (like Oedipus) who is likely to be subjected to the most powerful impact of the parental lack of emotional development.

In contrast, the later-born has the advantage of a ready-made observation post, a third point of a triangle that it becomes against the duo of mother and older sibling; and from here the later-born can make a different choice of route. The first-born, who had no such choice, can provide a buffer zone for the later-born. If, on the other hand, the first-born has had a relatively benign experience of infancy, then she or he is all the more likely to be available to form a mutually gratifying sibling relationship with the later-born.

So must it always be an advantage to be later-born? Frank Sulloway, in his fascinating tome *Born to Rebel* (Sulloway, 1996) traces through the biographical accounts of a range of historically famous creative pioneers (admittedly almost exclusively male), how many were later-borns. They appeared to have been able to leave their older first-born siblings to maintain throughout their lives a rigid adherence to a parentally sustained family system in which they could predominate the niche they had first sought out when displaced as the sole baby by the later-born. If first-borns, like Freud, were creative pioneers, they would become so from within such a hierarchical system, which they would seek to maintain, resisting criticism or attack from outside. In contrast, later-borns could leave their original systems and enter "virgin" territory.

But there are, of course, an almost infinite number of variables that can interfere with these generalized stereotypical scenarios. The mother who has never been able to move from her own primary vertical unit, into a genuine stand-alone lateral relationship where she could give birth to a child whom she can allow first to attach, and then detach, is likely to remain cocooned in a similar unit with her first-born. This would mean that her later-born children are excluded, together with their father, who may be equally unable to gravitate and develop.

As a juvenile court probation officer in the 1960s, I noted what a high proportion of my delinquent probationers were from the middle of large, working-class, socially deprived families. They fulfilled the well-worn observation that when there is little parental attention to be had a child would generally do better to be the oldest or youngest of the family.

And there is, of course, the massive cross-current of gender differences, which cannot be ignored. It is well recognized that to find the comfortable unique niche in its family of origin, a child can be at an increasing disadvantage the longer the run of earlier-born siblings of the same gender. The predicament becomes worse when the *next* sibling born is, at last, the parentally longed-for other gender. Even the younger of a two-child family has often a better chance of thriving if she or he can be the opposite gender of the first-born. "If I am not the sole Majesty the Baby, I am at least the sole Princess/Prince."

Couple choice

I have written at length elsewhere (Morley, 2006) about the way in which the mutual projective identification of couple choice can so often be seen to contain the partners' same or opposite experience of their siblings. In forty years of psychotherapy practice, my co-therapist husband and I have noted, perhaps more frequently than any other such repetition, that first-borns seek mutually in later-borns a partner who will be the younger sibling she or he loved or envied, or felt guilty at displacing, and wanted to make contact with as part of her/his inner world. The youngest may reciprocate in wanting to unite with the originally loved or envied powerful oldest. With the heterosexual couple, the choice allows the male to coalesce with his female (external or internal) lateral self, including his female sexuality, and vice versa. Or the mutual choice may be of another who has also felt propelled towards fulfilling, for the parents, aspects of the opposite gender role.

My own parents' "idyllic-till-death-do-us-part" marriage would seem to have been of this order. My mother was the second-born of three, with an Oxford graduate older brother drowning himself at twenty-two at the despair of being unable, in the face of a cold unmaternal mother, to fulfil their sea-captain father's requirements of male prowess. My more masculine mother could amply displace her brother from the niche of becoming their father's *male* favourite, leaving her younger sister to be the more feminine non-academic counterpart.

My father was the first-born of two children to his mother, but with an older half-brother, whose mother had died giving birth to him, *her* first-born. He, my uncle, had dealt with this initial trauma by becoming, overtly anyway, a genial, extrovert, macho Anglo-Catholic priest, leaving my father to be the shy, sensitive, introvert writer (his beautifully written novels filled with idealized Christian solutions to the, often war-torn, relationship problems they posed), the darling of his evangelical British–Israelite mother. My father's younger sister was left to occupy the niche of an unfeminine spin-ster agnostic social worker, a pioneer of the Probation Service.

My twenty-year-old father spotted the fellow PPE undergradu-ate girl who was to become my mother cycling down the High at Oxford, with a masculine freedom like and unlike his Oxford undergraduate sister. And my mother will have found in him, I think, a replacement brother; but this time one who was comfortable with his femininity and in close touch with his mother, with whom she could unite ecstatically, not lethally displace. Following that initial sighting, my father pursued my mother to put anonymous notes and a lamp on her bicycle. On their third meeting, a University-permitted chaperone-free country walk, she did not recognize the tunes he whistled to her of "Tea for Two", "Daisy, Daisy, Give Me Your Answer, Do", and "If You Were the Only Girl in the World"; but nevertheless she accepted his overt proposal of marriage at their fourth meeting. Sixteen years and four children later, they were still exchanging daily passionate love-letters while my father sojourned in Baghdad in 1945, writing the official history of Paiforce, the British Middle-East Second World War campaign.

[But it is not necessarily without its problems to be the children, above all the first-born, of such a repetition-demanding idyllic marriage, particularly where the Truby King child-rearing method (no contact for baby between four-hour breastfeeds) was *de rigueur* for the unmaternal Oxford woman graduate of the 1920s. Of the four of us, only the second-born, my much-loved older brother, succeeded in repeating the parental pattern to the letter, becoming a confidently masculine Anglican vicar, who has just celebrated, with his four children and many grandchildren, his Golden Wedding to the girl, with a loved older brother, whom he also met as a fellow Oxford undergraduate . . .]

A multitude of other possible mix-and-match commitments may, of course, be chosen. The only child looks for the partner with many internalized sibling relationships who seeks the experience of singularity embodied by the only child. Both parents may have struggled to replace an idealized dead sibling, one apparently successfully, but at the expense of their own identity, the other always failing to fulfil that often remorseless parental pressure in the face of the unmourned dead sibling. Or both may be twins, who have sought a partner who understands that special experience, particularly when identical, of lateral relationships.

It must here be reiterated that it is not that some couple choices can be seen to embody the same or opposite internalized vertical relationships, while others reflect early experiences of lateral relationships. All such choices will embody both dimensions. There is no emotionally valid short-cut from the original vertical baby–mother unit to the next emotionally developed mother–baby duo that will allow the child of the next generation to attach and detach; no short-cut that can dispense with the growth into the lateral dimension of siblings, peers, and the new couple capable of attachment and detachment. Hence, the adult initial choice of partner will unconsciously reflect the shared same and opposite developments of the emotional journey. The unconscious hope is of making progress together, but also finding the same defences against growth. If the couple flounders and breaks, it is likely to be from the very same reasons as those for which the couple originally chose each other.

The shared couple dilemma that seeks to avoid the lateral dimension of the staircase altogether will be found when neither partner has previously internalized a viable non-fused couple that allows the individuals to co-exist intimately without fear of engulfment or separately without fear of abandonment (R. Morley, 1984). The fragile mutuality of such a choice can be all too readily fractured by the arrival of a child, imposing its triad on the duo. If the new mother then retreats into an exclusive pair with the baby, the new father may retaliate by setting up his own new duo with a sexual relationship which excludes mother and baby. He may be feeling this to be either, "You have your new baby; I have mine"; or, "You have your new fused partner; I have mine".

The task of the couple therapist/counsellor, should the couple seek outside help, has to be to understand these seemingly endless permutations of couple choice. The couple may indeed want and try to move forward. However, they may also defend against reliquishing the original idealized phantasy of a duo, the fused couple unit, which would never need to suffer the pain of becoming a trio. The intrusive third may be seen as the lateral sibling, or as *mother's adult partner*, who interrupted the original vertical pair with the mother; or, she or he may be seen as the new vertical relationship of the mother–baby, interrupting the blissful lateral couple of the adult partners.

Psychoanalytic neglect of sibling relationships

I shall now address the question of why, psychoanalytically, we have so long neglected these repetitions of the *lateral*, as opposed to the *vertical*, relationships of childhood as they appear in our clients' couple choices. Why are psychotherapists sometimes very quick to spot the "split *mother* image" of the man who must separate his sexuality from the woman who is the mother of his children, but not to see the same incestuous fear underlying the split *sister* image? Do we not notice in the transference the stereotypical hallmarks of oldest children, such as their dislike of encountering any patient who follows them into the consulting-room, rather than the one who precedes them, which will be the more likely sibling transference of the later-born?

It is, I think, an important relevant observation of the psychoanalyst Alice Miller's (Miller, 1983), that psychoanalytic therapists are drawn disproportionately from the ranks of first-born children, who are then more likely to be "parentified", presenting the aspects of themselves the parents need to find. Psychotherapists analysing patients individually put a strong emphasis on the parental transference. Often this must be a necessary stage, which may be prolonged, before the patient is able to cope with the demands of reciprocal lateral and couple relationships to which she or he can attach–detach without loss of self. I have drawn attention (Morley, 2006) to the problem occurring when the patient has entered a couple relationship, or is hoping to do so, and the therapist fails to analyse the individual patient's track-record of lateral relationships, or to look for the emerging "couple fit". In these situations it becomes all too possible for the comparatively undemanding therapeutic relationship, with its continual focus on the vertical, to be preferred, like an affair, destructively to the lateral couple. Alternatively, the therapist may be unable to compete with the patient's partner who resists any change in the unconsciously mutually chosen couple fit.

The couple therapist/counsellor has potentially greater hope of avoiding these pitfalls when she or he is seeing the couple together. But despite the enabling recognition that it is the *couple* that is the patient, the third point of the triad the two individuals are needing to attach–detach, it is still insufficiently recognized that the *trans - ference* to be interpreted is often above all to the couple, rather than to the therapist. The complex countertransference, of which I have written elsewhere (Morley 2006) is likely, whether recognized or not, to be suffused with sibling and couple lateral issues. The therapist is now one of three, perhaps feeling like the hapless parent, or like an older sibling of quarrelling younger siblings, or the unheard younger sibling excluded by the older pair. The acute discomfort then experienced by the therapist can make it hard not to act out the countertransference; to split the couple into their individual components and become the vertical–parental judge, however even-handedly trying to support first one and then the other. The focus can now be lost on the couple-as-patient, containing the transferred interlocking sibling, as well as parental issues of the two individuals. Although it may sometimes be useful to work individually with the couple seeking therapy, rather than to refer them elsewhere, this is a very different matter, working always with the couple-in-mind, from seeing only the individual patient.

The basic rules of individual psychoanalytic work can seem sometimes ill-adapted to couple therapy. A once-weekly fifty-minute session can be pitifully inadequate and a longer session may be more appropriate. The requirement to keep rigidly to the same session times, to charge for missed sessions, to focus heavily on the impact of breaks; all tend to prioritize the therapeutic relationship, when this may be at the expense of the couple. The "parent" therapist needs perhaps to become the "parent-in-law", giving pride of place to the lateral couple that needs to detach from the vertical. Both Freud and some of his followers may have been in the first-born's predicament, anticipating no joy from the impact on the maternal duo either of the parental couple or from the birth of younger siblings. Even the use of two therapists, helpful as this may be in resolving some of the transference dilemmas of the vulnerable, single couple therapist, may not escape the autobiographical limitations of our psychoanalytic founders, or of their disciples.

Summary

This chapter has given further thought to the question of why psychoanalysis has been neglectful of exploring "lateral" (sibling) relationships in favour of the overwhelming concentration on "vertical" (parent–child) relationships. I dispute Freud's assertion that the oedipal–castration complex is the universally inescapable "strong" trauma of all *vertical* relationships; together with Juliet

Mitchell's proposition that it is the equally universal trauma of *lateral* relationships to be displaced by a sibling, real or phantasized. I propose that the only universal trauma for all mankind is the fact of the initial total helpless dependence for life on the mother. The only route upwards on the relational developmental staircase of alternate vertical and lateral steps, with "the couple" at each intersection, depends on a capacity to relinquish the original symbiotic mother–baby duo in favour of a trio, a triangular space that allows for thought, independent movement, and choice. To make this move depends quintessentially on how the mother has been experienced in the original vertical duo.

Within the context of that relationship, the single most important influential factor is likely to be the position in the family of origin. It is the first-born who is most likely to have her/his first exposure to the "third", the "not mother", in the father. She or he is likely to be exposed to the parents at their least experienced vulnerability. She or he then may go on to confront a second manifestation of the trauma, on the lateral dimension, from displacement by a later-born sibling.

A later-born is more likely to have an older sibling as her/his first "third", from birth, so that neither the impact of father, nor displacement by a sibling, is likely to be so traumatic. But since all childhood experience is based initially on the quality of the first pairing with mother, this "vertical" relationship is always going to be the foremost all-important reference point. Even if, within that context, lateral relationships play a different role, benign or malign, from the vertical, they cannot equal that first dimension at the immutable start of life.

The couple is seen as the crucial transition point from one dimension to the other, depending on its capacity to create and maintain its integrity while allowing a third, the child, to attach vertically and then detach laterally. It is questioned whether a greater than average number of psychoanalytic practitioners may be first-borns, and, perhaps as "parentified" children themselves, may want to ward off threesomes, both privately and professionally. This may include a preference for working in the one-to-one transference–countertransference of individual psychoanalytic therapy rather than accepting the demands of threesome couple therapy, where the impact of siblings may be harder to ignore.

References

Miller, A. (1983). *The Drama of the Gifted Child: The Search foe the True self.* New York: Basic Books.

Mitchell, J. (2003). *Siblings: Sex and Violence.* Cambridge: Polity.

Mitchell, J. (2006). Sibling trauma; a theoretical consideration. In: P. Coles (Ed.), *Sibling Relationships* (pp. 155–174). London: Karnac.

Morley, E. (2006). The influence of sibling relationships on couple choice and development. In: P. Coles (Ed.), *Sibling Relationships* (pp. 197–224). London: Karnac.

Morley, R. (1984). *Intimate Strangers.* London: Family Welfare Association.

Sulloway, F. J. (1996). *Born to Rebel.* London: Little, Brown.

CHAPTER FIVE

Ghosts of early sibling relationships in couples

Jody J. Leader

Introduction

I n this chapter I consider the impact family-of-origin sibling relationships can have on couples. After reviewing the literature
on sibling relationships, I use clinical examples from couple
work to illustrate how these issues might manifest in the consulting
room. Finally, I offer some thoughts on technique and make some
suggestions for future work in the field of couple therapy.

I have been inspired to focus on siblings and couples, in part,
because of my experience of psychoanalysis. My first task in analysis was working through issues that sprang from my early relationship with my mother, and after a few years I started to engage
with issues rooted in my relationship with my father. It was only
then that I felt secure enough to look more closely at my relationship with my younger sister. I was surprised to discover that some
of my most entrenched ways of looking at myself, family, friends,
and the world around me were coloured, often in broad strokes, by
my childhood relationship with her. The fact that it took so many
years of analytic work to reach this realization speaks to the psychoanalytic discipline's nearly singular focus on parental attachments,

almost to the exclusion of the enduring influence of sibling relationships. My analyst, because of her training, focused more on
the maternal and paternal transference than on sibling transference.
Looking through the oedipal lens requires that therapists, analysts, and couple therapists focus on their patients' mature, adult
attachments as reflections of old parental imagoes, not sibling
imagoes.

Further motivation for writing this chapter came from the recognition from colleagues when I told them that I was studying the
impact of siblings on couples. They vividly recalled stories of their
own patients whose siblings had an enormous impact on their lives
and their ways of relating. They described how the impact of their
own sibling relationships was alive in their friendships and romantic entanglements. One colleague eagerly phoned to refer his individual patient for couple therapy and left a message saying, "She
wants some help with her boyfriend. They've been fighting bitterly.
She's feeling really stuck . . . Oh, and she hates her sister."

As couple therapists, we are all familiar with the bickering
couple who look more like a brother and sister fighting over the
television remote control than two committed and compassionate
adults having a disagreement. The very structure of the couple therapy situation encourages sibling dynamics. The therapist, in the
authority-figure role with the couple, replicates the power relationship of a parent with two siblings. But in this chapter I go further
and suggest that sibling relationships can infiltrate the very fibre of
our intimate relationships. For some couples, managing the impact
of family-of-origin sibling relationships in the here and now can
turn into a complex developmental challenge. For example, the way
we think about our partners, talk to them, the roles we play, the
assumptions, both unconscious or otherwise, that we have about
what makes a "good" relationship, and how we argue and fight,
may be rooted in our sibling relationships. This is not to say that
sibling relationships have more of an influence on couples than
primary care-giver relationships. Those very early attachments to
parental figures delineate future object choice and relationship
dynamics in a way that sibling relationships cannot. However,
when the parental attachment is limited, dysfunctional, or non-
existent, or when parents favour one sibling over the other, the
sibling relationship can become an influential force.

Literature review

Although Freud had an interest in sibling relationships (he was quite candid about the enormous impact of his sibling-like relationship with one of his nephews), he virtually ignored sibling issues in his major treatises. Many of his cases are peppered with instances of rivalrous sibling relationships, for example the "Rat Man" (Freud, 1909d) and the "Wolf Man" (Freud, 1918b), but, in the end, his theories gave more weight to the mother–child and father–child relationship. This legacy, which is the foundation of so much of our clinical work today, explains in part, why psychotherapists have generally not explored sibling relationships as a way to increase their understanding of their patients' psychology of relating in the present.

Children often spend more individual time with their siblings than with their parents. Sibling relationships impact on one's very sense of self (Sandmaier, 1994) and provide rich opportunities for mutual learning and teaching (Collona & Newman, 1983). It is through sibling relationships that the first understanding of group feelings develops, as well as the first stirrings of the importance of justice (Freud, 1921c). In their seminal book *The Sibling* (1970), Sutton-Smith and Rosenberg explained how differently gendered sibling pairs and birth order have a differential effect on personality and intelligence. Since the late 1970s, many authors have written about the importance sibling relationships can have on object choice (Abend, 1984; Sharpe & Rosenblatt, 1994; Toman, 1988).

The impact that sibling relationships have on adult love relationships is complex. Judith Lasky and Susan Mulliken (1988) have noted how healthy sibling relationships encourage the development of subtle empathic communications and the ability to authentically "get inside" another's experience. These early relationships influence each adult's preferred level of intimacy, as well as their distinct style of communication and the kinds of defences they employ. When sibling relationships are conflictual, and those conflicts remain unresolved in adulthood, there is a compulsion to repeat. Klagsbrun (1992) states in her book *Mixed Feelings* that

> We repeat rivalries and jealousies, self-images of inferiority and sometimes of grandiosity, guilt and fears, power plays and

> struggles for separateness. We turn others in our lives into the siblings we had or wish we had or wish we had handled differently, and see ourselves as we once were or wish we were or wish we had not been. In a dozen different ways with a dozen different people, we re-enact strains or difficulties or unfulfilled desires of our sibling history. [p. 333]

For instance, a partner may have played a circumscribed role with their sibling throughout childhood, for example as rescuer, controller, pseudo-parent, companion, torturer, or competitor, only to grow up and expect the same of, or project the same on to, their adult partner.

Transference is one major way through which these repetitions reveal themselves in the consulting room. But while transference has traditionally referred to the way a patient "transfers" his/her unconscious and conscious feelings about significant people from his/her past, usually parental figures, on to the therapist, transference in couple therapy is clearly in evidence in the transference between the partners. That is to say, a partner "transfers" his/her feelings about past significant figures on to the partner, instead of the therapist. The idea of partner-to-partner transference was first alluded to by Skynner (1980), who described the ways partners perceive and manipulate each other as if they resemble important figures from childhood. Reich (1999) and Newmark (2004) revived this concept to describe partner-to-partner transference reactions that occur in a session in which both partners are present. Newmark emphatically states:

> I believe it is the early recognition and identification of partner-to-partner transferences and the exploration of the origins and current manifestations of those transferences that enable successful psychotherapy with the most destructive and intransigent relational patterns. [p. 4]

Sibling transference is a relatively little known and unexplored phenomenon. It was first alluded to in Freud's seminal work on transference (1912b), but only as a passing reference. Sixty-six years later, Lesser (1978) urged analysts to systematically explore sibling transference to free rigid life patterns. Others followed, writing about the importance of sibling transference in individual therapy and sometimes noting the impact of childhood sibling relationships in partner choice (Klagsbrun, 1992; Kivowitz, 1995; Moser, Jones, Zaorski, Mirsalimi, & Luchner, 2005; Shechter, 1999). None specifically articulated this phenomenon as a force in couple therapy. In an article on sibling relationships and mature love, Lasky and Mulliken (1988) note that sibling relationships can be helpful in excavating "the hidden recesses of repetitive neurotic behaviour in intractable contemporary love relationships" (p. 85), but they stop short of directly applying their work to couple therapy.

Klagsbrun (1992) has argued that internalized childhood sibling images can have an even greater impact on couples than parental images. Morley (2006) writes how "the couple's relationship [is] one of transference to the couple of their lateral sibling relationships, the quality of which had been dictated by their experience of their vertical parent–child relationships" (p. 213). In my experience, the ghosts of early childhood sibling relationships often loom large in the space between partners who experience conflict. Sibling relationships are not necessarily more important than parental relationships, but they can be very influential and this chapter is built on my contention that couple therapists can help embattled, entrenched couples by paying attention to partner-to-partner sibling transference reactions.

The nature of partner–partner sibling transference

The sibling transference between partners becomes manifest when one unconsciously perceives traits of her sibling in her partner. A personality trait, a tone of voice, or a habit may trigger the transference reaction. Even the partner's silences may unwittingly offer a blank screen on which to project sibling characteristics. Sometimes the pull of the past is so prevailing that just the very act of committing to an adult partnership is enough to trigger sibling transference. A spouse may also unwittingly project the well-rooted and circumscribed sibling role she experienced in her family of origin on to the partner. The role may be so familiar to her, so engrained in her unconscious, that she "sees" the other playing the role too.

How are clinicians able to recognize sibling transferences? The intensity of a couple's interactions in couple therapy can be an indicator, especially in a kind of push–pull power struggle. Reich (1999) emphasized the importance of noticing the partners' idealizations of each other. In my experience, partners' denigrations of the other can also be signposts of sibling transferences. Lasky & Mulliken (1988) have noted that the childhood sibling situation is most directly replicated in the adult love relationship when the partners are generally unaware or insistently denying or repressing the influence of their childhood sibling relationships.

Sibling relationships appear more likely to impact on adult couple relationships, positively or negatively, if the childhood sibling bond was strong and enduring. Bank and Kahn (1997) found that the conditions necessary for the development of this bond include a high degree of accessibility between siblings or, if separated, fantasies of contact between siblings, ineffective or absent parental presence or influence, and siblings playing a part in the development of personal identity. A strong sibling bond is also likely to develop when the opposite-sex parent has qualities that make him or her difficult to admire. In these instances, opposite-sex siblings may often act as oedipal stand-ins, making the sibling relationship that much more potent (Lasky & Mulliken, 1988). Factors that mediate the impact of a sibling bond on adult love relationships include the age of siblings, family constellation, and parental fantasies about each sibling.

Clinical cases

The following are some examples from my clinical work with couples. I have changed identifying details to protect the confidentiality of the patients, all of whom have given their permission to use aspects of our work together for the purpose of this chapter.

Fiona and Harry

With this couple, manifestations of the sibling transference were already present in the very first session. Fiona and Harry are both accomplished, articulate, graduate students who had been together for five years. They contacted me for short-term couple therapy. "We fight a lot," Fiona explains in the first session, and adds, "He's uptight and controlling." The couple then explains that they find themselves engaged in verbal sparring over trivial matters, such as the correct pronunciation of a word. Harry talks about the arguments as if they're annoying inconveniences. Fiona admits that the content of their fights may be trivial, but she is clearly distressed. The conflicts shake her at her core and she's not sure why. She wonders why Harry doesn't seem to be as affected by the disagreements as she is. "Do you think about these fights, in between the fights?" she asks him. I ask them to relay their respective personal histories, directing them to focus on familial and love relationships, including relationships with siblings. Fiona tells me about her older, estranged sister, whom she "hates". "My sister is rigid, deeply controlling, and cannot admit she's wrong," Fiona says. She continues, "This manifests in shockingly unpleasant personality traits: she is a bully." Fiona then talks about the sister with a bitterness tinged with longing and says "She plays a large role in my life and I position myself to be the opposite of her."

I now pay attention to Fiona's question to Harry about whether he thinks about their fights, in a different light. The question now appears more as a plea, not just to her partner, but to her sister, wondering if she, too, feels hurt and wounded by their estrangement. I realize she has also used the same words to describe both Harry and her sister. Shreds of hope and a longing for reunion with the sister appear to have kept many painful feelings alive for Fiona in such a way that they have infiltrated her relationship with her partner.

Victor and Betty

With some couples, a partner's role as a childhood sibling may have been to "over-function", or, in other words, to act as a pseudo parent to a sibling. If feelings about being relegated to this role remain unacknowledged and unprocessed, the couple relationship will suffer.

Victor, a forty-five-year-old health care professional, adopted over time a role with his wife that he once played with his brain-damaged older brother. Before the boating accident that left him disabled, Victor's brother was full of promise, smart, ambitious, and athletic. The morning of the accident, Victor, then eleven, had begged his mother to let him and the brother to go canoeing. Their mother was reluctant, saying the water was too cold, but Victor had pleaded until she finally relented. Victor's brother, then seventeen, nearly drowned when the boat accidentally capsized. He fell into a coma. There ensued long weeks in the hospital in which Victor and his guilty feelings were never attended to by his parents. Over time, it was discovered that his brother suffered brain damage that caused impulsivity, insecurity, and some cognitive deficits. To this day, Victor feels he had a part in his brother's injuries. The brother he knew died that day and a part of Victor believes that if hadn't pleaded with their mother, his brother might have gone on to fulfil the promise of his youth. Wracked with guilt, young Victor gradually took on the role as his brother's protector, coach, cheerleader, and pseudo-parent. While at college, he spent long hours with his brother on the phone, cajoling and advising, trying to keep him safe.

Now as an adult, with his new wife Betty and a baby, he finds himself in a similar role. Despite Betty's obvious sensitivity and competence in childcare, Victor feels he has to tell her what to do. "This sponge goes here", he might say, or "Don't put it on the counter, it has just been on the floor", or "You have to wash that before it gets near the baby." In other words, he treats his active, healthy and educated wife as if she was disabled, and complains bitterly about having to do it. He is enraged that he feels he is the one to do and think of everything. "I'm always the voice of reason," he says bitterly, and "I feel like I'm her mother." Victor never felt safe enough to voice his frustration with his disabled brother. Because of his guilt feelings, he has repressed and swallowed his anger. With Betty he now finds himself thrown back into the role he played with his brother. In the course of our work together, we were able to understand that this was a way for him of trying to master his past experiences.

The power of Victor's sibling transference is much more intense because, as an only child, Betty, for her part, was both overindulged and plagued by an intrusive mother. In a sense, she was "disabled" by her mother. Traits, such as to nag and to pester, feel safe and familiar to Betty, even though it "disables" her wish to become more self-sufficient and self-motivated. A consequence of this impasse is that as much as Victor nags, Betty feels no motivation to modify her stance. Victor, through the sibling transference, imagines that what he witnesses in his partner is his brother's disability, and as his wife apparently does not contradict this perception it has turned into an irrational but firm belief. This interaction between Victor and Betty serves as an illustration of how the system created between the two has rigidified the sibling transference.

Hector and Wanda

Conflictual, sibling-like, childhood *peer* relationships can also have a searing impact on adult relationships. An example of this particular type of transference is demonstrated in the case of Hector and Wanda, a recently married couple who have been attending couple psychotherapy for one year. Both feel stuck and pessimistic about their relationship.

> Wanda complains that Hector doesn't attend to her as much as, or in the same way, that he attends to his siblings. She constantly feels as if he prioritizes work and family over their relationship. "I saw you having an intimate conversation with your brother at the reunion," she complains, "and you never talk to me like that." Occasionally, Hector plays in an amateur basketball club and will stay out late. Wanda then feels lonely and feels he's treating her as second class, prioritizing others over her. These feelings persist despite Hector's exasperated, yet heartfelt insistence that he loves and values her. He just wants to play basketball every once in a while.
>
> As I have done many times in previous sessions with this couple, I probe into Wanda's past by asking if this feels familiar. She says she always felt on the fringes of the popular girl groups in school, being included in some activities, but not invited to all the parties. At that moment she recalls a traumatic event from when she was a ten-year-old schoolgirl, when girls from her soccer team, whom she always regarded as close friends, vandalized her locker while she was on vacation. They covered it with misogynistic slurs and decorated it with feminine hygiene products. She remembers not only the devastation and humiliation, but also the fact that she had no one to talk to about it. Her mother knew about it, but did not ask her about her feelings. The trauma of humiliation was reinforced by her mother's disinterest. I put it to her that I think she is seeing Hector through the lens of these old, painful relationships that she experienced with her friends and her parents. I suggest, "When you were growing up, there wasn't the emotional space and support to process all the frustration you experienced as a little girl. You still have mountains of feeling inside you about being a part of this difficult family constellation and difficult friendship constellation, and it's coming out in your relationship with Hector. He can do nothing right in your eyes, because your past is impairing your vision." Wanda's eyes filled with tears as I was saying this and she said, "You know, you're exactly right. I know you've been

saying this for months, but now I get it. It feels like a relief." She was beginning to see how their difficulties were related more to these unprocessed feelings from the past rather than directly with her husband.

There are other ways that sibling dynamics impact on this couple. Hector often fends off his wife's attempts to get to know how he feels. He becomes defensive when she talks about wanting to have "deep" conversations about their relationship and claims that there is nothing to talk about. Wanda appears hungry for more intimacy. She knows "it's there", but she feels unable to reach it in Hector. In a recent couple session, an off-hand remark by Hector about his older brother led to a discussion that illuminated a powerful sibling transference. After his father's tragic death, when Hector was eleven, his oldest brother assumed a paternal role that involved affirming, encouraging, and emotionally supporting his younger siblings. This always rankled with Hector, who felt uncomfortable with the brother's overly emotional style. The family had never talked much about feelings, and Hector wanted to keep it that way. As an adult, Hector now feels that anyone who campaigns to get him to talk about his feelings is annoying. Consequently, he fears that if he were to become a more emotional and vulnerable person with Wanda, *he* would be annoying. This powerful imago has stood in the way of greater expressive and psychological intimacy with his wife.

Some thoughts about technique

Talking to couples about transference issues can be tricky. One has to have a firm belief in the significance of transference to be able to talk about it in a compelling way. It can feel forced if the therapist is unconvinced that the transference dynamic is alive. Handling of the transference requires setting the stage in the very first session. One might say "I wonder if you're talking to, or about people who are not in the room", or "Who does he remind you of?", or "Is this a familiar feeling?" The therapist thus lets the couple know the currency of the therapist, so that later, when sibling transference is evident and vivid, bringing it up is not so awkward.

A thorough history gathered at the beginning of the treatment is essential. It is important to listen carefully to the "feeling" words each partner uses to describe their siblings. Often the words will be similar to those used to describe their partner. When one believes sibling transference is alive during a couple's entrenched, fiery, or repetitive conflict, each partner could helpfully be asked to explore their feelings in the moment. At such a point, it is not contraindicated to do some individual therapy during the couple session. To mirror, empathize, and encourage each partner to go deeper into their feelings, models to the couple how each needs to see the other as a separate person. Along those lines, one might ask each partner to describe their feelings from different perspectives; how they feel about their partner, how they feel about themselves in the situation, how they imagine their partner feels about them, and, if indicated, how they imagine the therapist feels about them. If echoes of old sibling relationships seem active in the room, that may be the time to gently offer an interpretation of sibling transference to the couple as a way of helping them to appreciate the power that drives their current feelings. Sometimes this can dissipate the intensity of the conflict immediately. At other times, the interpretation may need to be repeated over a number of sessions, or explained in different ways before it has an impact.

In certain situations sibling transference may develop towards the couple therapist. A partner may unconsciously recruit the couple therapist to play a sibling role. During the third year of treatment of Victor and Betty, I began to feel uncharacteristically "disabled" during sessions. I felt stuck and at a loss for words. The progress we had made in the early months, before the birth of their child, slowly ground to a halt and a sense of hopelessness pervaded the sessions. It was only through consulting with colleagues that I began to understand how Victor's intense, unconscious, split-off feelings of anger and frustration, intended for his disabled sibling, instead were disabling both Betty, the treatment, and me. I interpreted this to the couple to help them begin to understand the roots of their sense of despair.

It is natural that a therapist's own sibling relationships may have a huge impact on couple therapy. The triadic nature of the situation is fertile ground for the therapist's own transference feelings, perhaps perceiving the couple as her own siblings. For instance, if a couple is quarrelling in the session and the therapist feels unable to get a word in edgeways, she might be unconsciously transported to, say, her family's dinner table when she was silenced by her own bickering siblings (Pizer & Pizer, 2004). The more the therapist knows herself and the impact of her own sibling relationships, the more equipped she is to help her couples know themselves. Bank and Kahn (1997) describe this phenomenon occurring also in family therapy. Some therapists may be resistant to looking at sibling issues. Bank and Kahn speculate that some traditional family systems therapists are less likely to see sibling transference in their couples because they are focused on returning the balance of power in dysfunctional families back to the parents. The supremacy of the children, and logically, siblings, must always be lesser than the parents' authority. Sibling issues are thus rarely explored. They also speculate that therapists are often first-borns who were necessarily robbed of exclusive maternal attention by their siblings and thus are less likely to be tolerant of sibling issues and less likely to explore them. One might ask, what is the relationship between sibling relationships and parental relationships and how does one disentangle the influence of each? This topic is beyond the scope of this chapter; however, Lasky and Mulliken (1988) have noted that "the sibling relationship may be a new edition of the oedipal relationship, but this time with a less dangerous, more available, yet still taboo object" (p. 85). They characterize sibling relationships as having a more "ghostly resonance" when compared with more obvious parental influences. They acknowledge that in many instances, sibling and parental influences are intertwined, making disentangling them impossible.

Suggestions for future work

In addition to looking at the differences and similarities between parental and sibling transferences, much more needs to be explored in the area of sibling transference in couple work. For example, what happens when a conflictual sibling relationship continues into adulthood? How does that sibling's adult partner position themselves *vis-à-vis* the sibling conflict? How does this impact on the love partnership? Is sibling transference manifested differently in same sex couples? What is the impact of positive sibling transference on couples? The answers to these kinds of questions will lie in our work with couples, especially when we are able to be open to see and hear the ghosts and echoes of childhood sibling relationships in our consulting rooms.

References

Abend, S. M. (1984). Sibling love and object choice. *Psychoanalytic Quarterly, 53*: 425–430.

Bank, S., & Kahn, M. (1997). *The Sibling Bond*. New York: Basic Books.

Collona, A., & Newman, L. (1983). The psychoanalytic literature on siblings. *The Psychoanalytic Study of the Child, 38*: 285–309.

Freud, S. (1909d). Notes upon a case of obsessional neurosis. *S.E., 10*: 153–249. London: Hogarth.

Freud, S. (1912b). The dynamics of transference. *S.E., 12*. 97–108. London: Hogarth.

Freud, S. (1918b). From the history of an infantile neurosis. *S.E., 17*: 7–122. London: Hogarth.

Freud, S. (1921c). Group psychology and the analysis of the ego. *S.E., 18*: 67–143. London: Hogarth.

Kivowitz, A. (1995). Attending to sibling issues and transferences in psychodynamic psychotherapy. *Clinical Social Work Journal, 23*(1): 37–46.

Klagsbrun, F. (1992). *Mixed Feelings: Love, Hate, Rivalry, and Reconciliation Among Brothers and Sisters*. New York: Bantam.

Lasky, J., & Mulliken, S. (1988). Sibling relationships and mature love. In: J. Lasky & H. Silverman (Eds.), *Love: Psychoanalytic Perspectives* (pp. 81–92). New York: New York University Press.

Lesser, R. (1978). Sibling transference and countertransference. *Journal of the American Academy of Psychoanalysis, 6*: 37–49.

Morley, E. (2006). The influence of sibling relationships on couple choice and development. In: P. Coles (Ed.), *Sibling Relationships* (pp. 197–224). London: Karnac.

Moser, C. J., Jones, R. A., Zaorski, D. M., Mirsalimi, H., & Luchner, A. F. (2005). The impact of the sibling in clinical practice: transference and countertransference dynamics. *Psychotherapy: Theory, Research, Practice, Training, 42*(3): 267–278.

Newmark, J. (2004). Partner–partner transference in couple therapy: the storm before the calm. Paper presented at the Spring Meeting of Division 39 of the American Psychological Association, Miami, Florida.

Pizer, B., & Pizer, S. (2004). The gift of an apple or the twist of an arm: negotiation in couples and couple therapy. Paper presented at a fall workshop sponsored by the Massachusetts Association for Psychoanalytic Psychology, Cambridge, Massachusetts.

Reich, K. (1999). Nature of therapeutic action in psychoanalytic couples therapy. Paper presented at the Spring Meeting of Division 39 of the American Psychological Association, New York.

Sandmaier, M. (1994). *Original Kin: The Search for Connection Among Adult Sisters and Brothers*. New York: Dutton.

Sharpe, S., & Rosenblatt, A. (1994). Oedipal sibling triangles. *Journal of the American Psychoanalytic Association, 42*: 491–523.

Shechter, R. (1999). The meaning and interpretation of sibling-transference in the clinical situation. *Issues in Psychoanalytic Psychology, 21*(1–2): 1–10.

Skynner, A. C. R. (1980). Recent developments in marital therapy. *Journal of Family Therapy, 2*: 271–296.

Sutton-Smith, B., & Rosenberg, B. G. (1970). *The Sibling*. New York: Holt, Rinehart.

Toman, W. (1988). Basics of family structure and sibling position. In M. D. Kahn & K. G. Lewis (Eds.), *Siblings in Therapy: Life Span and Clinical Issues* (pp. 46–65). New York: Norton.

CHAPTER SIX

Dysfunctional aspects of couple relationships observed in a therapeutic group

Barbara Bianchini and Fabio Monguzzi

Introduction

The aim of this chapter is to describe our method of treating dysfunctional couple and parent–child relationships by means of group therapy.

We describe our experience of conducting a group consisting of parental couples who requested help in dealing, not with disturbances in their marital relationships, but with problems concerning their adolescent children. Moreover, they presented as parents, who, when facing difficulties in managing their relationships, experienced a profound sense of bewilderment, impotence, anger and inadequacy.

The presence of an adolescent in a family often reactivates unresolved problems in his or her parents. They find themselves grappling with the phantoms of their own adolescence while simultaneously, as parents, they feel ill-equipped to respond to the educational needs of a son or daughter who is increasingly less like the "child" they once knew. The children of the couples who come to us do have objective difficulties in their own right, and are perceived as being more fragile and less autonomous than their contemporaries. For them the organisation of the family is based on a suffocating tie of dependence and reciprocal control.

This dynamic is perhaps mirrored in the kind of conflicting demands with which we often find ourselves having to cope in our clinical practice. We see the couples' request for help as signalling an urgent need to restore relationships that are currently in a critical state, and which remain essential for the good functioning of family life. We refer, for example, to the ties of alliance and intimacy in the couple and the bond of attachment between parents and children. At the same time, we are also aware of the risk that any proposed therapeutic intervention may be neutralized by the power of deep-rooted relational dynamics. Furthermore, parents who seek help in this way give therapists a difficult task, due to the implicit urgency of the request itself and the untrusting feelings that accompany it, because they very frequently see their children as irreparably damaged and therefore as "not normal". As therapists, we are aware that what has in fact been damaged at that moment is the capacity to resume caring for oneself and the other, and that restoring this capacity takes time and a lot of hard work (Norsa, 2004).

Our first therapeutic commitment is therefore to construct a setting that can act as a container for anxiety, and thus perhaps transform alarm and urgency into concern and an ability to listen.

The value of group therapy

We believe that group therapy can respond to some important needs of couples and allow the creation of a model of sharing and communication, which up until that time has proved to be precarious, if not totally inadequate, or non-existent. Our groups consist exclusively of parental couples. This choice of therapeutic focus is based on the centrality of the couple as the founding nucleus of a family, and the consequent therapeutic need to observe its interactive dynamics and understand its organization.

The principal objective is to establish a meeting place in which the group's participants can stimulate and confront each other, and perhaps recover their ability to acknowledge and use their emotions as a means of understanding and communication. The attendance of both partners provides an invaluable opportunity to demonstrate in a tangible way how the parents' interaction and behaviour and the way they represent their adolescent children to the group is linked with the projected affect. As a result of its function of recognition and mirroring, the group can allow partners to rediscover themselves in a conjugal and familial historical–affective continuity that may become lost during periods of significant transition, such as happen with the emergence of signs of their children's emancipation.

It is also important to point out that it is often only thanks to the presence or absence of their partner at a session, and to the containment of the group, that some parents can be aware of previously unexpressed emotional experiences relating to their partner, and can thus find it possible to express themselves in a place where they are listened to and welcomed.

Patients in a group may be more able to confront the challenge of seeking their own "truth", which corresponds less to an obsessive search for cause–effect relations and more to self-liberation from coercion, as well as the adoption of responsible planning for one's own existence. All of this can take place in a constant dialectic that permits an exchange of experiences, not only between fusional and individuational movements, but also between what happens inside and what happens outside the group.

Our group model

The groups that we run may comprise up to six parental couples. Each group meets, as part of a public service, for an hour and a quarter once a week for three years. They are co-conducted by two therapists representing a heterosexual couple. The decision to conduct the group "as a couple" seemed to be particularly appropriate as a means of activating transference and countertransference dynamics, so as to facilitate the better articulation of identifications and projections in the participants.

The presence of two therapists, a man and a woman, working together in couple psychoanalytical therapy, is itself rich in significance, as has been pointed out, for example, in Dicks (1967), Losso (2000), Norsa and Zavattini (1997). The work of the therapeutic couple, provided that they are capable of continuously interpreting between them the themes that progressively emerge during the course of the sessions, has a value that is, *per se*, reparatory and containing, and also provides a model of bonding. The importance of this tie is evidenced by the patients' attacks, the envy it arouses, and patients' attempts to ally themselves with, or to seduce, first one and then the other therapist.

It is not difficult to imagine that such a configuration mobilizes powerful exclusion anxieties and, in some cases, phantoms of persecution, not to mention curiosity and fantasies concerning the "secret life of the therapists" beyond the therapeutic scenario. These curiosities and fantasies are phantoms of the primary scene brought to life during group sessions by the joint attendance of the therapists, who also represent the image of a parental couple at work.

Parents in the group have an opportunity to experience a particular range of identifications: with the other parents, with their own parents, both internal and external, with their children, with the children of other parents, with the husbands and wives of the other members, and with the therapist couple.

It is important to underline the fact that, although the parents often invite the therapists to meet the children, this does not happen. Instead, the therapists prefer to relate to them as they are presented by their parents, within the context of the sessions.

The parental partners' feelings of having been damaged and their related sense of hurt drive them to project these feelings on to one another in the hope of eliciting concrete responses. This way they do not have to respond personally to their hurt feelings. This dynamic is often repeated in the countertransference and manifested in the relationship between the therapists. We have observed in our clinical practice that the defences which are employed in the dysfunctional relationships between parents and children entail particularly the offloading of hurt and suffering on to the other. The same defence is adopted in relation to the therapists, who also frequently find themselves caught up in feelings of impotence and anger, or in a conflict concerning their respective therapeutic interventions. In this regard, it is necessary to stress that an important part of the therapeutic work involved in the treatment of dysfunctional parental relationships is done outside the group setting, in the intrapsychic dialogue of each therapist and in the interpersonal dialogue between them.

Clinical illustrations

We now describe some of the sequences that are characteristic of the three-year life of one particular group.

The initial phase

In the initial phase, when the group was attended by four couples, we faced a number of difficulties. For the first few meetings, group members' participation in the sessions was irregular, due to contingencies such as hospitalization, road accidents, and illness. The most painful issues were thus communicated very concretely, as a physical body that had become suddenly fragile.

At first, participation in the sessions was justified, on a conscious level, by the problems exhibited by the children and their parents' request for advice. Thus they asked us directly, "How should we behave?" and the fact that we did not give any direct answers of the kind, "You should act like this", progressively aroused reactions of profound anger, such as, "What are you here for?"

In this phase, the group was not seen as a shared space for reflection, but rather as a place in which to receive "recipes". At a deeper level, group participants were characterized by a marked sense of inadequacy, as if to say, "We are here because we are incapable". Participants also identified with each other, on the basis of their common experiences and the recurrent difficulty of being a parent, which might be expressed as, "My child does the same as yours".

As therapists, we perceived the anguish aroused by trying to communicate in close relationships, as the group progressively revealed their difficulties of communicating both within their couple relationships and with their children. We witnessed their desire for a magical fulfilment of omnipotent wishes, their collusion with their children's reaction to the absence of there being room for expectations and the lack of a structure that would offer adequate emotional dependability.

Dario and Marina

Dario and Marina described the pressures they felt subjected to by their children, who pursued them with continuous requests for money for clothes and consumer goods and then denigrated them because they could not afford to meet these demands. Their daughter attended a state-run classical high school in the centre of town, and felt inadequate because her parents did not have as much money as the parents of her schoolmates, money to which she claimed to have a "right".

The parents continually brought to the group their deep anger and apprehension about their inability to respond immediately to her requests. They seemed to be imprisoned between a slavish tendency to respond to any request and a violent refusal to comply with it. Thus, the reference values of their children were not questioned, and no form of mediation seemed to be possible. We noted that, in a situation of role reversal, their children were seen by Dario and Marina as judges of their abilities as parents; in such a relational model, it is only possible to play the part of the accused or the accuser.

The group culture during this first phase was prevalently one of impotence versus omnipotence with a primitive–narcissistic basis for relating; the children's affective needs were not listened to either because of their parents' helplessness, or because they were considered as being impossible to listen to.

The unconscious request aimed at the therapists was to offer a model of omnipotence, whereas we tried to appeal to the parental couples' actual resources. Anxieties about being inadequate were also current, along with an inability to identify and access personal potential. The apparent perceived fault lay somewhere between impotence and omnipotence (Corbella, 2003), and it was lobbed from one partner to the other, without either seeming capable of assuming responsibility for it.

The intermediate phase

Subsequently the group started to develop a narrative and historical awareness; members' absences, entrances and exits led to the emergence of a different dimension of thinking that was prospective and to the acquisition of a more complex and articulated temporal awareness. Group members began to see the possibility and potential of gaining access to depressive position thinking. The dimension of time can be transformative, and seeing something in greater perspective may also change subjectively the way it feels. The group's participants began to notice the differences between one another and, at the same time, there was an emergence of an increasingly deep emotional discomfort.

The parental couples found it difficult to call their children by their names and talked about them as if their internal images of the children were vague and obscure. It became clear to the therapists that it was necessary to bring the children more into focus. The therapists also found it difficult to call the group members by their names, and to be more curious and interactive in relation to what was emerging in the group.

Francesco and Rosaria

> Several months after its beginning, a new couple joined the group. Despite their agreement, however, to attend on a long-term basis, Francesco and Rosaria only came to a few sessions. Nevertheless, their presence made us see increasingly clearly how the children's relational attitudes were represented and re-enacted by the parents in the group.

> In particular, Francesco enabled us to highlight more clearly the impact of poor communication when he behaved in the group just as his son did towards him, by antagonistically demonstrating his difference. He seemed to say, "You must accept me as I am", and then he fled from the group, terrified at not being accepted.

At this point, the group wondered, "What will the therapists do with this couple?" or in other words, "How do the therapists treat rebellious children?" and "How do you become parents?" Group members became preoccupied with asking themselves detailed questions about the therapists as a couple, wondering what they might be like together, and what roles are and how power is assigned between them. Their answers to these questions were inclined to stereotype, such as "Women dramatize and men do nothing", although there was also a search for other models.

On this occasion, in response to the projective identifications of the group, the therapists countertransferentially felt reciprocal distrust and feelings of inadequacy. Through projective identifications with the therapist couple, the group members' were able to question themselves as parents and adults. For example, they wondered among themselves how the therapists might manage these kinds of conflicts. By doing this they were able decisively to relinquish some omnipotence, and in this search for authentic inner strength, based in reality rather then in omnipotent phantasy, they were also more available to be helped.

They started by distinguishing the roles of father and mother, with their respective differences, and seemed satisfied with their findings. Interestingly, the therapists also began to differentiate themselves, feeling that it was possible to expound their thinking more clearly, even when they differed.

Group members started to think about their roles and began to glimpse some distinctions. Initially, these differences were not seen as enriching, but as conflictual and thus still falling within the primitive and dichotomic logic of a compulsory choice. Partners therefore started to argue with each other and reciprocally to project blame. A group dynamic emerged by which every time there was an evolution towards a distinction or new relational modality, it took place within the framework of archaic reasoning dominated by splits and lacking in complementariness (Corbella, 2003).

The therapists worked on these projective aspects, trying to accompany the group to a moment of identification, and helping it to move on from bandying about blame to accepting personal responsibility. As a result, members began to see themselves as individuals who could change: they had arrived feeling inadequate in relation to their sick children, and had become individuals with real and arduous histories.

We want to emphasize that, for these couples, dealing with the children together had, at first, seemed to be impossible. This was because they saw themselves either as a couple or as father and mother, but not as a parental couple who could together identify with the children. Thus, the fathers left the privileged mother–child relationship intact, regressively identifying themselves with the Oedipus-like victory of a triumphant child.

The partners were afraid of confronting oedipal conflict, colluding with infantile positions that deny the *generative couple*. The third, therefore, seemed to be born of a couple who did not understand creativity and had not reached the genital stage, thus feeding the fantasy of an omnipotent mother who procreates alone.

It seemed to us as therapists that the couples were incapable of assuming parental responsibility *together*, dominated as they were by the fear of perceiving themselves as a parental couple and lacking the benefit of peer relationships. Furthermore, there was collusion *within* and *between* the couples over the idea that "the couple does not contain the child", in the sense that the child is not internalized by a couple relationship.

In the absence of a "conjugal triangle" (Britton, 1989; Ruszczynski, 2005), it is likely that the third is seen as uncontainable, thereby evoking unresolved primary oedipal conflicts. As a result, the third was seen as intrusive and persecutory. We observe that this additional anxiety can become paranoid, and the defences against it may include splitting, projection, omnipotent projective identification, idealization and denigration.

Claudia's parents

> About two years into the life of the group, the parents of Claudia, a seventeen-year-old girl with seriously provocative and hostile behaviour, found it increasingly difficult to manage their situation and openly expressed the deep conflict between them. They reported their acute conviction that the group could not help them at all and that it would therefore be necessary to call on the Juvenile Court. As a superior body it was capable of ordering their child to undergo joint family therapy, which they perceived as the only possible means of communication.
>
> At this time, a new couple, Carmelo and Maria, joined the group. The other couples in the group had begun to instruct them, pointing out the need to begin with the couple's internal relationship rather than to expect an external miracle. This message was also decidedly aimed at Claudia's parents, who seemed so unwilling to put themselves on the line.

The personal and family crisis for Claudia's parents gave rise to pain and paralysis in the group, and the idea that only an omnipotent intervention could improve matters. The therapists repeated that every resource and capacity is limited, interpreting the desire to flee in the face of difficulties and to wait for a magical solution, rather than commit personal resources to address them.

Over several sessions, Claudia's father and mother induced a disturbing state of confusion in the group. Everyone had been afraid of causing confusion and of not being listened to. It had become impossible to think. All we heard were descriptions of behaviour, chronicles, actions, counter-actions and impulsiveness, constituting an attack on the possibility of thinking.

Even in this climate of great agitation however, new elements continued to emerge. Dario and Marina, who had previously found themselves in crisis, managed to speak more to each other and to reflect on their past situation with more distance. At the beginning of the therapy, they had felt confused, inadequate and poor, and had neglected their appearance. Now they appeared better at every session, simply, but very carefully dressed. In another couple, who had recently found a more satisfactory equilibrium, the wife began to realize that she reacted angrily when feeling excluded and humiliated by the relationship between her husband and their son. They recounted the fact that, when faced with the sudden illness of her brother, they managed to help each other to try to look after him as best they could by trying to understand his most important needs.

The latter phase

The mutual support enabled the couples to break with old reference models and schemas, and the development of the perhaps unknown experience of being able to help others, even through the simple description of their own negative experiences, and their consequent reflections upon them, added to a sense of valuing themselves as couples. Simultaneously this development made it possible to realize that they had indeed acquired new parental skills.

On reflection, the group increasingly became a network of mutual support (Schermer & Pines, 1994) in which each could use the resources of all the other members. Thus, one part of the group might regress while the other retained contact with reality; one part might be passive while the other was active; one part might lose control while the other maintained it. The group thus became an entity in itself, and its members could begin to avail themselves of various emotional resources in exactly the same way as happens in a marital relationship.

Concluding thoughts: group functioning as a model for couple relationships

As we show above, the group demonstrated in this way an exportable model of relational functioning that can also be adopted by couples. It illustrates how a couple relationship can become a place that allows for a mutually constructive and maturational exchange, where the two partners reciprocally engage and encourage each other. In this way it becomes what Dicks (1967) calls a "natural therapeutic relationship" in which the partners can reciprocally use each other to tend and repair aspects of their own selves, and work on their respective unresolved object-relationships.

This movement towards a more mature relational modality requires not only tolerance of the loss of omnipotent and narcissistic aspects, but also the capacity to mourn them. Participation in a reasonably healthy, intimate couple relationship requires each partner to reunite him or herself with the distressing aspects of a self that were previously split-off and projected into an ever-present other. This loss of a previous psychic equilibrium may be experienced as disturbing, traumatic, and undesirable, and can make the relationship extremely unstable (Bianchini, Capello, Dallanegra, Monguzzi & Vitalini, 2005). We have seen that, if this instability can be contained, both by the more mature aspects of the partners and by the group therapeutic process, omnipotent projective identification and narcissistic relating can release its hold over the couple relationship and the lost projected parts of the self can be recovered.

In conclusion, it seems to us that a group can function as a thinking space in which it is possible to foster processes of identification and separation that concern parents as much as children. The interplay of recognitions and mirroring not only allows the partners to develop their roles and behaviour, but also enables them to become aware that their way of relating as a couple has had a negative impact on their parental function and role. What initially seemed to be exclusively a problem of the adolescent is additionally revealed as being an inherent part of the conflict within the parental couple relationship.

References

Bianchini, B, Capello, M., Dallanegra, L., Monguzzi, F., & Vitalini, L. (2005). Moments de souffrance psychique chez le couple en thérapie. *Le Divan Familial*, 14: 27–38.

Britton, R. (1989). The missing link: parental sexuality in the Oedipus complex. In: J. Steiner (Ed.), *The Oedipus Complex Today: Clinical Implications* (pp. 83–101). London: Karnac.

Corbella, S. (2003). *Storie e luoghi del gruppo*. Milan: Raffaello Cortina Editore.

Dicks, H. V. (1967). *Marital Tensions, Clinical Studies towards a Psycho - logical Theory of Interaction*. London: Karnac, reprinted 1993.

Losso, R. (2000). *Psicoanalisi della Famiglia, Percorsi teorico-clinici*. Milan: Franco Angeli.

Norsa, D. (2004). Disfunzioni della genitorialità e ansie riparative. In: N. Neri & S. Latmiral (Eds.), *Uno spazio per i genitori* (pp. 15–30). Rome: Edizioni Borla.

Norsa, D., & Zavattini, G. C. (1997). *Intimità e collusione. Teoria e Tecnica della Psicoterapia psicoanalitica di Coppia*. Milan: Raffaello Cortina Editore.

Ruszczynski, S. (2005). Reflective space in the intimate couple relationship: the "marital triangle". In: F. Grier (Ed.), *Oedipus and the Couple* (pp. 31–47). London: Karnac.

Schermer, V.L., & Pines, M. (1994). Ring of Fire: Primative Affects and Object Relations in Group Psychotherapy. London: Routledge.

CHAPTER SEVEN

Love in a warm climate: a partnership between object relations theory and attachment theory

Noela Byrne, Jenny Berg, and Penny Jools

"Until one has experienced the power of this psychotic process to lock two people together in what feels like hell to both, it is, I acknowledge, difficult to credit"

(Fisher, 1999, p. 456)

Introduction

Our aims in writing this chapter are to explore the source of the insecure couple attachment with reference to our two major theoretical frameworks:

1. The level of object relations functioning of the couple.
   We have previously described a sequence of developmental anxieties faced by couples when involved in a therapeutic struggle to develop a more mature relationship (Berg & Jools, 2004).
2. Attachment styles in couple relationships.
   Like Clulow (2001a) we have a particular interest in the impact of different attachment styles on the couple relationship.

Were the couples' attachment styles fixed or did they change over time in parallel with changes we had previously observed in the capacity for more mature relating? How did the therapy facilitate the development of a more secure attachment?

Therapeutic work with a couple with a longstanding, entrenched, and dysfunctional relationship can seem a daunting if not impossible task. We examine how two different theoretical orientations, object relations and attachment theories, contribute to the understanding of conflict in a couple's relationship. This relationshipcould be conceptualized as a "projective gridlock" (Morgan, 1995), woven out of entrenched mutually unsatisfying interactions over twenty-seven years. Countertransference feelings of impotence and hopelessness were experienced by the therapist when caught up in the "malignant third" (Pickering, 2005) that the couple had created from repeated excessive projective identifications withthe other. We postulate that viewing these dynamics from different perspectives is helpful for the therapist and ultimately for the couple, as it helps create a benign third position (Britton, 1989). In addition we shall show how achieving this third therapeutic dimension was facilitated in a "sentient" (Miller & Rice, 1967) peer group, which expanded the thinking space for the therapist and the couple.

Case illustration

The first few sessions

Three years ago, Wilma and Harry, both overweight, unfit, and close to sixty years old, clambered upstairs to their first session. Wilma was neatly and conservatively dressed, her husband wore track pants, with his shirt half hanging out. The couple was referred by the wife's analyst, who felt couple therapy was "their last hope".

Wilma and Harry had been married for twenty-seven years and had not had sex for the past eight years. They had many physical and psychological problems. Harry had a "drinking problem" and he suffered from panic attacks and high blood pressure that led to his early retirement on medical grounds. Both physical symptoms were probably due to his alcoholism. Wilma had been diagnosed with bipolar disorder, mainly depression, and had a history of several suicide attempts. They both suffered with migraine head-aches and Harry was also asthmatic. Their degree of somatization was of an overwhelming nature.

Initial attraction

The couple had met while professionally acting in the theatre. Wilma had initially thought, "Here's trouble!" because Harry, who drank heavily, was "tipsy", so she resisted becoming involved. Harry thought Wilma was "gorgeous", outgoing, sociable, and funny. He "wore her down" over the next year and she later admitted that she had liked his "twinkling eyes", his sense of humour and liveli-ness. So initially, each was the idealized, exciting object for the other.

Soon, however, "like a glove turning inside out", the repressed, hated, persecuting object relation appeared (Dicks, 1967, p. 66) and they were full of complaints about each other. Harry complained about his wife's rages and depression, which resulted in Wilma retreating to her bed for several days, bombed out on a "cocktail" of psychotropic drugs prescribed for both of them. He was always terrified of Wilma making another suicide attempt. Wilma com-plained about Harry "pathologizing" her whenever she was angry or expressed any of her needs. She felt she could ask nothing of him, saying that he became instantly defensive. She also protested about his huge collection of videos and DVDs that filled every available space in the house. When Harry disappeared to the pub, however, she was enraged by his perceived abandonment. She felt that both his drinking and his watching movies were activities that excluded her. They argued about the money Harry spent on drink and his movie collection, and about housework. Wilma, working full time, thought she did more than her fair share. Harry retorted that he did a lot for Wilma and she didn't appreciate it.

Their sexual relationship had deteriorated as soon as they moved in together. Harry said he withdrew from Wilma because she was always angry with him and Wilma had given up making sexual overtures because she was so often rebuffed.

At the end of the assessment it seemed as though the couple were "weighty", not only in their physical presentation, but also in the level of hostility between them. The therapist and the sentient group questioned whether the situation was indeed hopeless.

Family background

Harry was an only child whose father was absent "at sea" during and after the Second World War. His parents fought regularly, ostensibly because the father was a drinker, a gambler, and a poor provider. Harry experienced his father as a frightening, sadistic figure. An early memory is of his father holding him over the rails of a ship and threatening to drop him. His only connection with his father was being taken to the movies to escape his mother's wrath. Clearly, Harry has followed his father's passive–aggressive model of escaping into movies or drink, rather than deal with emotional difficulties. His mother was given to frequent, unpredictable outbursts of rage, which left Harry feeling persistently anxious. He has an early memory of her packing her bag and threatening to leave him because of some minor misdemeanour. The thought of threatened abandonment terrified him.

Wilma was the younger of two daughters. Her older sister was born after the death of a three-year-old sibling who had been "damaged" at birth. As a result, the sister was considered precious and was over-protected by her mother. Wilma, on the other hand, was expected to be strong and make allowances for her sister. She felt isolated and shut out from the family. Wilma also experienced her father as a frightening figure, because he regularly used the strap on her. He died when she was eleven years old, and she recalled feeling nothing but relief. In therapy, however, she has realized that there were aspects of him she loved, such as his humour. This may have been the basis for her initial attraction to Harry, with his "twinkling eyes". Although Wilma's parents appeared to have a happy marriage, Wilma believed that her mother's dependence on her father caused her to "fall apart" after her husband's death, never fully to recover.

The source of the insecure attachment

Harry and Wilma shared family backgrounds of abandonment, deprivation, and abuse and these experiences dominated their shared internal landscape. Their lack of childhood nurture led to a continual struggle to be the "nurtured child" in the marriage.

Harry was denied much of his early childhood as he was expected to act as the surrogate partner to his mother in his father's absence. Harry was not valued in this role, however, bearing the brunt of his mother's depression and anger towards her absent husband.

Wilma was dubbed the "strong" one in her family, thereby being deprived of her rightful dependency needs. In addition, her mother's collapse after her father's death led Wilma to fear that to depend on another exposed one to unbearable loss and vulnerability. Moreover, similar experiences of childhood abuse and deprivation left Wilma and Harry believing that to be vulnerable risked exposure to sadistic attacks.

Developmental anxieties: narcissistic object relating and shared unconscious phantasy

Wilma and Harry's relationship was of a narcissistic nature, operating with a phantasy of fusion with an ideal object. James Fisher (1999) defines narcissistic object relating as a denial of difference. This intolerance of difference frequently involves an intolerance of parts of the self. He says, "It is not the state of identification or oneness that is problematic, but the rigidity that cannot allow for the reality of difference" (*ibid.*, p. 220).

Conflict or difference brings disillusionment of the phantasized union and exposes the loss of the ideal self and object. The unacceptable parts of the self that have been projectively identified with in the other are now perceived as hateful aspects of the partner. They are not recognized as disavowed aspects of the self, and the partner, who is no longer seen as ideal, is therefore rejected and sometimes even mercilessly attacked. Reintrojection of projected aspects is not possible at this stage, as the couple is stuck in a "projective gridlock" (Morgan, 1995, p. 33) and is therefore unable to move on to the depressive position.

The therapist was often struck by the hurtful things that Wilma and Harry could say or do to each other, and wondered at the power of this process that seemed to hold them together. Fisher (1999) notes that in narcissistic coupling, coming together is often "impregnated with cruelty". Applying Bion's (1959) ideas to narcissistic relating in the couple, Fisher argues that there is a psychotic process at work that attacks linking so there is no ability to think about the emotional experience of oneself or the other.

This couple's sexual difficulties demonstrated the disillusionment of the phantasy of oneness and the consequent cruelty. After a sexually exciting courtship, Wilma asked Harry to do something different in their lovemaking. Harry, feeling wounded and inadequate, withdrew from her. He continued to withhold sexually as a way of remaining powerful in the relationship. Wilma protected herself by responding in kind.

This cruel cycle of projection and attack was also illustrated after Wilma went to a writers' workshop, but came home early:

> *Wilma*: "I feel so disappointed. I just realized my dreams of becoming a writer and earning money that way was just a fantasy."
>
> She then began to attack Harry, saying: "I never believed I would end up having to support someone else. Harry has done nothing to get a part-time job."
>
> *Therapist*: "Wilma, when you are feeling bad and a failure, you attack Harry. You prefer to see him as the one who is hopeless and a failure."

When their collusive phantasy of an ideal fusion (Dicks, 1967) broke down, they were confronted not only with their inevitable differences, but also with a deeper issue, their shared unconscious phantasy. Despite attacking and blaming each other for the loss of the idealized state, they also accepted that this was what they deserved, because they both believed that they were unlovable, that no one else would ever care about them, and that they were therefore stuck with each other. This left each of the couple vulnerable to sadistic threats of abandonment that stirred up primitive anxieties of disintegration. This dynamic is illustrated in the following vignette:

> The couple began arguing about how much housework each did. As this progressed, Harry became more and more enraged. Nevertheless, there was a repetitive feel about it, as though they had embarked on a well-worn path. Finally Harry stood up, saying that he wasn't going to stay and listen to this and stormed out.
>
> The following week, Harry reported that Wilma had taken an overdose that same night.

Therapist: "Is this what happens when Wilma's anger isn't heard?"

Harry angrily replied, "I'm not taking the blame for her overdose!"

It seems that at the point when Harry walked out, Wilma was put in touch with her vulnerability and her need for Harry, which she found both shameful and intolerable. Overwhelmed by her panic that Harry was abandoning her, Wilma tried omnipotently to control her anxiety by taking an overdose. Also, through the process of projective identification she was forcing Harry to feel his need for her *and* his fear of losing her.

Wilma and Harry's mutual, rigid, defensive styles functioned to ward off knowledge of their need for each other and their terror of abandonment, but at the same time kept them locked in an unsatisfying relationship. As will be elaborated later, there seems to be a link between shared unconscious phantasy and oscillations in attachment behaviour.

The attachment styles of the couple

In the early sessions, Wilma seemed more dismissive while Harry was more fearful (Bartholomew, Henderson, & Dutton, 2001). Wilma saw herself as independent and self-reliant to avoid knowing how much she depended on Harry. However, she was angry and desperate at times when he was unavailable to her.

Harry was untrusting of a close relationship because he was afraid of being hurt or rejected. In the face of Wilma's anger he would retreat to the pub or the movies to avoid her. He, too, became desperate, however, when she was suicidal. Their "dance" of approach and retreat in the therapy, was illustrated in the following material occurring after a three-week break in the therapy.

Harry began by saying he thought they were all right and that they had been OK in the therapist's absence.

Wilma said she was unhappy in her job and so was applying for another position in another Government Department. Wilma expanded on this by saying that if she got the new position; she would apply for a Churchill scholarship, which would mean she could be away for two months, travelling overseas.

Therapist: "How will that be for Harry?"

Wilma: "I don't care."

Therapist: "You don't care how Harry might feel about your being away for two months?"

Wilma reluctantly agreed that, of course, Harry would miss her.

Therapist: "Harry, how did you feel when Wilma said she didn't care?"

Harry: "I thought she was joking."

Therapist: "But if you thought she was serious?"

Harry: "Well, I would feel really hurt."

Therapist: "I think it is often hard for you to know where you stand with Wilma, and whether she does really care about you, and that makes you very anxious."

Wilma's dismissive stance was well illustrated here, reinforcing Harry's fear of close relationships. Harry's largely fearful stance was demonstrated later in the same session.

Wilma had developed cardiac symptoms during the break and Harry suggested that Wilma had been so anxious that she had virtually overdosed on his anti-anxiety medication. This aroused Harry's abandonment anxiety and his fear that Wilma might take another overdose. Wilma did not recognize that her behaviour had caused him concern, and retaliated with an accusation regarding his unavailability to her.

Wilma: "You don't realize how unavailable you become when you have had more than a couple of drinks."

Then, with escalating anger, "Oh what's the use? You never listen to what I'm really saying. You just think I'm criticizing you. There's no point in coming here any more. We might as well separate."

This couple's dance, particularly in the early stages, demonstrated the meshing of their dismissive/fearful styles of attachment, which was problematic because each of them behaved in a way that reinforced the other's insecurity. Their denial of need for the other meant they maintained a powerful invulnerable position, but threats of abandonment perpetuated their insecurity in an oft-repeated "tango". As with Dicks' concept of the couple's "dyadic joint personality" (Dicks, 1967, p. 114), disowned or disavowed aspects of the self were projected into the other, and could then be related to in the other.

Similarly, Clulow comments: "Viewing the couple as a unitary system . . . each partner can be said to have an identification with or investment in, the defensive strategy of the other" (2001c, p. 146).

This dance of advance and retreat was also experienced in the countertransference. The therapist often felt uncertain whether Wilma and Harry would continue, as the therapy seemed to move two steps forward and then two steps back. The "sentient" peer group also felt bewildered and despairing at times and wondered whether any change was possible. We assumed that Wilma and Harry must have felt the same.

Were the couple's attachment styles fixed or did they change over time?

There were two findings of note here. First, in the course of therapy it seemed that the attachment styles changed. Over a period of three years, Wilma moved from a dismissive style to a more secure way of relating, hovering between preoccupied and secure. While this was due in part to the work of couple therapy, the change was also facilitated by her work in her own analysis. Harry also moved towards a more secure way of relating, although not to the same degree as Wilma. The changed attachment styles were less prob-lematic, as their mutual attachment was no longer undermined. The couple's movement through the therapeutic process to a more secure form of relating could be seen to correspond to a movement from a paranoid–schizoid position to a more depressive position (Klein, 1987).

Second, an interesting and unexpected finding was that of *oscil-lations* in attachment organization within the individual, even in the course of a session. Significantly, these oscillations appeared to follow a period of disorganization, which exposed extreme anxiety of a disintegrative kind and associated with a dramatic increase in psychosomatic symptoms (Ogden, 1989). After these crises, Harry seemed to move from a fearful to a more dismissive attachment organization and Wilma moved from a dismissive to a more preoccupied organization.

What caused this oscillation? As already suggested, what brought Wilma and Harry together was their shared experience of deprivation and loss. This was accompanied by a phantasy of themselves as unlovable and a perception of their vulnerable, needy selves as shameful. We postulate that the *trigger* for this cycling in attachment occurred when one of the couple was put in touch with their fear of abandonment and the associated disintegrative anxiety. Thus, when Harry walked out of a couple session, Wilma felt her own vulnerability, and "fell apart". With her insecurity exacerbated, she then became more preoccupied. The overdose she took was perhaps in part an attempt to control her feelings of disintegration.

When Wilma was angry and/or critical of Harry, he felt he had lost his idealized sense of self, as well as the idealized couple union. Overwhelmed, he angrily pushed away his despair, walked out and went to the pub. He then "became" his own abandoning father. Thus, Harry appeared to move from fearful to dismissive organization. His drinking bouts may be seen as related to periods of disorganization.

The oscillation between dismissive and preoccupied attachment organization in Wilma's internal world, following a period of disorganization is illustrated in the following session:

> Harry arrived first. Wilma was late. She said she had been having a hard time at work because she felt that too much was being asked of her. She had lost her temper and told off the boss. He had said, "Never mind, we love you,"

> Wilma said contemptuously, "How patronizing!"

> When Wilma returned home from work, she had wanted to tell Harry what had happened, but he had been drinking because an audition had gone badly.

> Wilma said, "I felt that there was no point in my talking to him when he's like that. He went on for hours about how he was worried he's lost his singing voice."

> The next morning she had tried to tell him, but he had minimized it and walked away. As a consequence she felt devastated and stayed in bed for the rest of the weekend. Finally, on Sunday night, she had asked him why he hadn't come up to talk to her.

Harry had replied, "Because you were angry and I was afraid that would only make it worse."

Wilma then angrily turned to Harry and said, "How do you think that made me feel? I'm a bad girl for losing my temper with the boss and you don't want to spend time with me either. I feel abandoned by you!"

Harry: "There have been so many times when you've been angry and it only made it worse when I tried to talk to you. I felt abandoned by you when you went upstairs to bed."

Therapist: "It seems that the fear of abandonment is something you share, but in this case you both made it happen. Harry was not prepared to take the risk and Wilma was not prepared to persist, to make sure she was heard."

How did the therapy facilitate the development of a more secure relationship?

It is hard to overestimate the importance of the "sentient" peer group in containing the anxieties that this couple generated and in providing a crucial space in which it was possible to think constructively about them. Initially, it was important for the therapist to provide containment and a "safe haven" by being consistently available and reliable. Thus, when Wilma became angry with the therapist and refused to return, a phone call reassured her that her anger had not destroyed the relationship and she was able to attend the next session.

Harry responded well to transference interpretations, particularly about his anger. He agreed to continue the therapy after the therapist suggested that he used going to the pub as he did his movies, as an escape hatch. When she suggested at one point that he might feel that she and Wilma were "ganging up on him", he agreed and recalled feeling the same with his parents when they would join in attacking him "like two pit bull terriers". This information had not been disclosed before. Later in the therapy, an angry Wilma was also able to respond to a transference interpretation when the therapist suggested that she might feel that Harry was being favoured by the therapist, as her mother had favoured her older sister.

Couple therapy, because of its very nature as a threesome, can bring Oedipal anxieties into consciousness and provide the couple with an opportunity to tackle these issues. When the therapist offered her perspective, there was an opportunity for the couple to experience a "third position" (Britton, 1989). Harry initially used the therapist in a narcissistic way that excluded Wilma, and it was necessary for the therapist to make a conscious effort to include her. Later on, after having experienced the therapy as a secure base, Wilma was able to speak up for herself and at times would give Harry a playful slap if he dominated the session or interrupted her.

As object relations therapists, we believe that for a major change to occur, containment at a deeper level needs to be achieved. We postulate that this happened when the couple experienced therapy as a secure base, where each could acknowledge their own unconscious phantasy and together process their shared experiences of abandonment and feelings of unlovableness.

In the final session Wilma and Harry owned their shared backgrounds of abandonment and alienation as they acknowledged how much they identified with their three stray cats, for whom they had provided a home. This seemed an appropriate metaphor for the warm nurturing environment they had begun to create for themselves.

In the course of entertaining friends, something they had not been able to do for years, Harry had drunk too much. Instead of getting angry, Wilma felt anxious, but in the end, she just went to bed.

The next morning Harry said he was angry with himself. The therapist pointed out that by Wilma not being angry, Harry was able to take responsibility himself for his excessive drinking.

Harry: "Yes, I was so angry with myself, I have to cut down on my drinking, for my health, for my weight . . ."

Wilma cut in and said, "For our relationship." Harry ignored her comment.

Therapist: "Did you hear what Wilma said? She wants to know that she is also an important reason for you to cut down your drinking."

Harry: "Yes, of course that's an important reason."

Wilma: "I told him the other night that I love him and I want to be with him, that he is a great companion and my best friend."

Therapist: "And what about you, Harry, can you tell Wilma what she means to you?"

Harry: "Yes, I sometimes say it, especially in bed, I say I love you."

Conclusion

Within an object relations framework, we acknowledge the value of working with the attachment styles of the couple. Wilma and Harry exhibited a commonly troublesome attachment pairing, i.e., fearful–dismissive (Fisher & Crandell, 2001). The therapist was able to work with the here and now by pointing out how each avoided the closeness they craved. Towards the end of the therapy they gained more insight into how their defensive behaviour destabilized the other, thus contributing to ongoing feelings of insecurity in their relationship.

Over the course of the therapy, we noted a change towards more mature and secure levels of functioning in the couple when viewed from either theory base. As well as a change towards more secure attachment styles in both Wilma and Harry, we also noted changes in attachment behaviour, even within a session. Our hypothesis is that these oscillations in attachment style occur as a result of the activation of psychotic disintegrative anxieties (Ogden, 1989). These regressive anxieties are activated when the unconscious shared phantasy of abandonment, based on a belief in their individual feelings of being unlovable, is exposed. A period of disorganization is followed by a switching or oscillation in their attachment style. This is where work at a deeper emotional level in exploring internal objects is crucial in order to effect lasting change. As the shared unconscious phantasy was understood by the couple, they were then able to find the strength to recognize what united them as partners rather than what divided them.

In the course of this therapy we witnessed a marked change in the couple's internal world. The need to dominate and powerfully exclude feelings of dependency was gradually replaced by compassion for that aspect of themselves. When that level of mutual containment was reached, Wilma and Harry were able to move out of the prison of their "projective gridlock" (Morgan, 1995) and a warmer climate was created in their relationship.

References

Bartholomew, K., Henderson, A., & Dutton, D. (2001). Insecure attachment and abusive intimate relationships. In: C. Clulow (Ed.), *Adult Attachment and Couple Psychotherapy*. Hove: Brunner-Routledge.

Berg, J., & Jools, P. (2004). Holding on and letting go: developmental anxieties in couples after the birth of a child. *International Journal of Applied Analytic Studies*, 1(3): 224–233.

Bion, W. R. (1959). Attacks on linking. *International Journal of Psychoanalysis*, 40. Reprinted in *Second Thoughts*, New York: Heinemann, 1967 [reprinted 1987, London: Karnac].

Britton, R. (1989). The missing link: parental sexuality in the Oedipus complex. In: J. Steiner (Ed.), *The Oedipus Complex Today: Clinical Implications* (pp. 83–101). London: Karnac.

Clulow, C. (Ed.) (2001a). *Adult Attachment and Couple Psychotherapy*. London: Brunner-Routledge.

Clulow, C. (2001c). Attachment, narcissism, and the violent couple. In: C. Clulow (Ed.), *Adult Attachment and Couple Psychotherapy*. Hove: Brunner-Routledge.

Dicks, H. V. (1967). *Marital Tensions: Clinical Studies Towards a Theory of Interaction*. London: Karnac.

Fisher, J. V. (1999). *The Uninvited Guest: Emerging from Narcissism to Marriage*. London: Karnac.

Fisher, J. V., & Crandell, L. (2001). Patterns of relating in the couple. In: C. Clulow (Ed.), *Adult Attachment and Couple Psychotherapy* (pp. 15–27). Hove: Brunner-Routledge.

Klein, M. (1987). *Envy and Gratitude*. London: Hogarth.

Miller, E. J., & Rice, A. K. (1967). *Systems of Organization: The Control of Task and Sentient Boundaries*. London: Tavistock.

Morgan, M. (1995). The projective gridlock: a form of projective identification in couple relationships. In: S. Ruszczynski & J. Fisher (Eds.), *Intrusiveness and Intimacy in the Couple* (pp. 33–48). London: Karnac.

Ogden, T. H. (1989). *The Primitive Edge of Experience*. New York: Jason Aronson.

Pickering, J. (2005). The interlocking model scene. *Australian Journal of Psychotherapy*, 24(1): 32–56.

PART III

COUPLES IN RIVALRY: POWER IMBALANCE IN COUPLE RELATIONSHIPS

CHAPTER EIGHT

An impasse in power relationships: an intersubjective view in a South African socio-cultural context

Rika van den Berg

Introduction

The marriage between culture and psychology has been recognized, reviewed, and described in philosophical debates (for example, Barcinski & Kalia, 2005; Iborra, 2005; Tappan, 2005), but it has not been sufficiently researched and described systematically through empirical work. Theorizations of socio-cultural variables are not integrated as strands in psychoanalytic formulations or in explanations of patterns of attachment. Individual, internal psychoanalytic theorizations are expanded to account for social phenomena such as racism or sexism (for example, Straker, 2004). The defence mechanisms of splitting, denial, and projection are most often applied in such explanations.

Through presentation of case material, this chapter begins by providing empirical evidence to substantiate an argument that racism may be viewed as the product of an interaction between the internal and the social world. The social and the internal world play an interactional, causal role in the construction of racism. Secondly, the chapter illustrates how these social phenomena intrinsically affect the development of the individual self and patterns of attachment. These phenomena similarly have an effect on the attachment between the couple, the attachment to the therapist, and the therapeutic process. In this case, it was manifested in an impasse in the therapeutic process with the couple. Thirdly, the concept of the intersubjective field has facilitated an understanding of the complex relationship between the individual and social world. The case material illuminates the multi-dimensional and multi-layered nature of the intersubjective field between the couple and the therapist. Finally, I argue that each of the layers of the intersubjective field is historically based. A view of the marriage between the socio-cultural and intrapsychic variables has to be considered within the specific meanings of the historically constructed categories of race, class, and gender for a particular individual, dyad, triad, or group, at a specific time in history. The specific meanings will lead us to understand the ways in which power was internalized in the formation of the identities of the participants. These meanings are articulated in the therapeutic process and the dynamics that are played out in the therapy room.

Conceptualizations: attachment, culture, psychoanalysis, and discourses

Winnicott (1951, 1971) formulated the concept of the transitional object. He theorized that the differentiation of the self from the mother is facilitated through transitional objects. This process becomes the source of the infant's play, and the template of cultural experience (Yates & Sclater, 2000). Winnicott's understanding of the subject-in-culture, although not explicitly stated, was the first conceptualization of intersubjectivity. It allows for the formulation of the dialectical link between individual self and cultural discourses. In the dialectic relationship between mother and baby, meaning is co-created and re-created to produce the subjective experience of the infant self. Through differentiation and the development of the self, the intersubjective field between mother and baby widens to incorporate more and more of the external world— the world of cultural experiences. The object relationships internalized by the baby in the dialectical relationships with care-givers contain representations held by the care-givers that are imbued with the unique meanings of the specific contexts in which the representations of care-givers were shaped.

Culture encompasses difference, giving meaning to and forming shared representations where there are differences in communities due to race, ethnicity, gender, and class. Attitudes and values are communicated via language and other symbolic representations and woven into the social identities of group members. Cultural group practices, or discourses, such as etiquette, racial and gender stereotyping, embody representations that contain shared traditional and communicated meanings about the meaning of, for example, being black. These meanings are shaped in the history of the cultural group and are communicated and assimilated in the care-givers' internal world, and become part of the care-givers' social identity. The meanings related to, for example, race, are articulated in the relationship with the infant. These representations both articulate and simultaneously construct meaning for the infant in the interaction between the care-giver and the infant/child. These representations therefore determine the nature of the interactions in the interpersonal field, and shape the identity of the infant/child. The representations are imbued in the patterns of attachments that are shaped in these early relationships between the infant and his/her care-givers. These patterns also form the templates for marital and therapeutic relationships.

How do all these representations form a coherent whole? The ego integrates psyche and soma, mediates between and integrates conscious and unconscious experiences. The ego interprets and integrates in a unique and individual way the messages from the social environment, while also co-creating the socio-cultural representations of the external world. The ego can be said to be a third intersubjective space: a reflective space where representations of the internal and the external social world are interpreted, mediated, and integrated.

Representations are historically specific and create a specific intersubjective context for each couple

The representations in the internal world of the individual are shaped in specific contexts. Different historical, socio-economic, political and familial contexts lead to different representations. For example, the practice of apartheid, which consciously concretized racial prejudice and institutionalized racism, created a context for the formation of different internal representations in South African white people compared with white people in other countries. Within South Africa, the whiteness of white Afrikaans speakers carries a different meaning from that of white English speakers. During Apartheid, Afrikaans people were typically stereotyped as the perpetrators in their discrimination against black people, while English speakers often viewed themselves as white liberals trapped in a political situation. The Afrikaans' psyche, shaped in these representations, is potentially more prone to white guilt and negative self-representations. The differences in the South African social contexts of the meaning of whiteness illustrate the existence of multiple cultural realities within one socio-cultural context.

The multi-dimensional and multi-layered nature of the intersubjective field

The personal historical layer of the couple

I will call the couple that I am describing Susan and Andrew. Susan is a dark-skinned English-speaking woman; Andrew is a white English-speaking male. Susan and Andrew shared representations of emotionally depriving objects, related to their experience of submissive, absent mothers. The critical, harsh, male voice and lack of mirroring by a loving father was also a shared experience. Due to the emotional deprivation and lack of mirroring by care-givers, both were narcissistically wounded and had a sense of being persecuted by the other.

The personal historical, socio-cultural contribution of the therapist to the intersubjective field

Although bilingual, I identify with my first language as being Afrikaans. I trained at an Afrikaans university as a teacher, worked in the field, and then went back to training in psychology. My awareness of differences in culture influenced my decision to study psychology at an English university, although at the time that I made this decision I was not conscious of the extent to which Afrikaaners were scapegoated as the perpetrators of apartheid. Raised in the split between the white groups, I chose a supposedly liberal, non-racist English university. An example of a research project on racism conducted at the English university where I trained is that of Kottler and Long (1997).

The historically specific socio-cultural layer of the intersubjective field between the therapist and the couple

The couple and I historically share a socio-cultural environment of male dominance, submission of women, and subordination of people of a dark colour through the legislation of apartheid. During our adult years, there was a transition to a new political dispensation with all the specific adaptations that this required.

The intersubjective field of theory and training

The process that the therapist-in-training undergoes is similar to the process of the growing child. The trainee forms internal representations based on the discourses conveyed to him by mentors; for example, the psychoanalytic discourse of narcissism. The presence or absence of social theory in training determines whether the trainee integrates different discourses, such as the psychoanalytic and the social. The therapist develops an "analytical ego" in integrating theory. The analytical ego observes the intersubjective field in the therapy room and interprets and helps the couple to integrate the specifics of their experience in a unique and individual way.

Supervision—another layer in the intersubjective field

I am part of a peer supervision group where I have been through a process that impacted directly on the work with this couple. The group meets regularly to discuss case material and theoretical papers. There are ten people in the group, each with a personal and socio-cultural history that informs the interpretations made about a couple. I will illustrate the impact of this intersubjective field in my discussion of the therapeutic process.

*The case material: applying the integration of social and
psychoanalytic thinking to the relational field between
Susan, Andrew, and myself*

The clinical material chosen for this presentation is organized to demonstrate the impasse that can occur if social and psychoanalytic theorizations are not integrated. The case material illustrates the presence of the narcissistic constellation between Susan and Andrew, but also the social discourses of race and gender that were at play. The relevance of the impasse for the development of a secure attachment in the couple is demonstrated.

Psychoanalytic understandings of the concept of narcissism vary. Kohut (1971, 1977) theorizes that, in narcissistic forms of arrested development, a split in the self might occur that may manifest in swings from idealized to denigrated perceptions of the self. A very vulnerable ego–self may be easily overwhelmed by the swing between the two poles. This phenomenon of two poles—the idealized and the denigrated—described by Kohut can be observed in the couple relationship. The idealized–denigrated narcissistic constellation may be split between the couple in different ways. Both may be carrying the idealized image consciously, while the denigrated part is hidden in the unconscious. This could result in competitive power struggles and displays of superiority by both partners. Alternatively, one may consciously carry the idealized part, while the other carries the denigrated part. The opposite pole is then unconscious for each of the partners. One consciously carries the insecurity, while the other carries the strength and competence.

The dynamic of perpetrator-versus-victim is prevalent in the therapeutic relational field where the participants have been exposed to a racist or sexist socio-cultural environment. The roles of aggressor and victim shift between the participants. The psychic representations of what it means to be a perpetrator in a racist or sexist environment, however, is so unacceptable that all participants abdicate the role of perpetrator. In the racial dynamic, no one wants to be the perpetrator/aggressor and the arguments centre around who is to blame and who was the aggressor. The perpetrator/victim dynamic is different from the narcissistic constellation where there is identification with the grandiose or the inferior self.

The content of the arguments differ. The grandiosity might, for example, manifest in complaints about the incompetence of the other. The inferiority might manifest in reports of the overly demanding neediness and insecurity of the partner.

In the narcissistic constellation in this couple, Susan was consciously the keeper of the power while Andrew was viewed, by both of them, as the fragile, insecure partner. Andrew embodied and expressed the insecure attachment between them, while Susan had the overt power and dismissed him as an unsuitable partner in interactions. The presenting problem was that she found his neediness overly demanding and a hindrance in her academic pursuits. Both are highly intelligent, but her initial superior capacity for reasoning served as an effective intellectual defence against vulnerability and intimacy. Her confusion, related to having multiple cultural identities, while being in an insecure symbiotic relationship with her partner, was largely unconscious. She could only voice her need for separateness and her own identity through her attacks on him for his lack of boundaries, accommodation, and need for affirmation from her. They would, for example, have an argument about her not wanting to affirm him in his choice of a jacket. His ambivalence about the symbiosis was initially more unconscious because he needed desperately to be idealized by her, yet at the same time he felt abandoned by her.

The relational field was fraught with persecutory attacks and power struggles. The struggles reflected the narcissistic power constellation between them, but also the racial and gender issues that were expressed in the themes of "who is the perpetrator, and who is the victim?" Who is the victim: Susan in not wanting to endure smoking or Andrew in having to give up? What is at fault when he misses their child's swimming gala? Is it his lack of proper communication skills in telling her about work obligations, or her listening skills? Who, then, victimized the child? In another incident he was on the toilet, and she became very angry with him for not silencing their dogs, as she had already gone to bed and was being disturbed. She felt she was the victim in not being cared for. He then became angry and attacking in return. She became the perpetrator in her attack and then he became the victim, injured by her suggestion that he had been behaving badly. In this instance, Susan struggled to accept that she could be an aggressor, who could be persecutory of Andrew. They recounted the passive–aggressive power struggles that they got into outside the therapy room, which could result in days of no emotional contact and a hostile distance between them.

I was conscious of social discourses around gender, but I was not then able to link these with the discourse around narcissism in an integrated way, and make the dual interpretations required. I was not aware enough when Susan defensively used gender issues to mask her own fragility and deep wounding. She frequently attacked Andrew about role divisions, such as his work being more important in the balance of household chores, or being a weak male in not standing up to the lawyer, or a typical male when it comes to party preparations, or a sexist male when he didn't stand up to the teacher in supporting his daughter's wish to play cricket.

At another time, however, the gender discourse would be in the background and she would want his support. There was, for example, a disagreement when Susan bought a new car. She raised it in the session that Andrew had not supported her in confronting the salesman on her behalf for not fulfilling the contractual agreement. Susan felt very let down and "on her own" in this. She felt she would always have to be the strong one, and do it for herself, portraying the narcissistic wounding of not having been seen by him, the parent. He felt narcissistically injured in that she was saying that he was not good enough, that he would never be good enough for her, "the rejecting parent". The multiple layers of complexes and projections between them are illustrated here. While there was merit in some of her accusations, the representations developed in gender discourses that she had been exposed to in her career were not integrated with another part of her, that of the weak, fragile self covered up under the intellectual, coping, and successful woman. The attacks about gender inequality were often attacks also about Andrew's limitations in mothering Susan. The dynamic oscillated between her being the narcissistically wounded child, and a sexist dynamic, where she demanded equality as a woman. He would then become the perpetrator, and she the victim of his sexism.

The narcissistic dimensions of Susan and Andrew's internal worlds and the manifestation in the power constellation between them, were in the forefront of my mind in understanding what was happening in the room. I was aware of how this narcissistic constellation was split between them, and I could hold them through interpretations centred on these understandings. The social discourse that was unconsciously at play in the intersubjective field between us, however, featured the social stereotypes of what it may mean to be an Afrikaans speaker. These stereotypes unconsciously impacted on my authority as a therapist, and contributed to the impasse that we reached in the process of establishing a secure attachment between Susan and Andrew.

An impasse in the therapeutic process due to socio-cultural representations

In my practice in treating very narcissistically wounded individuals, the first phase of the therapy centres round the strengthening of the self in order to be able to face the shadow aspects of the personality. I will interpret the depriving object that the patient has been subject to, but not as an internal object. In some instances the actual interpretation of the internal objects is unnecessary, as the trauma is healed in a corrective emotional experience in the attachment formed between patient and therapist. In some instances, however, the new patterns of attachment and corrective emotional experiences are not enough. An interpretation of the depriving internal object is needed, as the resistance against experiencing goodness is more dominant. This seems to be when there were intense hateful feelings in the early social environment and in the care-giver's relationships with the developing infant.

Initially, I acted as a good container for the projected, hateful, persecutory internal objects that this couple could not contain for each other. During the first phase, before the impasse, both shifted in their experience of their sense of self. Susan became more in touch with her feelings and vulnerability, while Andrew's ego strengthening allowed him to separate from her more, to hold his own ground, and to be more direct in his expression of anger. She could then start to look at her own split self, the needy and the coping self. The process of Andrew becoming more separate led to a distancing physically and emotionally from her. This brought transferential feelings related to the hateful, depriving, and abandoning object introjected in her early environment in relation to him more to the fore. She had previously consciously experienced him very much as unable to care for, or really see, her needs. Susan's experience of Andrew as being the depriving hateful object was now central as the complex surfaced further, triggered by his increasing separateness. This mirrored Susan's experience of an unconscious, hateful object relationship, an object that she felt wanted to rid him of her. This anxiety made her unable to take any of the good things that he was offering in a real way.

A recurring theme was Susan's insistence that Andrew ought to come to bed at the same time as her, because she feared that he did not want to be with her. My attempts at looking at the feelings that it stirred for her, and looking at his need for separateness at times, fuelled her conviction that she was on her own, and that no one wanted to hear her. I was emotionally in touch with her agony and desperation, but I was unsure where to direct my interventions. In this phase, Andrew was, at times, equally stuck in an internal object relationship where Susan became the antagonist in the projection on to her. Her attacks on him sometimes left him convinced, when his complex was triggered, that he would never be good enough. This left them unable to receive the goodness from each other and to develop a secure attachment in their relationship.

While hateful feelings were in the room, I was immobilized in interpreting the constellation of the hateful object in my dark patient. I could see, relate to, and nurture the weak part of her self, but "because I did not want to see her colour" I was blind to another side to her, that of the hateful aggressor internalized in the racist and sexist surrounds of her upbringing. She would alert me to it in the incidents that they brought. For example, a fight that they had about him not wanting to make a phone call on her behalf. He had said that he felt bullied into it. She was devastated that he had thought that she "*was* a bully". I was able to interpret her hurt and defensive anger, but neglected the interpretation of her own fear of being a bully. Unconsciously, what I feared was becoming the perpetrator myself, through being a stereotype of Afrikaans speakers. This mirrored Susan's fear of being a perpetrator.

During the impasse in the therapy, I briefly referred to the couple in my peer supervision group, without giving a proper context to what I was saying. While the comment made by one of the male group members was not fully accurate as to the dynamic that was going on, it started a process of self-reflection for me. I was shamed by the comment. In self-analysis I reflected on my impotence in the confrontation of this hateful object in each of them. I had to acknowledge that I had made myself blind to her colour in an attempt to make things equal. There was a hitherto unconscious part of me that saw her as different. My fear of being the Afrikaans aggressor, the perpetrator, and of attributing stereotypical notions of her being lesser, made me protective of her. An unconscious part of an object relationship gets hooked in the material that the patient brings if the therapist is not conscious of it. Some of my feelings were possibly related to a projective identification with her internal unconscious representations of white therapists. I had to re-examine fully my fear of being a perpetrator in the racist environment that I had grown up in. Altman (2004) argues that we have to be able to bear the pain of having caused damage in a real way, in order to really make reparation. Otherwise we may engage in pseudo-reparation or condescending care, such as being patronizing. I could not fully assert my therapeutic authority and make potentially attacking interpretations when I was not in touch with the parameters of my own potential internal perpetrator. The projections informed by racial perceptions in the couple and in relation to me could also not be interpreted. These were obscured by my unconscious fear and understanding of their constellation as mainly narcissistic in nature. My fear of being a perpetrator mirrored the persecutory fears between the partners in the couple, which prevented them from forming a secure attachment.

Conclusion

Effective analytic practice requires the integration of social and psychoanalytic theory and ongoing self-analysis. The integration of the psychoanalytic understanding of the narcissistic constellation in the couple relationship, and the unconscious racial representations in them and in myself, shifted the impasse in the therapeutic process. The impact of the racial representation on their attachment to me and to each other is self-evident.

In South Africa, there has been an attempt at working through people's experiences related to the atrocities of the apartheid era. A series of hearings, the "Truth and Reconciliation Process", in which victims could reveal the extent of the traumatization during apartheid, took place after the first free elections. This was not sufficient, however, to raise consciousness and heal the wounds. The suppressed feelings and injuries to all races continue to be acted out within the South African political and social context. We may have a consciousness of differences between us, but we have work to do in healing wounds and integrating remnants of the past.

References

Altman, N. (2004). Whiteness uncovered: commentary on papers by Melanie Suchet and Gillian Straker. *Psychoanalytic Dialogues*, 14(4): 439–446.

Barcinski, M., & Kalia, V. (2005). Extending the boundaries of the dialogical self: speaking from within the feminist perspective. *Culture & Psychology*, 11(1): 101–109.

Iborra, A. (2005). Beyond identity and ideology: processes of transcendence associated with the experience of conversion. *Culture & Psychology*, 11(1): 89–100.

Kohut, H. (1971). *The Analysis of the Self*. New York: International Universities Press.

Kohut, H. (1977). *The Restoration of the Self*. New York: International Universities Press.

Kottler, A., & Long, C. (1997). Shifting sands and shifting selves: affirmation and betrayals in the process of institutional transformation. In: A. Levett, A. Kottler, E. Burman, & I. Parker (Eds.), *Culture, Power & Difference. Discourse Analysis in South Africa* (pp. 44–61). London: Zed Books.

Straker, G. (2004). Race for cover castrated whiteness, perverse consequences. *Psychoanalytic Dialogues*, 14(4): 405–422.

Tappan, B. (2005). Domination, subordination and the dialogical self: identity development and the politics of ideological becoming. *Culture and Psychology*, 11(1): 47–75.

Winnicott, D. W. (1951). Transitional objects and transitional phenomena. In: M. Khan & R. Masud (Eds.), *Collected Papers: Through Paediatrics to Psychoanalysis* (pp. 229–242). London: Hogarth Press.

Winnicott, D. W. (1971). *Playing and Reality*. London: Routledge.

Yates, C., & Sclater, S. (2000). Culture, psychology, transitional space. In: C. Squire (Ed.), *Culture in Psychology* (pp. 135–146). London: Routledge.

CHAPTER NINE

Touching the void: the impact of psychiatric illness on the couple

Christopher Vincent

Introduction

Since starting clinical work in a department of psychotherapy attached to a general psychiatric service, I have become increasingly interested in exploring the clinical and theoretical implications of what I wish to describe as "couple voids". The particular "voids" I would like to explore arise between couples where one or both partners suffer from psychiatric illness. These situations convey a power imbalance between the couples where questions about self-interest, the quality of their attachment, and altruism arise. So far as I know, this idea has not been developed in relation to couple relationships but it has been explored in relation to intrapsychic functioning (Emmanuel, 2001). In developing my ideas about this concept, I draw from attachment theory in describing two types of couple void. Both have properties drawn from the classification linked with the Adult Attachment Interview; one couple void is linked to the "preoccupied" category, while the second is linked to the "dismissing" category. In conclusion, I make some tentative suggestions about why one couple seemed to benefit far more from therapy than the other couple.

What is a couple void?

The term refers to the quality of interaction between partners emerging either at assessment or during treatment. The hallmark of these voids is a sense of emptiness between the partners that results from an angry emotional engagement which excludes the survival of good experience. It is this angry interaction that I suggest has characteristics of preoccupied attachment. Alternatively, the void can result from a lack of emotional engagement between the couple, and I suggest that this interaction is linked to the dismissing category.

The idea that a void has opened up between a couple who present for treatment will be familiar to couple therapists. Sometimes the void will be described quite explicitly, as, for example, when one or both partners talk about "living parallel lives which don't touch"; but sometimes the sense of emptiness will be implied. For example, the anguished plea of a woman that "I want back the man I married" can signal that a gap has opened up between the couple and, seemingly, cannot be bridged. Or the couple who come for help with arguing over their children can hide from themselves the reality of having lost contact with each other. Often an awareness of a void becomes apparent when, at assessment, the therapist invites the couple to explain what attracted them to each other in the first place. The contrast between liveliness in the relationship *back then* with the emptiness *now* can draw attention in a helpful, but painful, way to what has gone missing over the years.

Why should working in a psychiatric setting require that the psychotherapist should get to grips with the dynamics of emptiness? The answer seems related to the extent and depths of depression found among psychiatric patients who seek help with their relationships. Depression is often associated with emptiness and despair, as Freud explained in "Mourning and melancholia" (1917e), when angry feelings are turned against the self and these can extend into an interpersonal world barren of good experiences or objects.

I was also prompted to think about the idea of couple voids after I had read the gripping book by Joe Simpson entitled *Touching the Void* (Simpson, 1997), which subsequently was used as the basis of a film. This book deals with the relationship between two young male mountaineers, Joe Simpson and Simon Yates, who decide to climb a daunting peak in the South American Andes on their own with the minimum of equipment. The dramatic crisis in the book comes at the point when, on the descent from the peak, Joe falls and breaks his leg very badly. The climbers are roped together, but Joe loses his hold and slips into a massive cavernous void, where he is suspended from the line attached to Simon, above. Simon's dilemma is to decide what he should do next. If he stays he reckons they will both die of hypothermia, even if Joe has not already been killed in the fall. If he cuts the rope and seeks to save his own life by disregarding Joe's welfare, he will betray a basic human instinct and one of the unspoken principles of the mountaineering community. He elects to cut the rope, believing that Joe is probably dead anyway. In fact, miraculously, Joe has survived, and by a combination of luck, grim courage, and huge determination, manages to find his way back to base camp and a shocked colleague.

The moral and psychological dilemma faced by Simon is familiar in all couple relationships. How far and under what circumstances does narrow self-interest become more important than obligations to the interests of the other partner and to the relationship itself? And, ultimately, when does self-interest require that you sacrifice the interest of your partner either by cutting that person out of your life or preserving them in your life as a receptacle of hatred? Some couples resolve this dilemma by actually separating physically, but the dynamic tension between self-interest and concern for a partner can operate when couples stay under the same roof and attempt an emotional separation that is never utterly final. For them, distancing has to be preserved for fear that accommodating the other's interests would feel like a sacrifice too far. On the other hand, their partnership may have to be preserved, in part, out of recognition that there is a mutual dependency that includes the need to blame.

This dilemma is analogous to that part of Joe and Simon's crisis when Joe was suspended on that rope and Simon had to contemplate cutting it. Simon's decision to resolve the dilemma by cutting the rope was a bid for his own survival. In a psychological sense, many of the clients I see are unable to make that decision and remain paralysed by the conviction that they must remain gripped by the power of negative and anti-life forces.

Turning away or turning towards the partner who disappoints

Sometimes partners cope with the dearth of love between them by developing compensatory activity and interests outside the relationship. Under these circumstances the void can feel like a wasteland where nothing fertile takes place compared with the creativity taking place outside the home. And we might say of couples who structure their lives in this way that they really do *avoid* one another. The process of turning away from an attachment figure is captured in attachment theory by two important measures (Fonagy, 2001). In the Strange Situation Test, infants classified as anxiously avoidant seek "precociously" to control or to "down-regulate" emotional arousal at times of separation and reunion with key attachment figures. Adults who are classified as dismissing after taking the Adult Attachment Interview show parallel traits of emotional disengagement marked by being derogatory or idealizing about key attachment figures in their lives. These two measures of insecurity capture the way that infants and adults manage rejection at points of separation by creating the illusion of emotional self-sufficiency.

Sometimes, however, a reverse process occurs, so that in the face of psychological hurt the void itself becomes invested with much more emotional energy. For example, avoidance can be associated with passive hostility, as often happens when sexual intimacy is stopped or one parent's open intimacy with a child can stand as a constant rebuke and reminder to the other parent about the intimacy they lack as a couple. So, rather than the void being a wasteland empty of emotional life, it may have the paradoxical qualities of being both empty and full at the same time; empty of genuine affection, respect, and love and, instead, filled with hatred, confusion, and ambivalence. This quality of turning towards the partner who disappoints and being unable to let go of the attachment is also echoed in attachment theory. In the Strange Situation Test, the anxiously attached ambivalent/resistant infants show distress at separation, but are not comforted by the care-giver's return and appear to "up-regulate" affect in an angry way, in order to secure the care-giver's attention. Similarly, the preoccupied adult following an Adult Attachment Interview will convey a sense of never having separated emotionally from key attachment figures and will talk about them in angry or passive ways. Thus, while the avoidant infant and dismissing adult seek to create a state of mind valuing emotional self-sufficiency and separateness, the ambivalent/resistant infant and preoccupied adult convey a sense of being frightened of being separate and autonomous. Instead, they define themselves in ways that are inextricably connected to the minds and experiences of key attachment figures in their lives.

Of course, some couples do both things; they invest compensatory energy outside the relationship, as if to be dismissing of attachment. But they also imbue the void that has opened up between them with negative emotional energy, as if they remain preoccupied with each other. Psychiatric illnesses can function in both of these ways, mobilizing outside help from GPs, CPNs, psychiatrists, and hospital staff, but also serving to heighten couple tension, as happened with the male patient who threatened his wife with a manic episode and consequent hospital admission. Admission implied separating from his wife and family, but was also experienced by them as a punishment for over-stressing his coping resources.

A preoccupied couple void

The experiences of Joe Simpson and Simon Yates tracked directly on to my countertransference experience with the first couple, Sandra and Derek. I see this couple as being preoccupied in attachment theory terms and, not surprisingly, they evoked in me feelings of not being able to let go of them although they seemed unable to make use of the therapy with me. One example of being unable to let go was the trigger for writing this chapter. I had seen Sandra and Derek for a session and had returned home to be asked by my wife whether I would like to go the cinema to see the film *Touching the Void*. Rather testily I said I did not want to see it, although I knew in my head that I rated the book highly and that, on other occasions, I would have jumped at seeing the film. Further reflection made me suspect that thinking about the void in Sandra's and Derek's lives overlapped too closely with the awful experience I had been reading about in Joe Simpson's book.

Sandra and Derek are both aged fifty-four and they have three sons. Derek is a tailor and Sandra is currently out of work and somewhat phobic of public places. She first had psychiatric treatment for depression in her early twenties, but her most recent period of depression started in 1990 following her discovery of some critical notes Derek had written about her but which he meant to keep secret from her. Having read them, however, she was devastated, and fell into a depressive illness from which she has never really recovered. She has had two brief hospital admissions, but has mainly been seen as an outpatient or as a day hospital patient. Her psychiatrist described Sandra as having a resistant depression for which she has received the full battery of available therapies apart from couple therapy. The couple have been encouraged to start couple therapy in the past but, while it has been available, they have been unwilling to engage. Occasionally, when her psychiatrist has considered discharging Sandra as an outpatient, Derek has called to say that Sandra was too ill and needed further appointments.

Before seeing the couple, I discovered from the psychiatric notes that an uncle had sexually abused Sandra and, consequently, she became anorexic in her teens. I also noted that she was still anorexic and that this prevented the couple eating in public places. The notes also mentioned that, aged twenty-five, she had had an illegitimate baby by a much older man and that the baby was adopted.

On their questionnaires completed before assessment, they each gave a pen picture of their problems. Sandra wrote "It started in 1990 when I found a written report my husband made about me which listed all my faults . . . I was devastated. I tried to talk about it but he wouldn't. He blamed me and wouldn't discuss the notes for several years. We now have no relationship . . . I feel he doesn't care about me at all . . . he seems so cold and uncaring and I can't break through the wall he has built around himself . . . I want my husband back, the man I married." Derek described another list of problems: "Communication, sexual frustration, Sandra's eating disorder, Sandra's low self esteem, feeling being alone under the same roof. Not being able to solve the problem that goes back 14 years when due to possible frustration/depression on my part I wrote a list of uncomplimentary things about Sandra which [I] have regretted ever since."

When I first met the couple they came across as living separate, non-communicating lives. They did not sleep in the same bedroom, they talked about having separate seats from which they watched the television and they could not hold a conversation together apart from the most perfunctory of exchanges. However, with me they could joke painfully about their wish that life could have been so different if these notes had not been written and agreed that twelve years of married life previously had been largely good. They both said that, even now, they would like to share a bed together, but they each believed that the other had to change before any improvement at home could happen.

At the first consultation I understood something about Derek's background. He told me that he was an only child of parents who were very emotionally cut off. His father had been in long-term psychiatric care with depression for much of his childhood. Derek volunteered the thought about himself that he has never felt at ease dealing with emotionally charged matters for fear that he will lose control of them in a catastrophic way. He accepted in a rather flat way my thought that perhaps Sandra needs to hold all the depression for them both, much as his father seemed to hold inside him all the depressed feelings for his parents in those early years. In saying this, I had in mind that Derek had been so resistant to Sandra being discharged from the outpatients' list and that, to date, both had resisted couple therapy. The fact that Derek wrote in his questionnaire about being depressed and frustrated prior to writing his critical notes added weight to the idea that Sandra held a "double dose of depression". From Sandra's perspective I saw her as a person who unconsciously felt a need to be punished and in this connection, her experience of sexual abuse and of having a baby handed over for adoption were critical events. They thus matched each other well at an unconscious level: her need to be punished matching his need to project depression.

I offered to see them for twelve sessions, which is the standard offer in our service and, unusually, I agreed to extend therapy if, after review, we all thought it appropriate. I thought they were both very likeable people and I thought that their level of insight and wish for change augured well for therapy providing some help. Although I was conscious of the awful emotional void between them, I thought I could see good reasons why it had been constructed and the defensive purposes it served. I was wrong, however, in thinking I could succeed where others had failed. I have rarely, if ever, sat with a couple whose capacity to talk would end so quickly into a session and where the ensuing silence felt so unbearably negative. Under these circumstances, my interventions were powerfully informed by how they looked and moved in their chairs and by my countertransference.

Derek would invariably start the sessions, after nervously checking Sandra's face for permission, and his report would be about failures between them during the past week. He usually tried to make light of what he was saying, trying to draw a smile from Sandra. She might add a little to the report, but there was no reworking of the issues that had been so difficult. Each would give up in despair and look to me, as if I could get them out of their discomfort. An obvious theme underpinning my comments was of good things turning bad. I linked the instant collapse of optimism in the room with events in their lives such as Sandra's abuse, the loss of her baby for adoption, the loss of their good marriage following the notes being found. I talked about the sense that optimism could not prevail and that they lived fatalistically, as if having to suffer for terrible past wrongs. Nearly all of my interpretations were accepted as accurate but they did not promote a reciprocal response that took the conversations further. Rather, the response was to agree that this was the way things were and nothing could be done about it. Silence followed and the void opened up. I was a Simon Yates connected to a body, in my case a couple, whose life was in question and for whom I felt I could do nothing, or so it felt. My interventions appeared not to have the slightest effect on the quality of their marriage during the therapy. In short, I felt I touched their void, or, at least parts of it, but without changing it, and at the review of the therapy there was an agreement that we would not engage for further sessions. The rope was cut.

A dismissing couple void

The second couple, Ann and Gordon, were in their late fifties. Gordon had recently been admitted to hospital on three occasions, anxious and alarmed about his recurring impulse to kill Ann with a kitchen knife. During the previous autumn he had given up work because a benign tumour in his back was adversely affecting his ability to walk. He was eventually admitted to hospital and the tumour was removed successfully. The tumour meant that he could not work and he faced the prospect of permanently losing a prestigious and successful job. During the autumn, as his condition was being investigated, he became increasingly anxious and was finding it hard to sleep. He mentioned to the ward staff that for years he had a fear of seeking medical treatment, so that longstanding arthritis in his knees and hips went unattended. The hospital staff also learnt that for the past two years he had avoided seeking help for erectile problems.

I was asked to see this couple with a view to assessing their difficulties in a joint interview with the doctor who was involved with Gordon's care. We were given a history of couple difficulties that went back to the first year of marriage. Gordon explained that he entered marriage from living at home with his mother, who had spoiled him somewhat. It left him feeling resentful, however, that he had not lived a sufficiently independent life, as his brothers and his wife had done before marrying. In particular, he was from the outset envious that his wife had appeared more successful than he in having a varied and satisfying sexual life before marriage. In order to compensate for this sense of deprivation, Gordon was, from the beginning of their marriage, always on the look out for flirtation and extra-marital relationships. Six years after marrying, he left home to live with a lover. This met with a retaliatory response from his wife who, after getting over her initial sense of rejection, decided to have love affairs of her own. After several months they reconciled at Gordon's request, but Ann said that they never talked through what had happened. Instead they got on with their lives, as if the separation had not happened. However, beneath the outward appearance of "marriage as usual", Ann vowed never to put herself in a position with Gordon where she could be hurt again. Two strands to her life subsequently helped her do this. First, she committed herself to being a mother when they had a much-loved child. This experience offered an emotional closeness that she could not risk with her husband. Second, she developed a successful part-time career for herself and became an important figure in their local community.

Within the home she developed what she acknowledged to be a self-sufficient, bossy manner, rendering Gordon effectively redundant. When he talked about returning home after his operation, he said he sat and looked at the walls and realized that over the years he had contributed nothing to the house. Everything about the house had Ann's imprint on it. It was not difficult to see that in this marriage envy and its repression had played a central role. So long as Gordon had his work and the chance to have affairs with female work colleagues, he could repress and deny his envy of what he perceived to be his wife's greater success in life, which had become all the more pronounced following the crisis in their early marriage. She could manage her feelings of rejection by resolving never to place herself in a vulnerable/dependent position again. Both had denied the full emotional implications of their separation, and both had, in a manner of speaking, "dismissed" it from their minds. They had turned away from one another, having established a marriage where a huge void existed between them. This was made tolerable for Ann by investing her energies in parenthood, work, and community service, while Gordon invested all his energies in his career and his affairs. The present crisis came about because Gordon was threatened with the premature loss of his job and his sexual potency. This exposed him to the feeling that he had nothing left in his life, apart from looking in on Ann's success. We believed that it was this experience that provoked massive destructive envy such that he wanted to kill her.

My colleague and I were able to use this formulation of the problem to make a series of interpretations at the first interview, and Ann and Gordon continued meeting weekly with him. There have been significant changes in a very brief period. Gordon has been able to take on, and Ann to divest, some responsibility in the home for cooking meals. He has seen his GP for medical advice regarding his erectile problems and the couple have been away for a weekend together, which they both enjoyed. Moreover, he has been helped to review his employment situation and has been asked to return to part-time work. His recurring thoughts that he must kill his wife have abated.

Reflections

Allowing for the fact that this improvement may represent a flight into health and prove more illusory than real, why is it that the couple void between Ann and Gordon seemed possible to identify, work with, and change, and that between Sandra and Derek could be identified, worked with, but remained unchanged? I think that part of the answer lies in the nature of the voids that each couple had constructed and the purposes which each void served.

Put simply, the preoccupied void existing between Sandra and Derek was, in a manner of speaking, the centre of their lives, which, in turn, defined and reflected who they had become. The void was nurtured and preserved on a daily basis and stood as a constant reminder that life has to be built around a sense of personal failure and punishment. Derek's outside work as a tailor did not serve to generate an internal sense of goodness that might have shifted the negativity at home. To relinquish their void would have entailed dismantling and reconstructing their individual identities and this challenge was too much within the context of twelve sessions of couple psychotherapy.

By contrast, Ann and Gordon had established a dismissing void between them based on repression and denial. It is possible that once the emotional shutters had been erected between them after the separation, they have not required the same degree of psychological energy to keep them in place. In fact, once *in situ*, the defences have been relied upon to stay put and work, freeing both to apply energy in other areas of their lives. The void did not define who Ann and Gordon had become, and life outside the relationship gave them both a sense of positive self-image. Perhaps it was this experience of personal autonomy and separateness that gave them the strength to repair their relationship, helped by continuing their sexual relationship over the years. Moreover, both partners in this marriage seemed to have ego strength and a capacity for reflective functioning that enabled them to make use of the interpretive interventions made by all the professionals who worked with them.

Like the relationship between the two mountaineers, both couples struggled with the task of negotiating extremely painful predicaments. The couples' experiences of the "emotional void" created by one partner's psychiatric condition were different in each case. What they have in common, however, with the mountaineering couple, is the dilemma of being faced with a more extreme version of life events, where one partner's specific need places intense demands on the relationship. I have also demonstrated how Attachment Theory can offer a useful model for distinguishing between different types of "voids" and perhaps provide the establishment of a typology of "couple voids".

Acknowledgements

I am grateful to Sandra and Derek, and to Ann and Gordon, who, under other names, have given permission for me to write about their work with me in ways that would make them recognizable only to themselves.

References

Emmanuel, R. (2001). A-Void—an exploration of defences against sensing nothingness. *International Journal of Psychoanalysis, 82*: 1069–1084.

Fonagy, P. (2001). *Attachment Theory and Psychoanalysis*. New York: Other Press.

Freud, S. (1917e). Mourning and melancholia. *S.E. 14*: 239–258. London: Hogarth.

Simpson, J. (1997). *Touching the Void*. London: Vintage Books.

CHAPTER TEN

An exploration of the unconscious couple fit between the "detached" and the "adherent" narcissist: one couple's shared fear of madness

Viveka Nyberg

Introduction

> Whether in marriage or analysis, the physical space we share is also psychic space. It is a room housing the mind of the other, and it is furnished with thoughts of the other. It is not just material reality of the room that confines us; it is the psychic reality of the other person investing its contents with talismanic significance—that territory imbued with another's ideas, that room invested with someone else's good intentions, that couch or bed saturated with the other's desires, that domestic arrangement requiring acquiescence. [Britton, 2003, p. 166]

As couple therapists, we often talk about a couple's fear of intimacy, and in this chapter I investigate a more extreme degree or version of this anxiety. I present a couple with whom I worked for twelve months in weekly sessions. The couple shared an experience of having grown up with mothers who suffered from mental illness and fathers who were largely absent. I am interested in exploring what impact the experience of mental illness in the couple's parents may have on their interaction as a couple. I have found Britton's (2003) concept of narcissistic "detachment" and narcissistic "adherence" helpful and illuminating. Although he uses this concept primarily as a way of understanding the relationship between analyst and patient, I have found it instructive to apply it to interaction between couples.

Britton (2003) defines a narcissistic object relation in which something of the self is repudiated or attributed to the other. He draws a distinction between two different types of narcissistic disorders, based not on symptoms, but on the experience of the transference and countertransference. He defines one as *adherent narcissistic disorder*. This is what Rosenfeld (1987) refers to as "thin-skinned narcissism" (borderline disorder), where the transference is of an adherent kind. The countertransference is characterized by the analyst's inability to find a place outside the psychic reality of the patient. He defines the other type as *detached narcissistic disorder*, the "thick-skinned narcissist" (which is often described as schizoid personality). In this particular transference, the experience of exclusion is projected into the analyst, who is unable to find a place *within* the patient's psychic reality. Britton (2003) explores the experience of treating such patients and their difficulties in tolerating analysis because they are dominated by a dread of having to integrate someone else's separate mind. He states: "Instead of there being two connected, independent minds, there are either two separate people unable to connect or two people with only one mind" (*ibid.*, p. 171). This seems to summarize succinctly aspects of the psychological tension this couple experienced. I suggest that when the "detached" narcissist and "adherent" narcissist form a partnership, it creates an unconscious "couple fit", which becomes a defensive and pathological mental organization. This "fit" is characterized by a particular power imbalance where the detached and adherent aspects act as poles meant to repel the other and its defensive purpose is to prevent intimacy. The "fit" also allows for understanding a shared dread as a catastrophe that would happen if two separate minds were to be brought together. Although it is when the couple comes together that the "fit" takes shape, it is the unconscious recognition of what the other brings that creates a basis for the relationship. Within this "fit", the "thin-skinned" narcissist is able to project his or her detached needs into the "thick-skinned" partner, and vice versa. This brings about a defensive and polarized "fit" based on each partner carrying the split-off parts of the other.

The couple, Anton and Lin, were in their late forties. Anton originated from the Americas while Lin came from the Far East. They had met five years previously when they were both visiting scientists at a North American College. Lin had previously been in a long-term relationship, while Anton was twice divorced and had two grown-up children. Neither of them had had previous therapy. At the time of starting couple therapy they were both working for an international company in London on short-term contracts. Along with so many other aspects of their lives, this seemed to epitomize their experiences of uncertainty and temporary living arrangements. They also took some pride in feeling they could survive in an environment that was to some extent unpredictable and lacking in security. They were living separately and their presenting problem was an inability to feel safe together. Anton described his anxiety about Lin's propensity to "go into a tailspin" over some remark of his, which made her feel rejected. This was often related to his tangled relationship with his ex-wives and children. Lin, on the other hand, explained that she felt unable to understand the connections between Anton and his ex-families. To her they seemed mysterious, secretive, and threatening.

Both partners had experienced early and prolonged trauma, including maternal rejection and unpredictable separations. Lin was born into a diplomatic family, which meant that they moved at regular intervals. After Lin's birth, her mother suffered from severe postnatal depression and was hospitalized for several months. She was cared for by nannies and by her paternal grandmother, while her father was stationed abroad. Her mother experienced a further episode of severe depression three years later when Lin's younger sister was born, and was again hospitalized for a lengthy period. As the family was stationed abroad, Lin was sent to boarding schools from an early age and would, as she put it, "travel the world in the care of cabin crews", to visit her family during school holidays. Anton's mother suffered a psychotic breakdown when Anton was born and rejected her son, who was then cared for by his father and an aunt on a "rotational basis" for the first three years of his life. He did eventually settle with his mother, although there was an ongoing battle betwen his parents regarding custody.

The early phase of treatment

Secrets and separations were introduced as themes in the early sessions. Lin accused Anton of secretly thinking of buying a house for himself behind her back, and in so doing, of excluding her from his life. It seemed that houses and concrete objects had come to embody secrets, as well as representing something solid, as if emotional links between people had been translated into bricks and mortar. Anton presented himself as detached and a bit confused, as if he felt at other people's mercy. He referred to himself as a "plodder", while he appeared to lodge knowledge and dynamism in Lin, presenting himself as an innocent victim and therefore without responsibility. Lin appeared to be the driving force, the one who demanded knowledge and information, which she felt Anton with-held. They both wondered suspiciously whether the other wanted to be emotionally close.

My interpretations, which were directed towards the couple's anxiety about whether they felt they could trust the therapist, were ignored and met with equal suspicion. Anton expressed an anxiety that I might have a different agenda in the way I "brought myself into the room". This confusion was also expressed in their interaction, where the couple demonstrated how difficult it was for them to hear that the other felt something different, as if having a different reaction or thought was experienced as having "a different agenda". The early sessions were filled with material demonstrating how they both experienced themselves as getting lost in the other partner's mind. This was enacted in the regularity with which arrangements around their meetings would become confused because one of them would get lost or delayed or would forget the arrangement altogether.

It was already possible at this point to observe Anton's attempts to minimize Lin's anxiety and that this seemed to increase her internal turbulence. There were occasions when I felt under attack, as if I was put under intense pressure and I would be questioned over the choice of a particular word or phrase. It seemed that in the countertransference I was given an understanding through projective identification of the kind of experience to which they subjected each other, as well as reflecting early object relationships with a narcissistically preoccupied mother. During these first few months of treatment I frequently had an experience of trying very hard to understand what was happening in the sessions, while somehow not getting it quite right. I think this also reflected their own sense of trying to get things right with each other, for fear of the consequences, such was their feeling of persecution by the other. They would carefully weigh my words to figure out their relevance and meaning, as if they were trying to detect not only underlying ambiguous messages, but also as if they were trying to make the therapist doubt herself. When I addressed this they both agreed, and Anton declared that he used to experience this kind of confusion all the time with his mother. On the whole, though, my transference interpretations seemed to make them feel displaced, as if I had deprived them of their rightful space; instead I became a rival parental figure who "stole" the sessions for my own "agenda" and put my needs first. This led to my largely abandoning these types of interventions during this phase of the therapy.

The way in which communication between them could easily be seen as a means of "annihilating" and undermining the other was illustrated in a session three months into treatment. Lin arrived expressing outrage that Anton had entertained an overseas work colleague over the weekend and that this had meant he turned up late for their meeting. Anton sulked in the session, saying that he tried very hard to "please everyone" and he refused Lin's attempts to talk about what had happened. I commented on his attempt to detach himself from what he felt was an emotional demand. He agreed, and said that he could also feel unwanted and rejected by Lin. Lin, unable to hear about Anton's experience, protested that this was "nonsense", she certainly did not reject him. This interchange seemed to illustrate a re-enactment of a situation when the other's emotional experience, and also their significance, had to be denied and invalidated.

Middle phase of treatment

As we moved into the middle phase of treatment, I began to observe their different ways of dealing with the anxiety engendered by the other's unwillingness to make a statement expressing commitment. Lin would become increasingly anxious and feel persecuted by Anton's detachment. He, in turn, would perpetuate the cycle by withdrawing further, as if he experienced Lin's demands as a kind of impingement. As the therapist, I was faced with the task of trying to find and maintain a therapeutic relationship that did not feel persecutory. I continued to refrain from "bringing" myself into the sessions, commenting on their experience that words could be used as a way of "trapping" the other, rather than to create understanding.

Six months into treatment, they announced that they had decided to try to live together and that Anton was moving into Lin's house. The increased intimacy intensified their anxiety, which was acted out in the ways in which they undermined one another's trust. For example, on the day he moved in with Lin, Anton had a long, involved phone conversation with an ex-girlfriend, while appearing to ensure that Lin could hear every word. Lin, of course, immediately felt rejected.

During this time, the couple presented a great deal of material expressing their fear that closeness for them was a fragile state of affairs where you could easily end up feeling "dumped" or "sent packing", not only by each other, but also by the therapist. After all, their early relationships had been characterized by appalling separations.

There followed some sessions where I was permitted glimpses of the feared "madness" that was for them both part of their mental inheritance and, hence, their mental reality. I had the impression of a couple who could be supportive of each other during the session, but in the following week a psychic distancing emerged between them, as if an experience of good intercourse would invariably be followed by abandonment. At one point, Lin developed what she referred to as her "firm belief", which seemed closer to a conviction, that I, as the therapist, had been "perverted or seduced" into perceiving her as unreasonable and into siding with Anton against her. This anxiety seemed rooted in a fear that she could be misunderstood in catastrophic ways. She felt isolated and seemed to take pleasure in extracting new confessions from Anton about his convoluted business dealings, which she experienced as secret and exclusive. The more she tried to "get to the bottom of" these "secrets", the more Anton seemed to withdraw into secrecy. As Lin seemed to become increasingly out of touch with reality, Anton, on the other hand, seemed to become increasingly calm and reasonable, as if his own feared disintegrated feelings were projected into Lin. Simultaneously, there were emerging indications that Lin was beginning to recognize that certain feelings did indeed belong to her, rather than to Anton, while he, in turn, began to question his compliance with Lin's version of events. In so doing, he acknowledged his fear of upsetting Lin by confronting her "unreasonableness".

Final phase of treatment

This slight shifting of positions between the couple seemed to be reflected in my experience of them. I began to feel less intimidated by Lin and freer to offer challenging interpretations from a less entrenched position. Anton seemed to become less deferential towards Lin, who in turn spoke more directly about her fear of "going mad". There were signs that they were using fewer mutual projections. It was as if, momentarily, it was possible to be on the "same planet", as they put it, where they could experience each other as less mysterious. It appeared, however, that as they experienced greater emotional connectedness Lin voiced increasing fears that a person could be driven mad through "distortion". This anxiety was enacted in the transference when Lin experienced me as having "distorted her reality" by suggesting that a part of her wanted to "destroy" the therapy. Lin returned to this comment, accusing me of persecuting her. In the countertransference I experienced her projections very forcefully, feeling trapped like a butterfly pinned to a board, unable to think or move. There was an overwhelming sense of needing to be of one mind with her. I suggested that perhaps Lin wanted me to know how hard it is to hold on to a sense of self when under an emotional onslaught. She was unsure about this interpretation, but at the same time she seemed more contained.

This material perhaps confirms the formulation that Lin's mental reality had been "distorted" through traumatizing emotional events. At the same time, these and other similar experiences allowed Anton the opportunity to observe that what Lin could do to him, she could also do to others. Perhaps the plain fact that the therapist survived the projections provided an experience of "reality-testing" for the couple. Although Lin seemed to be the one who expressed the anxiety about an internal state that felt out of control, it was increasingly evident in the material that she carried Anton's projected fear of his own "mad" parts. Anton now began to question the value of therapy, which he experienced as "gnawing away at each other's bones". Through the image of mutual cannibalism, he seemed to express a deep-seated worry that therapy could develop into a sadistic attack. Despite his detached demeanour, however, it might be that he also felt threatened by the sense of progress in the therapy.

Shortly before they decided to end therapy, they spent a long weekend away together. In the following session Lin told us that Anton had taken the car and driven back to the airport, leaving her stranded at the hotel and having to make her own way back. They both felt the relationship was now over. It became evident in the session that they had unconsciously conspired to destroy the intimacy afforded by the holiday and that neither of them was able to prevent this from happening.

Lin gave her perception of the week's events. Anton said that he was sure she was "right". I suggested that Anton seemed to feel that it was not sufficient just to listen to Lin but that he also had to agree with her thoughts and analysis, as if he did not have a mind of his own. He seemed to take this on board and said to Lin that he ought to be able to contain her when she was angry and unreasonable, but that he could not. He said, "Someone else would say, 'Shut up you bloody idiot'", but he could not do this. Instead he felt he had to run away, like when he drove off to the airport. They continued talking together in a less defended way, such that Lin appeared to feel more understood and Anton was more assertive.

This exchange demonstrated a different quality, where they seemed to have an increased capacity to hear each other in a real and thoughtful way and to allow for the other's separate and different experience. In the following session, they continued to "test out" their own internal perceptions and phantasies, using the other as an external reality "mirror". For example:

Lin told Anton that she had felt crowded out of his mind. He responded that she could have taken more space herself, that the space had been there, available for her. She asked him if he felt she had created her anxieties about his business dealings and ex-families from nothing. Anton replied that there had been enough to feed her fears, but added that she was not wholly rational in her suspicions. He was fearful there was also something disturbed in Lin.

This brief interchange, when Anton was able to confront Lin with the aspect of her demands that was not rational, provided a significant glimpse of the couple's potential for containing each other. Rather than "pouncing" on Anton in retaliation, Lin appeared to feel held and understood by him. The following week they told me they had decided to stop therapy, as they were now separating.

> In the penultimate session, I wondered whether their manner of leaving therapy, mirrored the way they had experienced frequent abandonment by their parents. Lin agreed, and she came back to Anton's fears about her "madness" and how this was something they had not really talked about. Anton said this fear played a big part in his life, too, and that his own mother had always been on the edge of "normal life". He went on to say that he also lived with a fear of his own madness.

It then appeared as if the couple's attempt to separate was not so much about anxiety regarding increased separateness within the relationship, but rather about psychic survival. In leaving therapy, it seemed that Anton was, for the first time, able to own some of his equally fragmented early experiences and his feelings of depression. He did not need to depend on Lin to express his own fear that madness was "part of the fabric" of both their parental relationships. By not consulting the therapist over the ending, moreover, they also triumphed and conveyed their contempt for my endeavours as a useless parental object. Nevertheless, it emerged that they had gained a certain tolerance of the other's experience of exclusion, neglect, and emotional pain. Interestingly, it appeared that, during the final sessions, the couple related to me more as a separate individual rather than as a merged, undifferentiated, "one-minded" therapist. Perhaps this did, to some extent, reflect the couple's experience of a tentative and less confused separateness.

Discussion

Although Britton's (2003) theoretical model about the relationship between the adherent and the detached narcissist is primarily based on the relationship between analyst and patient, his ideas suggest the potential of a relationship, or marriage, between the adherent and the detached narcissist. Anton seemed to represent the qualities of the "thick-skinned" narcissist with his detached manner. This was manifested in the transference to the therapist, as he appeared to absent himself through his silences and slow and deliberate communications, as if he were holding something back in order to make the therapist feel excluded. In the countertransference I frequently had an experience of not being able to connect with Anton's internal mental world, as if he were forcefully pushing the therapist out. In relation to Lin, this was expressed through his difficulties in acknowledging her anxiety, as if her feelings were not "real" to him. In childhood, he had found ways of hiding through secrets, as if he were looking for a secret space where he could go missing. The consequence for his adult intimate relationships was that it was not easy for the other to find a place within his internal world. However, there were also moments when the therapist's interventions reached him emotionally and he allowed me to take his distress seriously. He experienced these occasions as extremely painful.

In contrast, Lin, in sharing the characteristics of the "thin-skinned" narcissist, appeared to try to get inside Anton through her relentless demands and her accusations of his deceitful secrecy. She seemed to fill the space, as if she were trying to control any bid for independence made by Anton, as well as by the therapist. The emotional power she asserted was manifested through projections and projective identification. The countertransference in relation to Lin felt radically different, as I, as the therapist, often felt pulled into Lin's internal world, like being drawn into a spider's web. Britton suggests that, although the two situations are very different, they are both organized to avert the same catastrophe. The catastrophe is about the fear of what might happen if two separate psychic realities are brought together to occupy the same psychological space.

Britton argues that such patients have experienced being misunderstood in such a catastrophic way that they fear the very extinction of their identities. He suggests that, if this failure is experienced as an attack rather than a deficiency, the patient may believe that a force exists that destroys understanding and meaning. Hence, this experience is repeated in the transference when the therapist's failure to understand the patient is experienced as an attack on the patient's psychic integrity. The dread that the couple's internal worlds were incompatible and, if brought together, might create something catastrophic, can perhaps best be understood as based in the partners' experience of early traumas.

Both Lin and Anton had mothers who suffered from mental illness; they had experienced separations from the parental objects as well as having parents who were themselves separated. It would seem they both had early object relationships that were dominated by narcissistic object relating with mothers who may have been primarily preoccupied with their own mental survival. The pathological aspect of Anton's detachment is a manifestation of his need to deny the importance of the other. Lin's unconscious response is to demand to be the epicentre of her partner's life. This way they both ensure that there is little risk of emotional closeness and intimacy.

I am suggesting that both Lin and Anton shared an early experience where it felt that to join in a relationship with the maternal object would have been to experience something truly devastating. It would have meant confronting a damaged and disintegrated mind, incapable of containment, but capable of psychic attack. This was perhaps evident in Lin's attempts to force her thoughts into the therapist, as if the alternative would have been for the therapist to force something destructive inside her. As Anton felt able to begin to know about his own fear of madness, it seemed that he took flight from this knowledge by leaving therapy.

The couple's experience of feeling increasingly understood by the therapist was felt as a threat to their psychic equilibrium. Although Lin expressed a reluctance to terminate therapy, she nevertheless colluded with Anton's wish. If the couple had remained in treatment, she would have had to recognize that Anton's fears of madness were as fundamental as her fears, but also to accept that Anton had a mind that was separate from her own. Lin attempted to negate this anxiety by trying to "recruit" Anton into her world as if they could merge and be of one mind. As Britton suggests, when there is no expectation of understanding, the need for agreement is absolute.

As the clinical material illustrates, the categorization into "detached/thick-skinned" and "adherent/thin-skinned" narcissism is by no means exclusive or rigid. There were overlaps between the partners that allowed for some flexibility. I am suggesting that, when "thin-skinned" and "thick-skinned" narcissists form a partnership, this allows for the opposite mental function to be projected into the other. In Lin's case, this allowed her not to know about her "thick-skinned" part, where she could also experience herself as an outsider. In this way, she could perhaps maintain a phantasy that she was available for an intimate relationship, if only Anton would change his ways. Similarly, Anton could remain unknowing about his "adherent" needs and aspects. His "thin-skinned" and adherent needs were manifested in his inability to open up a separate space with his elderly and dependent mother, as if he were trying to merge with her. By allowing Lin to express his longing for a more exclusive relationship, he could maintain his stance as unreachable and detached. This bears out the observation that unless a couple is able to withdraw some of their mutual projections, it is likely that their relationship will remain based in a defensive relating. Although there were moments when there were glimpses of something less persecutory opening up between the couple, the tendency towards polarization dominated, and, in the end, the fear of relating more intimately gained the upper hand.

References

Britton, R. (2003). *Sex, Death and the Superego*. London & New York: Karnac.

Rosenfeld, H. A. (1987). *Impasse and Interpretation*. London: Routledge.

CHAPTER ELEVEN

Sex as protection against intimacy and closeness: working with buyers and sellers of sex

Gullvi Sandin and Anna Kandell

Introduction

In this chapter we share our experiences of taking part in a study (Boman & Green, 2004) where we worked, as psychotherapists, with men and women involved in the buying and the selling of sex. The chapter outlines how specific psychological needs were satisfied through the relationship between the men and the women and how the transaction was an attempt to resolve complex emotional dilemmas around power, dependency, devaluation, and shame.

In Sweden, attempts have recently been made to combat the sex trade by various social programmes and through legislation. Arguments for and against making prostitution illegal have often been debated, as well as the question of whether this should concern both the buying and selling of sex, or if it should apply only to the person buying sex. The Act of Prohibiting the Purchase of Sexual Services (1998: 408) stated that a person who is paying for sex shall be sentenced for the purchase of sexual services to a fine or imprisonment for a maximum period of six months. This law was revised in 2005 and was then included in the Criminal code.

Arguments in favour of this law include the suggestion that it is an effective tool, in the first place to protect women, but also as a means of defeating prostitution. Arguments opposing the law claim that it will not reduce prostitution, but will merely move the activity from the streets to more hidden places. A further claim is that not only the sellers of sexual favours, but also the buyers, can be considered victims in a psychological and emotional sense. In Sweden, it is officially acknowledged that prostitution is a form of exploitation of women and children and that it constitutes a significant social problem, which is harmful not only to the individual prostituted woman or child, but also to society at large. This objective is central to Sweden's wider goal of achieving equality between women and men, and it is considered that gender equality will remain unattainable as long as men buy, sell, and exploit women and children by prostituting them.

The law has not yet been evaluated. It seems, however, to be a fact that selling or buying sex is now considered to be unacceptable and wrong, even among young people. It is evident that the law and the discussions about the law have had an impact on public opinion.

Experiences from therapeutic work with the sellers and buyers of sex

As part of the project we worked both with men who bought sexual services and with women selling them. The project was based at the RFSU Clinic, the Swedish Association for Sexuality Education, in Stockholm. The RFSU Clinic in Stockholm is similar in outlook to the Portman Clinic in London, but it also has a remit to educate the general public on sexual matters. The project took place over six years between 1998 and 2003. During this time six psychoanalytic psychotherapists worked with twenty-five women who were involved with the selling of sex, and thirty men who were buying sexual services. This chapter is based on our work in the project and our thoughts about the relationship between sellers and buyers of sex. The work with the men and women, and the psychotherapists' experiences, is described in detail in the report *What's Love Gotta Do With It?*, written by psychotherapist Suzanna Boman and psychoanalyst Elisabeth Green (2004).

A fundamental principle for clinical work at the RFSU clinic over the past thirty years has been to examine problems from different perspectives. During 1998–1999 we met an increasing number of men who suffered from obsessive sexual behaviour and who wanted help with their problems. We also found that women in prostitution sought help for various symptoms. In planning clinical services and work with prostitution this meant meeting with both sellers and buyers of sex. The RSFU clinic decided, as part of the study, to offer psychotherapy to this group of patients as a way of focusing on their specific difficulties. The aim was to increase awareness and knowledge of the particular psychological issues driving men and women to buy or sell sex, as well as to find suitable methods for meeting, caring for, and treating this group of patients. Before we started the project we had several questions in our minds. A major aim was to increase our understanding about the emotional forces behind the behaviour and to try to comprehend some of the emotional intricacies involved in the relationship between the men and the women. It was initially announced that the clinic was prepared to give priority to this group of patients. Social workers, police, medical clinics, and newspapers are examples of channels that were then used to reach these particular groups.

It is relevant to note that none of the women asked for help because of being involved in prostitution. Instead they were concerned about their inabilities to make close relationships and worried about their self-destructive behaviour. Some were depressed and suffered from sleep disturbance. None of the twenty-five women in the project said they needed the money they earned from prostitution to make a living or in order to feed a drug habit. Eleven of the women had university education, fourteen were employed, and five were students. Three were receiving regular benefits from social services. Eleven women were either married or in a stable relationship.

With regard to the men, the most commonly presented problems were sexual obsessions or concerns that their relationships with their partners were unravelling. They were addicted to the viewing of pornographic films, to using internet pornography, to making sex calls, or to buying sex from prostitutes. With few exceptions, the men taking part in the research project were socially well functioning. Of the thirty men taking part in the project, many had well-qualified jobs and sixteen had a university education; nineteen were married, cohabiting, or in stable relationships.

The psychotherapists who took part in the project experienced some difficulties in establishing creative and stable working relationships with both the men and the women. The women were all seen individually; of those who commenced in long-term psychotherapy, nineteen terminated the treatment within a year. The remaining six women continued in treatment and these were the same women who had approached the clinic on their own initiative. Some of the men were offered group psychotherapy, as it was known from previous experience at the clinic that this form of treatment tended to work for men presenting with sexual symptoms. Of the men, twenty stayed in treatment for less then ten sessions. Out of the remaining men, six stayed in treatment for more then a year; four were in group psychotherapy and two in individual therapy.

Some thoughts about the relationship between seller and buyer: both sharing an internal couple constellation of victim and perpetrator

As the men and women were not seen together, the focus of the work was obviously not on the actual relationship between buyers and sellers of sex. In order to reflect on, and understand, some of the relational dynamic that takes place between these two groups, the therapists relied instead on what they were told in the course of the therapy, as well as the transference and countertransference relationships. It became clear that, contrary to common opinion, it is a simplistic notion to regard the women as being victims in relation to the men. Considering the psychological needs of both groups and the way their internal worlds appear to be structured, the most striking finding of the project was that we were able to understand that the women and the men are simultaneously both victims and perpetrators. The two groups appear to share an unconscious image of an internal couple that is relating to each other as victim versus perpetrator.

On the whole, the women do not describe themselves as dependent on the men. Rather they tend to express contempt and communicate a sense of triumph. The women experience that they are in possession of something that the men need so badly that they are prepared to debase themselves and to pay for it, even to the point of breaking the law, as buying sex is now an illegal activity in Sweden. The woman has the power to say yes or no. At times the woman also experiences a profound contempt for herself, as she participates in an activity that is damaging to both her emotional and physical well-being and one which she has to hide from her family and friends. The men, on the other hand, sometimes described a fantasy that they like to think that they—as men—are giving the woman something of value, besides the financial transaction. The men are also in possession of something the women want, i.e., the money. On the surface, the men want sex and are prepared to pay for it, and the women want money and are prepared to offer sex in exchange. The men taking part in the research project however, do not, in reality, need to pay to have sex and the women do not, in reality, need to prostitute themselves to have money. This raised for us the important question about the kind of emotional relationship the two groups were searching for.

Many of the men gave the impression of being in an inferior position in relation to the partner they were living with. In the course of therapy they often communicated a fear of dependency, expressed in daydreams of living by themselves or travelling around the world alone. As we understood it, there was a strong desire to be "close" without being emotionally involved, or "stuck". There was an anxiety about what might happen if they were to be dependent on only one woman and how they would manage if the woman left them. The thought of never having sexual access to more than one woman was a frightening thought for this group. This anxiety seemed linked, on the one hand, to a great fear of being abandoned and totally alone, while on the other hand there was an anxiety about being trapped in a form of closeness that would be too confining.

Dependence–independence

We will describe our understanding of the men and the women and their relationships with regard to dependence–independence.

The men

It seemed to us that, for the men purchasing services of a prostitute, this became an attempt to cope with an inner conflict characterized by a strong need and longing for a partner versus an equally strong fear of dependency. For those men who were in stable relationships, the buying of sex and use of pornography became a secret that created a distance from their partner. At the same time, when the intimacy with the partner became too intense and claustrophobic, it could be "diluted" through turning to the prostitute and this way the relationship with the partner might be "saved".

We also found through our work with the project that issues around dependency and independency for women is also "balanced" through acts of prostitution, though there appears to be a difference in the way it manifests.

The women

Unlike the men, women who were living with a partner, tended not to experience the division between "normal" life and a "secret" life. Instead, most of the women described their relationships with the partner as involving destructive and self-destructive elements and portrayed a strong dependency on a man they knew was "bad" for them. These women talked about how prostitution did come between their partner and themselves, both as a protection and as a hindrance. Those women who lived on their own without a stable relationship seemed on the whole to avoid close and intimate relationships. Perhaps for them prostitution represented a form of closeness, while at the same time this activity made it very difficult for them to achieve intimacy with a partner. On one occasion when a woman taking part in the project was asked about her work as a prostitute, she answered that the therapist should mind her own business and that she was not going to give the therapist ideas, as if the therapist was perceived as a prostitute colleague. When the therapist replied that she had asked the question out of concern that the patient might be doing herself harm, the patient was astonished.

The men and women we met in this study seem to share an internal fear of intimacy and closeness. This anxiety is re-enacted in their activities and in the relationships they establish with each other. To have some control over the choice of partner in this context seems to allow for some of their central psychological needs to be met.

Shame, shamelessness, contempt

The feeling that can balance out, and hence perhaps neutralize the experience of shame, is the feeling of contempt. Shame over one's own shortcomings can be transformed into contempt for someone else. Shamelessness is also related to shame: by behaving shamelessly the person may attempt to deny and hide their experience of shame. The experience of self-contempt is a shared feeling among both the men and the women who are part of our material, but it is expressed differently between the sexes. Men, besides the shameful secrets around the buying of sex and use of pornography, tend to talk about their personal shortcomings and problems. They express a feeling that they ought to be different; for example, more active, braver, and manlier. They experience themselves as deviant, perverse, and powerless in relation to their behaviour, which they tend to describe as obsessive. Their self-contempt seems linked to anxieties and feelings of inferiority that include their inability to "control" themselves and their need of other people. To us as psychotherapists, these anxieties manifested as constant feelings of shame, connected to a feeling of being unloved and not having their self-worth confirmed.

During therapy the men did not, on the whole, express pronounced contempt for the women—neither towards their partners nor the prostitutes. It was obvious, however, that the men viewed the prostitutes as objects; they were not allowed to become human beings with needs, feelings, and problems. Instead, they were treated more as fantasy objects, or bodies, or body parts—part objects—that enjoyed what they were doing and appreciated the man. One male patient told his psychotherapist towards the end of his treatment that he could no longer buy sex because the prostitutes "had got eyes": in other words, the prostitute was now seen more as a human being than as an object.

The women, on the other hand, expressed their self-contempt in different ways. They would often express a pronounced contempt for themselves and in particular towards their bodies and gender. They often seemed to feel that everything was wrong with their bodies; they were too fat, they needed cosmetic surgery, and they often expressed a sense that their bodies "deserved" to be indifferently or abusively treated. We were able to understand that some of the women had never experienced their bodies as an integrated part of themselves, but more like an object belonging to the outside world or even to someone else.

The women did, on the whole, express pronounced contempt for the customer; for example, they would talk about how pitiful, stupid, and disgusting he was and how easily he could be deceived. This unspecific contempt, however, can have a kind of boomerang effect; for example, what kind of person is the prostitute if *she* gets involved with someone like *him*? The contempt the woman feels towards the customer returns the moment he chooses her. One woman, with her face displaying strong disgust, explained to the psychotherapist how on one occasion when a female boss had hired a strip-tease girl for an office party, neither the patient nor the men in the office liked it.

Revealing feelings of shame—mission possible?

In our clinical work with these patients, the dimensions of shame and contempt have been greatly meaningful and helpful to our thinking and understanding of these patients. It is very hard indeed to talk about activities that are perceived as shameful and to expose one's self to humiliating feelings. This has been more noticeable with the women than the men. The women have often found it easier to talk about anything but the actual prostitution, and they would often draw a line about what kinds of things they were prepared to talk about. It appeared that the experience of putting feelings surrounding the prostitution into words would awaken deeper feelings of shame than the act itself. We have wondered if putting into words what previously has been acted out makes it "real", perhaps for the first time, and that the psychological experience of connecting the act to thought and feeling becomes too painful and has to be denied.

In order for the patient to communicate feelings of shame there must be a relationship in existence with the psychotherapist that is founded on trust. Exposing shameful feelings means running a considerable risk, like being seen and seeing oneself through the eyes of another person—not to mention the risk of not being understood and thereby losing all sense of hope. In our opinion this kind of dynamic is of great importance in understanding why some therapeutic contacts were prematurely terminated in the treatment process, apparently often following a productive session. In these cases it was as if the shameful experiences were "deposited" in the psychotherapist, and perhaps the confrontations with these feelings were felt to be too difficult and the psychotherapist then had to be avoided.

Power and control: a way to eliminate feelings of powerlessness

The buying and selling of sexual acts reflect power issues in several ways. The man, as the customer, has money, and therefore the power to purchase the right to use the woman's body to satisfy his desires. He can choose between different women based on his preference, without the need to consider the woman's feelings or needs. The woman, in turn, has power over the man, as she possesses what he so desperately wants. For a brief moment it is as if she can experience a feeling of being desired and wanted by one or several men, whom she can choose to accept or reject.

The patients often described feelings of powerlessness in many situations. Both the men and the women gave accounts of difficulties in asserting their own interests in an adaptive and constructive manner. Some said they often felt attacked and debased by others and they would try to escape these situations, feeling both hurt and humiliated. In the face of one's own shortcomings the experience of powerlessness can be total—the person is then helplessly exposed to their own manifested symptoms and/or to the oppressive and harsh judgement of society. The person may then be left with little or no feeling of being able to control his or her own life and fate and to make his or her own choices.

With the two groups we worked with, the issues seemed to be about having power and being able to dictate the conditions for what is allowed to happen in relationships. It is important not to be caught by surprise and to be powerless in the face of someone else's needs, or to be overwhelmed by one's own needs. This theme was equally important for both the men and the women. Both groups lacked experience of being able to trust another human being and to feel safe within a relationship. One might conceptualize this as a shared unconscious phantasy that to be close and dependent on another exposes one to being despised, disgraced, isolated, anxious, and depressed. The main defence against this phantasy is to ensure that relationships with others remain under one's control. From these shared experiences, the two gender groups were able to intuitively understand each other's needs. There seemed to be an unspoken agreement and understanding that the needs of the other person were not to be challenged, but instead met and, in a way, even respected.

One of the women taking part in the project told her therapist of a situation when she had been to visit her parents for a long weekend. Her two brothers were also visiting, and she was aware that her father took no notice of her, but instead directed the conversation to her brothers. She also felt that her mother appeared to favour the brothers and take more of an interest in them. She found herself making attempts to attract attention to herself, telling them about her life in the city and contributing her views on different topics, but to no avail. The patient recalled to the therapist her growing sense of feeling abandoned and helpless, as if she didn't exist. When she returned to the city she went to her apartment to leave her bag and then immediately went out on the street looking for a customer. She then felt that an internal balance had been restored, as she was the one with power and control when cars with prospective customers stopped next to her. In the session it was not difficult for her to connect this experience to an attempt to manage the anger and sadness left over from the visit to her family.

In the treatment setting, the themes of power and powerlessness can be observed in the acting out around boundaries. For example, arriving late for sessions, cancelling, or failing to attend, can be seen as attempts to negate the experience of powerlessness in relation to the therapist. By coming and going as one pleases, the situation is redefined and a sense of control is reasserted. In the patient's fantasy it is now the psychotherapist who is waiting helplessly for the patient.

By carefully controlling what is or what is not divulged to the psychotherapist, the patient is also avoiding taking any risks in the therapeutic relationship, sometimes to the extent that sessions become reduced to the point of triviality. In this kind of situation the psychotherapist's countertransference sometimes reflects feelings of despair and powerlessness regarding the possibility of positive change. At other times the countertransference mirrors feelings of being controlled and feeling unable to think and speak freely.

Conclusion

In this chapter we have described our experience of working as psychotherapists with men and women involved in the buying and selling of sex. We have outlined how perhaps the most striking finding was that, contrary to popular opinion, it is simplistic to consider the women as victims of the men. Instead, we found considerable overlap in the psychological needs and internal psychic worlds of the two groups, which led us to think of both groups as simultaneously victims and perpetrators. We have also outlined how the different dimensions of the complex relationship between buyers and sellers of sex can usefully be summarized in relation to shame versus shamelessness and power versus powerlessness.

References

Boman, S., & Green, E. (2004). *What's Love Gotta Do With It?* RFSU, Stockholm, Sweden. http://www.rfsu.se/publications__rfsu.asp

PART IV

THE POWER OF THEORY
AND RESEARCH:
THE PSYCHOTHERAPIST'S
AIDS TO THINKING ABOUT
THE COUPLE

CHAPTER TWELVE

The power of our attachment to theory—or Oedipus meets Ganesh

David Hewison

Introduction

We are accustomed to the idea that couples who come to see us for psychotherapy are caught up in their own "theory" about their relationship—a theory that is structuring their relating and which we might otherwise call a "shared unconscious phantasy" (Bannister & Pincus, 1965; Ruszczynski, 1993). The purpose of therapy is then to modify destructive versions of this and enable developmental versions to evolve. What we talk about less is the therapist's relation to their own versions of theory, particularly when it is something to which we might have a powerful attachment.

"Nothing is so useful as a good theory" is a saying variously attributed to Kurt Lewin, Donald Winnicott, and Jock Sutherland. Wilfred Bion suggested that theories should only be used for the first few sessions of an analysis, but that then they should be discarded in favour of an openness to the material consequent to an absence of memory, desire, and understanding (Bion, 1970). Some people suggest that this means that theories are not important in psychoanalytic work—as though the statement that one should eschew "memory, desire, and understanding" is not itself a theory. Michael Fordham proposed his own version, suggesting that one may have a kind of mental filing cabinet for theory to which it should be returned once it had done its job of enabling the analysis to begin, and that it should then be replaced by what he called "not knowing beforehand" (Fordham, 1993). Apparently, Fordham had an actual filing cabinet in his consulting room and it may have been this that inspired his image. It seems (Urban, 1996) that at some point in its life one of his child patients had scrawled upon it the phrase "Dr. Fordham is a nit-face"—which, of course, is another theory! Jung wrote that in psychology "theories are the very devil" (Jung, 1946, par. 7), while simultaneously attempting to construct the unified theory that would connect all psychologies together into one psychological Theory of Everything, if we follow Sonu Shamdasani's reading of him (Shamdasani, 2003). Elsewhere, Jung wrote succinctly that "every theory is a subjective confession" (Jung, 1931, par. 774).

We all know what is meant by theory, though in the *Shorter Oxford English Dictionary*, "theory" is defined as being two nouns, not one. The first "theory" is familiar and has four different variants. These are:

> A mental scheme of something to be done, or a way of doing something; a systematic statement of rules or principles to be followed.

> The knowledge or exposition of the general principles or methods of an art or science, especially as distinguished from the practice of it. In mathematics, a set of theorems forming a connected system.

> (The formulation of) abstract knowledge or speculative thought; systematic conception of something. Frequently opposed to practice.

and last:

> An unsubstantiated hypothesis; a speculative (especially fanciful) view. [Little, 2002]

It is interesting that this meaning of theory implies that it is something that is separate from "doing", or practice, and we know that psychoanalysis is a practical matter. Might the second definition of "theory" capture this more active, non-abstract, quality? It does, although in a striking and rather unexpected way.

The Shorter Oxford Dictionary offers the following definition for this second version of theory: a theory is "a group of theors who are sent by a State to perform a religious duty or rite". "Theors" are themselves defined as ambassadors, sent "especially to consult an oracle or perform a religious rite". The root of both versions of "theory" is the same, that is, *theoros*, or spectator. So it seems that in the midst of the idea that a theory is a rather abstract, pale, and bloodless thing, we find that it is something concrete, with agency, and immersed in occult mystery and religious devotion. It involves gods as well as nit-faces, and we know from the history of the Delphic oracle that interpreting the message conveyed by a theory is no easy matter. Theory, then, is a very personal affair, engaging us in rational and non-rational ways, and involving action as well as contemplation. The power of our attachment to theory becomes a bit clearer. It is not just an idea, but also a meeting with the divine. Little wonder, then, that theoretical disagreements can take on the stamp of religious battles.

In this chapter, I explore aspects of Freud's theory of Oedipus, suggesting that in his powerful attachment to Sophocles' play *Oedipus Rex*, he did more than just blur the distinctions between the two different meanings of "theory" outlined above. I suggest that for Freud, for a variety of reasons, *Oedipus Rex* was the divine oracle that he consulted and that psychoanalysis has a quality of religious ritual as a result. I reflect on elements of the Oedipus myth missed out by Freud, and contrast the Sophoclean story with that of the story of the elephant god of Hindu belief, Ganesh, touching on some contentious issues between Freud and Indian psychoanalysts. I conclude that psychoanalytic work needs both Oedipus and Ganesh, as well as both versions of "theory", for practitioners and for the couples who consult us. This is for the obvious reason that couple relationships involve people who are in the relationship and people who are, therefore, outside it. Both positions raise feelings of inclusion and exclusion, closeness and distance, attachment and separation, which are touched on in both the Oedipus and Ganesh stories. In addition, the added factor of children puts the adult couple into a very particular emotional position. This occurs whether or not children are actually a part of the life of the couple, as dynamics of twosomes and threesomes abound in all adult couple relationships and they have to be managed and come to terms with in order to enable emotional development to continue.

Of Oedipus

The story of *Oedipus Rex*, as told by Sophocles, is an exceptionally well-structured piece of drama, with the tension escalating despite periodic relief, culminating in an extraordinary climax of revelation, horror, heroism, and omnipotence. The outline of the basic story is well known: Oedipus attempts to discover the source of a plague that has been visited on the city of Thebes, the kingship of which he won when he defeated the Sphinx who had been terrorizing the city. In defeating the Sphinx by solving her riddle, he also won the hand of Jocasta, Queen of Thebes, and widow of King Laius, who was murdered by a stranger shortly before Oedipus arrived in the city. Oedipus is trying to escape from a curse, delivered by the Oracle at Delphi, which says he will kill his father and sleep with his mother. As the play unfolds, it becomes increasingly clear that this is just what he has, unwittingly, done. He is the son of Laius and Jocasta, abandoned by them on a hillside, because Laius knew of another curse from the Oracle saying he was destined to be murdered by his own son. Oedipus was rescued, however, and brought up in Corinth, believing himself to be the son of its King and Queen. It was he who killed Laius, a man unknown to him, in a fight at the crossroads and who thus caused the plague that he is now attempting to relieve.

The play charts his increasing self-knowledge and his determination to get to the bottom of things, despite all the warnings from those around him. It also shows him as cruel and vicious and blind to his own faults. Sophocles has Oedipus blind himself and be made to wander off in banishment at the end of the play. This further tragedy is a departure from other versions of the story, which have him continue to reign in Thebes. For Sophocles, Oedipus' downfall was that of a man "who knew the famous riddles and was a man most great", yet who insisted on discovering the truth, despite the cost.

Some authorities have suggested that the play is about the absence of free will and the need to give in to divine fate. Other, more contemporary, interpretations suggest that it is about actions of free will in the face of fate, noting that Oedipus did not have to discover the truth about himself, his parents, his marriage, and his children. Rather, he was the agent of his own discovery, not a passive victim manipulated by the gods (see Knox, 1984, for a survey). Freud, in the *Interpretation of Dreams*, takes a psychological view, that the power of the play is its universality of content; that Jocasta is right when she tries to allay Oedipus' suspicions about their relationship by telling him that men often dream of sharing their mother's bed. We *do* dream of such things—that is the point. Freud, however, disagrees with Jocasta's interpretation of these dreams, in that they are not just "shadows, nothing at all". Indeed, for Freud, *Oedipus Rex* writes our innermost fantasy life large on the stage for all to see, and we are fascinated at seeing ourselves in it (Freud, 1900a).

Nevertheless, there is more to this than meets the eye. Why is it this version of Oedipus rather than any other that has such a powerful attraction for Freud? After all, Freud chooses not to rely on the Roman playwright Seneca's version, written some 400 years after Sophocles, or those of Voltaire, Schelling, or Schiller, although he does quote, approvingly, on three occasions the words of the eighteenth-century French *philosophe*, Diderot. As Freud puts it, building a case for the universality of the complex,

> [it should not] be allowed to pass unnoticed that the two criminal wishes of the Oedipus complex were recognised as the true representatives of the uninhibited life of the instincts long before the time of psycho-analysis. Among the writings of the encyclopaedist Diderot you will find a celebrated dialogue, *Le Neveu de Rameau*, which was translated into German by no less a person than Goethe. There you may read this remarkable sentence: "If the little brute were left to his own devices, and remained in all his ignorance combining the undeveloped mind of a child in its cradle with the violent passions of a man of thirty, he would wring his father's throat and go to bed with his mother". [Freud, 1916–1917, p. 338]

Ernest Jones gives us a clue as to Freud's singular devotion. In the *Life and Work of Sigmund Freud*, he describes a rather curious event. Jones and other followers of Freud presented him with a gift to mark the occasion of his fiftieth birthday. This was a medallion which had, on one side, a portrait of Freud in profile, and on the other a picture of Oedipus and the Sphinx, with the line from the conclusion of Sophocles' play, "Who knew the famous riddles and was a man most great". On seeing this, Freud had an extreme emotional reaction; he became pale and agitated, as though he had seen a ghost. Jones recounts that Freud was seeing a version of something that he had long yearned to see:

> as a young student at the University of Vienna he used to stroll around the great arcaded court inspecting the busts of former famous professors of the institution. He then had the phantasy, not merely of seeing his own bust there in the future, which would not have been anything remarkable in an ambitious student, but of it being inscribed with the *identical words* which he now saw on the medallion. [Jones, 1959, p. 15. cited in Rudnytsky, 1986, pp. 4–5]

In true Jones style, he later ensured that exactly such an inscribed bust was installed in the University.

We know, therefore, that Freud identified himself with this particular Oedipus when a university student. Further investigation reveals that Freud was fascinated with Sophocles' hero even at school, because, at seventeen, he was given the opening passage from Sophocles' play to translate from the Greek. In a letter of 16th June 1873 to his friend Emil Fluss, he indicates that he had already chosen to read it on his own account. In another letter of 15th October 1897 to Wilhelm Fliess, during the period of his self-analysis, he reveals that,

> I have found love of the mother and jealousy of the father in my own case too, and now believe it to be a general phenomenon of early childhood . . . If that is the case, the gripping power of Oedipus Rex . . . becomes intelligible. [Freud, 1954, cited in Rudnytsky, 1986, p. 7]

What turns out in the *Interpretation of Dreams* to be a general comment supported by reference to *Oedipus Rex*, has its origins in Freud's identification of himself as such an Oedipus.

Freud's own family background gives weight to this idea. His mother, Amalie, was his father, Jacob's, third wife, and she was the same age as Jacob's sons. Thus, Freud's mother was of the same generation as his half-brothers, a generation between Freud and his father. Rudnytsky, in *Freud and Oedipus* (1986), traces the impact of this confusion of genealogies and the particular closeness that Freud felt with his mother over the course of Freud's life and in the development of his early theories. He notes, also, that the death of Amalie's second child, Julius, only a few months after birth, when Freud himself was just over a year old, had left Freud with a "germ of guilt" following what he describes as his "ill wishes" towards the baby and his "real infantile jealousy" of him (Letter to Fliess, 3rd October 1879, cited in Rudnytsky, p. 19). Julius's place in Freud's public accounts of his childhood is taken by his nephew John, who was a year older than Freud, although Julius remained present in his private letters. Freud's first mention of a parapraxis was in a letter to Fliess and it concerned his dead brother. It does not however, make it into his list of parapraxes in the *Psychopathology of Everyday Life* (Freud, 1901b, pp. 291–296).

Rudnytsky (1986) suggests that Freud's struggles with the extraordinary facts and circumstances of his childhood not only led him to try to uncover heroically the "riddles" of nature, but also to hide his very personal involvement in it. In something of a whirlwind *tour de force*, Rudnytsky links Freud's periodic destruction of his letters and archives with a story that might be revealed in them, which Rudnytsky suggests is the repeating motif in various forms of Freud's emotional and erotic entanglement with his mother, and his need for a hated and an idealized male friend, preferably with both attributes in the same person. Freud's father's death triggered the satisfaction and the guilt associated with the death of Julius, and forced Freud into his self-analysis. This in turn led to the invention of psychoanalysis, which based both its subject matter and its process around the core myth of Sophocles' *Oedipus Rex*.

In *The Interpretation of Dreams*, Freud wrote,

> The action of the play consists in nothing other than the process of revealing, with cunning delays and ever-mounting excitement—a process that can be likened to the work of a psychoanalysis—that Oedipus himself is the murderer of Laius, but further that he is the son of the murdered man and of Jocasta. [Freud, 1900a, pp. 261–262]

He goes on to say,

if *Oedipus Rex* moves a modern audience no less than it did the contemporary Greek one, the explanation can only be that its effect does not lie in the contrast between destiny and human will, but is to be looked for in the particular nature of the material on which that contrast is exemplified. There must be something which makes a voice within us ready to recognise the compelling force of destiny in the *Oedipus* . . . His destiny moves us only because it might have been ours—because the oracle laid the same curse upon us before our birth as upon him. It is the fate of all of us, perhaps, to direct our sexual impulse towards our mother and our first hatred and our first murderous wish towards our father. Our dreams convince us that is so. King Oedipus, who slew his father Laius and married his mother Jocasta, merely shows us the fulfilment of our own childhood wishes. [*ibid.*, p. 262]

On the next page he writes,

Like Oedipus, we live in ignorance of these wishes, repugnant to morality, which have been forced upon us by Nature, and after their revelation we may all of us well seek to close our eyes to the scenes of our childhood. [*ibid.*, p. 263]

Rudnytsky suggests that it was Freud's childhood that needed to be shut out and yet simultaneously investigated. His attempts to manage this complicated process and his heroic, Oedipus-like determination to proceed steadfastly forward, gave psychoanalysis the radical task of looking at what could not be looked at and of determining the ways in which our patterns of repression and resistance try to keep our unconscious knowledge from ourselves. This also tied it down to a particular version of the family, and the relations between parents and children, in which infantile sexuality and the Oedipus complex were primary. In 1923 Freud stated, "no one who cannot accept them all should count himself a psychoanalyst" (Freud, 1923a, p. 247). It was recognized that other, non-psychoanalytic, schools of psychology were also interested in these areas, with the exception of the privileging of the Oedipus complex. As a result, as Freud himself put it, the Oedipus complex became the shibboleth by which true psychoanalysis and its opponents were recognized (footnote added to 1920 edition of *Three Essays on Sexuality*: Freud, 1905d, p. 226n). This point was repeated in a Scientific Meeting at the Tavistock Clinic only a few years ago as still being true, emphasizing that it is the commitment to the centrality of Oedipus that defines contemporary psychoanalysis.

You will note that Freud's language has moved from talking about Oedipus to talking about the Oedipus complex. He had made use of Jung's definition of a complex as a feeling-toned collection of mental contents, comprising images, associations, thoughts, and affects, part conscious and part unconscious, which is able to gather to itself a greater or lesser amount of psychic energy and so have the potential to dominate consciousness (Jung, 1948). The Oedipus complex allows Freud to move away from *Oedipus Rex*, to consider other related psychic states, desires, and identifications. Freud, however, moves away from it like a ship moving away from its home port; no matter how far it goes, it is always connected to its point of origin. We know that Freud was clear that the work of psychoanalysis is structured like the play of *Oedipus Rex*, which suggests that psychoanalysis will inevitably find its founding myth in every clinical engagement. But more than this, the power of Freud's attachment to Sophocles' play means that the psychoanalytic Oedipus complex, in its early versions at least, misses out not only the story of Laius, but also the story of the Sphinx.

Just why was Laius so cursed? Laius came to fame as one of the founders of the Greek practice of pederasty, the love between an adolescent boy and an older man, in which the older man serves as the younger one's mentor and patron. But he also came to infamy as the one who broke the bounds of this practice. While a tutor for Chryssipus, the son of Pelops, rather than practising "pedagogic pederasty", he kidnapped the boy and raped him, forcing him to be his lover in Thebes. In this version of the myth, as a result of this outrage, the goddess Hera sent the Sphinx to plague his city and he was forbidden to have children under pain of a particular kind of death and lineal humiliation, the curse that Oedipus came to know only too well. Freud's version of Oedipus omits the sexually violent father and the murderous qualities of both parents, and replaces them with a sexually transgressive and murderous child.

What of the Sphinx? The Sphinx was the subject of the clash between the different versions of the Oedipus complex as conceptualized by Freud and Jung. When they met for the first time in 1907, Freud impressed Jung with his conviction of the centrality of sexuality in psychic life. Over the next few years, Jung's growing objections to this were met by Freud's insistence that Jung simply lacked the experience necessary to understand it properly. In 1910, when they met in Vienna, Jung describes Freud saying to him,

> "Promise me never to abandon the sexual theory. That is the most essential thing of all. You see, we must make a dogma of it, an unshakable bulwark." He said that to me with great emotion, in the tone of father saying, "And promise me this one thing, my dear son: that you will go to church every Sunday." In some astonishment I asked him, "a bulwark against what?" To which he replied, "against the black tide of mud"—and here he hesitated for moment, then added—"of occultism." [Jung, 1983, p. 173]

Jung states that this began to move the two men apart. From this point, their friendship was heading towards its end.

The split between them finally came with the publication in 1912 of the second part of Jung's *Symbols of Transformation*. In this work Jung, who had been encouraged by Freud to mine the treasures of mythology and comparative religion, directly disagreed with Freud's version of the Oedipus complex, which, at this point, was about a four-year old boy's sexual yearning for his mother that is renounced because of the threat of castration by his father. Jung criticized the interpretation that Freud had made, and, in its place, pointed out that the important aspect of the complex was the presence of matriarchal incest. In other words, the mother in the myth was more important than the father. He suggested that this meant that the Oedipus complex was really about a much younger child's relationship to mother and not the four-year-old child's relationship to father. The inability to separate from mother, not castration, was the problem. To prove this, he went into the genealogy of the Sphinx, necessarily taking as his source the broader legend of Oedipus rather than *Oedipus Rex*, and wrote:

> In the Oedipus legend the Sphinx was sent by Hera, who hated Thebes on account of the birth of Bacchus. Oedipus, thinking he had overcome the Sphinx sent by the mother-goddess merely because he had solved her childishly simple riddle, fell victim to matriarchal incest and had to marry Jocasta, his mother, for the throne and the hand of the widowed queen belonged to him who freed the land from the plague of the Sphinx. This had all those

tragic consequences which could easily have been avoided if only Oedipus had been sufficiently intimidated by the frightening appearance of the "terrible" or "devouring" Mother whom the Sphinx personified . . . Little did he know that the riddle of the Sphinx can never be solved merely by the wit of man.

Jung goes on to talk about the genealogy of the Sphinx:

> . . . she was the daughter of Echidna, a monster with the top half of a beautiful maiden, and a hideous serpent below. This double being corresponds to the mother-imago: above, the lovely and attractive human half; below, the horrible animal half, changed into a fear-animal by the incest prohibition. Echidna was born of the All-Mother, Mother Earth, Gaia, who conceived her with Tartarus, the personification of the underworld. Echidna herself was the mother of all terrors, of the Chimera, Scylla, the Gorgon, of frightful Cerberus, of the Nemean lion, and of the eagle that devoured the liver of Prometheus. She also gave birth to a number of dragons. One of her sons was Orthrus, the dog of the monster Geryon, who was slain by Heracles. With this dog, her own son, Echidna incestuously begat the Sphinx.

He concludes, rather dryly:

> This should be sufficient to characterise the complex whose symbol is the Sphinx. It is evident that a factor of such magnitude cannot be disposed of by solving a childish riddle. The riddle was, in fact, the trap which the Sphinx laid for the unwary wanderer. Over-estimating his intellect in a typically masculine way, Oedipus walked right into it, and all unknowingly committed the crime of incest. The riddle of the Sphinx was herself—the terrible mother-imago, which Oedipus would not take as a warning. [Jung, 1912 pars 264–265]

Contemporary psychoanalysis is much closer to Jung's position than that of Freud at that time, putting mother and baby centre stage, with some seeing the workings of the Oedipus complex at a very tender age, and others not being so sure. The German psycho-analyst, Anna Ursula Dreher, writes of what she calls "Oedipal-ization", the turning of everything into a facet of the Oedipus complex (Dreher, 2000). I think we can see something of her argu-ment if we reflect on the ways in which some contemporary psychoanalysts use Freud's original concept to refer to a diverse range of developmental phenomena: infantile sexuality; managing the process of changing one's love object from mother to father (or vice versa); becoming a triad rather than a dyad; developing a mind; thinking thoughts; being able to be creative; reaching and/or resolving the depressive position; being able to observe another couple and being able to bear someone observing you in a couple; being able to reflect on such things from a "third position". It also refers to being unable to manage such processes, as well as to publishing a psychoanalytic paper or, indeed, to writing a chapter such as this! At the same time, we have to recognize that such concepts are both important and useful in the clinical encounter. But why do they all have to be called the *Oedipus* complex? Is it that, without the term, psychoanalysis risks no longer being powerfully attached to Freud's favourite play, and so to Freud himself? If we imagine seeing and doing things differently, are we going to be struck down like Oedipus, with all our productions, our clinical lineage, rendered obscene and unbearable to others? We can, no doubt, hear echoes of the work of the "Secret Committee", but might it also be valuable to try to imagine what might have happened had Freud been as powerfully attached to another parent–child myth?

Of Ganesh

It is time for me to introduce Ganesh. A couple of years ago, I spotted in a shop window a small figurine of the Indian god, Ganesh or Ganesha, a pot-bellied fellow with four arms and the head of an elephant. I think my attention, in fact, had not particularly been caught by him alone, but by the fact that he was lying down on what could, with only a little stretch of the imagination, be considered a version of Freud's rug-and-cushion-strewn consulting room couch. I was available for this kind of flight of fancy, because I have had for many years a drawing of Freud in his consulting room with none other than Mickey Mouse on the couch. In the picture, Freud looks appropriately serious and perhaps a bit puzzled, and Mickey looks radiantly delighted as usual as he talked away. I sometimes wonder what it is that he's saying.

When I saw the reclining Hindu divinity, it immediately reminded me of the Mickey Mouse picture, and I began to imagine Freud sitting behind this couch in turn, and so wondered idly what an analysis of Ganesh would have been like. Would he have an Oedipus complex and, if so, would it fit Freud's concept? When I looked into this more, I discovered that Ganesh was a fascinating character with a properly mythic story around his birth, including an extraordinarily close relationship with his mother and murderous battles with his father. So far, so Oedipal!

The story is that Parvati, wife of Shiva, and with him creator of all things, wished one day to bathe in privacy. In order to ensure that she was not disturbed, she rubbed the dust off her skin and formed a beautiful little boy from it. She gave the boy the task of guarding her doorway whilst she bathed. After a while, Shiva came home and tried to get in, but the little boy blocked his way. Shiva demanded. The little boy, obeying his mother, continued to refuse. Inevitably, they fought, and, after a struggle, Shiva decapitated the child. Parvati, distraught, demanded that Shiva make him live again, but his head was nowhere to be found, such was the force of Shiva's blow. Parvati continued to insist and so Shiva ordered that the head of the next animal to be found nearby should be used. The necessary means were found in an elephant sleeping nearby, and so Ganesh was reborn.

Shiva elevated Ganesh first among the gods, and decreed that he should be the first to be worshipped before all other manifestations of the divine. Ganesh became known as the "Lord and remover of all Obstacles", and the three are considered as the epitome of the loving parents and child. Interestingly, despite being a Hindu divinity, cults of Ganesh exist across religious divides in India, suggesting that there is something in his story too that "makes a voice within us ready to recognise [a] compelling force . . ." as Freud suggested of *Oedipus Rex*.

There are two further important aspects that show the qualities of this legendary being. The first is the story about an argument between Ganesh and his brother as to which of them should be considered the elder. Shiva decided that the question was to be resolved by a race between them. Whoever was first to travel around the universe could claim the honour. Off Ganesh's brother went, racing into the stars on the back of his peacock. Ganesh, whose means of travel was a mouse or rat, found his parents, circled them, and then claimed the prize. When asked how he could claim such a thing, he responded that his parents were, for him, the very representation of the whole universe and thus he was granted the status of the elder child.

The second aspect is that, in common with much Hindu mythology, there is no such thing as a single variant of Ganesh. In fact there are over 100 ways of naming him, depending on what attributes are to be emphasized, and there are thirty-two ways of depicting him, ranging from the familiar four-armed god, to one with a hundred arms, another with four heads, another with lions' heads, with a third eye, and so on. As a character, then, it is Ganesh rather than Oedipus, who is more suited to a multitude of meanings and developments in theory that all have one name.

Some Indian psychoanalysts and psychoanalytic commentators on Indian cultures have suggested that the story of Ganesh represents parent–child relationships in Indian cultures more particularly than the Greek myth, which it resembles. They suggest that in the Indian culture, unlike in Western cultures, there is a requirement for a standing up to followed by a surrender to the father, while simultaneously retaining closeness with the mother (Vaidyanathan & Kripal, 1999). Both castration and father–son murder are minimized, as, after all, Ganesh is brought back to life, and the feminization of men and their identification with their mothers are not considered problematic. There is a suggestion that, in India, Freud's version of Oedipus was seen only in Europeans. Obeyesekere, Professor of Anthropology at the University of Princeton (Obeyesekere, 1999), suggests that, had Freud followed up his interest in Indian culture, he could not have insisted on the version of Oedipus which is found in *Oedipus Rex* alone; another version would have had to be privileged. My description of Freud's entanglement with *Oedipus Rex*, however, suggests that Freud never really had any choice. Freud was too powerfully attached to his theory, and tended to treat his Indian psychoanalytic colleagues in similar ways to his European ones; that is, if they confirmed his version of Oedipus, they were correct; if they contradicted it, they were ignored. One commentator suggests that in the eleven-year correspondence between Freud and Girindrasekhar Bose, the founder and President of the India Psychoanalytical Society, who was trying to initiate an intercultural exchange about psychoanalysis, Freud

> was not ready for a dialogue, but insisted on a style of interaction that resembled a monologue. He considered taking only those pieces out of Bose's theory that he could appropriate without having to change anything in his own theory. [Hartnack, 1999, p. 100]

Bose kept trying to show Freud that his version of the Oedipus complex could not be applied in India, sending him numerous case examples and fully worked papers in which the identification with the mother, rather than her renunciation, was shown repeatedly in contradistinction to Freud's view. Freud had initially been resistant to this idea, but then appeared to soften, suggesting, some seven years in to their correspondence, that

> these phenomena have to be worked into our system to make us see what modifications or corrections are necessary and how far we can acquiesce to your ideas. [letter from Freud to Bose, 1st January 1933. In: Sinha, 1966, cited in Hartnack, 1999, pp. 99–100].

However, the same letter also contained the following statement:

> It needs more time and effort to overcome the feeling of unfamiliarity when confronted with a theory so different from the one professed hitherto and it is not easy to get out of the accustomed ways of thinking. So don't take it amiss when I say the theory of the opposite wishes strikes me as something less dynamic than morphological which could not have been evolved from the study of our psychopathological material . . . [*ibid.*]

It must have been hard for Bose not to take such a statement amiss, since he had been trying to show Freud that what he was saying *had* evolved from *his* study of "psychopathological material". Some four years later, Freud had still not worked Bose's findings into his system and in the last letter of their correspondence, suggested that "psychoanalysis is still young and will certainly progress uninterruptedly till no doubt can exist about the value of its contribution to the science of psychology" (Letter from Freud to Bose, 25th October 1937, in Ramana, 1964, p. 133, cited in Hartnack, 1999, p. 100).

Freud had not been able to relinquish *Oedipus Rex*, after all, leading Bose to write later that Freud's insistence on defining what was and what was not psychoanalysis, his shibboleths, "has led to the impression in certain quarters that the Freudian system is an esoteric one with Freud as the head of a church" (Bose, 1945, p. 254, cited in Hartnack, 1999, p. 97). Freud had been introduced to the world of Ganesh, to a non-European version of Oedipus, but it would appear he remained true to his dogma, just as he had asked Jung to do so many years before.

Conclusion

In these stories we come back repeatedly to the motif of a theory that is held on to, or returned to for guidance, in a way that can only be termed "religious", if we take that word to mean the scrupulous observance of something, as well as applying to something sacred. We see it in couples where neither party can quite give up their version of the "truth", their theory, about the other person, to the extent that, even when we are able to help them see that there is a shared problem, they seem to totter on the edge of acceptance and then return to a position of insisting that, even if the problem is shared, the solution lies only in the other partner's hands.

In Freud's powerful attachment to *Oedipus Rex*, he was able to apply his genius to a problem that is both universal and highly personal to him. It is to his credit, and to our benefit, that so much creativity has emerged from it. For example, psychoanalytic thinking about the myth of Oedipus has borne fruit in couple psychotherapy, as the recent *Oedipus and the Couple* (Grier, 2005) demonstrates. I am also suggesting, however, that in its performance as a "religious rite", Freud's oedipal theory, and so psychoanalysis generally, has had a necessarily difficult struggle to allow the co-existence of difference and development. Freud's struggles with his early colleagues, the "Controversial Discussions" in London between the followers of Melanie Klein and Anna Freud during the war, and the continuing strains between the variants of the depth psychologies today, all suggest that this is not something that we are going to be able to resolve. Instead, we have to find ways of tolerating difference and development pluralistically and even polytheistically; ways that may be more akin to Ganesh, with his multitude of aspects and attributes, than to Oedipus, with his single-minded determination. If we can be open to difference, including that in psychoanalytic perspectives from different parts of the world, we may already appreciate that we need the "Lord and remover of Obstacles" to dance with us as well as "the solver of all riddles". On reflection, perhaps this was what Mickey Mouse was talking to Freud about, all along.

References

Bannister, K., & Pincus, L. (1965). *Shared Phantasy in Marital Problems: Therapy in a Four-Person Relationship.* London: Institute of Marital Studies.

Bion, W. (1970). *Attention and Interpretation.* London: Tavistock [reprinted London: Karnac, 1984].

Bose, G. (1945). *Everyday Psychoanalysis.* Calcutta: Susil Gupta.

Dreher, A. U. (2000). *Foundations for Conceptual Research in Psycho - analysis.* Madison, CT: International Universities Press.

Fordham, M. (1993). On not knowing beforehand. *Journal of Analytical Psychology, 38*(2): 127–136.

Freud, S. (1900a). *The Interpretation of Dreams. S.E., 5.* London: Hogarth.

Freud, S. (1901b). *The Psychopathology of Everyday Life. S.E., 6.* London: Hogarth.

Freud, S. (1905d). *Three Essays on the Theory of Sexuality. S.E., 7.* London: Hogarth.

Freud, S. (1916–1917). *Introductory Lectures on Psycho-analysis.* Lecture 21, *S.E., 16*: 320–338. London: Hogarth.

Freud, S. (1923a). *Two Encyclopaedia Articles. S.E., 18.* London: Hogarth.

Freud, S. (1954). *The Origins of Psychoanalysis: Letters to Wilhelm Fliess, Drafts and Notes 1887–1902.* New York: Basic Books.

Grier, F. (Ed). (2005). *Oedipus and the Couple.* London: Karnac.

Hartnack, C. (1999). Vishnu on Freud's desk: psychoanalysis in colonial India. In: T. G. Vaidyanathan & J. J. Kripal (Eds.), *Vishnu on Freud's Desk—A Reader in Psychoanalysis and Hinduism* (pp. 81–106). New Delhi: Oxford University Press.

Jones, E. (1959). *Life and Work of Sigmund Freud: The Years of Maturity, 1901–19.* Vol. 2. London: Hogarth.

Jung, C. G. (1912). The origin of the hero. *Symbols of Transformation. An Analysis of the Prelude to a Case of Schizophrenia. C.W., 5.* London: Routledge & Kegan Paul, 1954.

Jung, C. G. (1931). Freud and Jung: Contrasts. *Freud and Psychoanalysis. C.W., 4:* 333–340. London: Routledge and Kegan Paul, 1970.

Jung, C. G. (1946). Psychic conflicts in a child. *The Development of Personality. C.W., 17:* 1–35. London: Routledge, 1954.

Jung, C. G. (1948). A review of the complex theory. *The Structure and Dynamics of the Psyche. C.W., 8:* 92–104. London: Routledge & Kegan Paul (2nd edn), 1969.

Jung, C. G. (1983). *Memories, Dreams, Reflections.* London: Flamingo.

Knox, B. (1984). Oedipus the King. Introduction. In: Sophocles, *The Three Theban Plays. Antigone. Oedipus the King. Oedipus at Colonus* (pp. 130–153). Harmondsworth: Penguin.

Little, W. (2002) (Ed). *Shorter Oxford English Dictionary.* Oxford: Oxford University Press.

Obeyesekere, G. (1999). Further steps in relativization: the Indian Oedipus revisited. In: T. G. Vaidyanathan & J. J. Kripal (Eds.), *Vishnu on Freud's Desk—A Reader in Psychoanalysis and Hinduism* (pp. 147–162). New Delhi: Oxford University Press.

Ramana, C. V. (1964). On the history and development of psychoanalysis in India. *Journal of the American Psychoanalytic Association, 12:* 133.

Rudnytsky, P. (1986). *Freud and Oedipus.* New York: Columbia University Press.

Ruszczynski, S. (Ed.) (1993). *Psychotherapy with Couples: Theory and Practice at the Tavistock Institute of Marital Studies.* London: Karnac.

Shamdasani, S. (2003). *Jung and the Making of Modern Psychology: The Dream of a Science.* Cambridge: Cambridge University Press.

Sinha, T. C. (1966). Development of psychoanalysis in India. *International Journal of Psychoanalysis, 47:* 431.

Urban, E. (1996). Book review of M. Fordham, *Children as Individuals* (London: Free Association Books 1994). *Journal of Child Psychotherapy, 22*(1): 153–156.

Vaidyanathan, T. G., & Kripal, J. J., (Eds.) (1999). *Vishnu on Freud's Desk—A Reader in Psychoanalysis and Hinduism.* New Delhi, Oxford University Press.

CHAPTER THIRTEEN

Marriage is a strange attractor: chaos theory, a paradigm shift for couple therapy*

David E. Scharff and Jill Savege Scharff

Introduction

C haos theory, the theory of dynamical systems, offers a new paradigm for understanding the dynamics of psychological, mental, and affective processes in couples and the development, maintenance, and therapy of couple relationships. The couple relationship forms when two individual psychodynamic systems combine in unpredictable ways to develop a system that is essentially chaotic and inherently self-organizing. This chapter demonstrates how couple therapy informed by chaos theory moves troubled couples out of their limit-cycle functioning and encourages the development of new strange attractor patterns that confer enhanced flexibility of response in the couple system, bringing couples new adaptability and confidence to meet developmental challenges.

Every intimate couple relationship has a unique personality. This personality is evident on the surface through the observable interaction of the partners; it is constructed at the depths from the

---

* This is an expanded version of a paper published in *Interazioni* 1 (2007).

individual and shared unconscious—a mysterious, unpredictable, and infinitely complex combination of brain interactions, attachment patterns, affective facial, bodily, and sexual signals, and verbal communication. Any approach to understanding and treating the dynamics of the couple relationship must take account of this complexity. We look to chaos theory (also called the theory of nonrandom chaos), complexity theory, or dynamical systems theory for a new way of thinking about unconscious communication, the development of psychic structure, coupling, and therapeutic action in the analytic treatment of couples.

Chaos theory: a paradigm for understanding couple dynamics

Iterated operations

Chaos theory derives from the mathematical study of the action of complex dynamical systems governed by continuous feedback. These systems *iterate* their operations, each time beginning with a situation that is the sum of all previous experience. Chaos theory, which has been applied to the study of diverse unpredictable systems like weather, population dynamics, aesthetics, biological systems such as heart rate and brain waves, applies to psychological systems as well. For instance, each of us uses our internal operating systems to proceed through life. At each moment, we are the sum of all our previous experience; and we use our internal systems to guide us through the next developmental stage.

Sensitive dependence on initial conditions

In such complex systems, infinitely small differences in starting points affect the outcome profoundly. The processes of growth and development are iterations of life's operating equations, and they show *sensitive dependence on initial conditions*. Small and seemingly inconsequential variations in constitution, temperament, and parenting are magnified or minimized under various circumstances, leading to unpredictable results.

The couple relationship is a biological system repeatedly adjusting to feedback, both cementing the form of the marital joint personality and introducing slight variations that modify the spouses' personalities in the light of shared experience. Couple relationships, like those of all biological systems, are complex iterated equations with *sensitive dependence on initial conditions* as they apply their daily operating equations to the next set of life challenges. Small differences in the beginning of a day can affect the next week's, or even a life's, course in unpredictable ways, while something that seems to loom large at one moment may defy prediction and turn out to be relatively inconsequential.

Tuning force for the self-organizing potential

The current interactions of members of a couple and their family histories recorded in each partner's internal object relations affect the patterns of the couple. In chaos theory terms, interactions, affect states, and object relations separately and together exert a *tuning force* on the individual personality (Quinodoz, 1997). They also act as a tuning variable affecting the marital joint personality and the family dynamics, some family members having relatively greater effects than others. For instance, a mother's internal object relations exert a large tuning force on her infant's developing mind, while a child who has left home may exert a relatively weak tuning force on the parental couple she has left behind. A therapist's affective attunement, conscious interventions, and receptivity to unconscious communication exert a tuning force on a couple dynamic.

The complex system of the couple relationship tends to enter periods of relative chaos, experienced as confusion and tension that are disorganizing. The unhealthy system gets stuck there. The healthy system enters chaos temporarily, experiences some turbulence, and then self-organizes as a more functional interactive system, under the influence of the tuning force of the interacting partners' personalities, or of a more organized interactive system nearby such as the healthy marriage of friends or relatives, or the technique of a thoroughly analysed therapist. When not hampered by histories of trauma or deprivation, a couple's self-organizing potential should lead to more complex and adaptive patterns over time.

Fractals

At different levels of magnification of a system, patterns repeat, appearing not exactly the same but similar at each magnification. In chaos theory terms, each pattern is a *fractal* of the other patterns found at different levels of scale (Galatzer-Levy, 1995). A couple's sexual relationship, speech patterns, relationship to extended families and children—all are fractals of their internal object relations and of their overall relationship (Scharff & Scharff, 1998). The transference–countertransference dialectic is also a fractal of all these elements of their relationship, a magnification that we experience and study together in therapy. All these elements both organize the system of the couple relationship, and at the same time are actually produced by the dynamic of the system. In chaos theory terms, the force that both organizes and is organized by the system is called an attractor. The attractor may be of one of three types: fixed, limit-cycle, and strange.

Fixed, limit-cycle, and strange attractors

A *fixed attractor* appears to move a system through a predictable pattern towards rest at a single spot, like a gravity-powered pendulum that eventually comes to a stop at a fixed point. A *limit-cycle attractor* appears to move a system through a fixed pattern continuously, like an electrically powered pendulum that moves back and forth in an arc. A *strange attractor* appears to move a system through a complex, apparently random pattern, out of which an organized pattern gradually appears—like a whirlpool that seems to pull water into the whirl, although it is actually the flow of the water that produces the whirl. Similarly, a couple's fights appear to pull their relationship into an aggressive mode, which at the same time is caused by the complex tension of their interacting needs and personalities. None of the movements of the system is exactly the same, but each contributes to a discernible overall complex pattern—the "whirl" of disagreement—that characterizes this couple's relationship. A strange attractor may exert an especially strong effect on the couple system and pull it, like a whirlpool pulls objects outside the whirl into the whirl, into its *basin of attraction*.

In the complex system of a couple with sensitive dependence on initial conditions, precise prediction of patterns of interaction is not possible. Like all self-organizing systems, we live life by looking forward and proceeding into the unknown, and can only understand when looking back. At times, life patterns shift under destabilizing conditions, just as a whirlpool may be affected by a strong nearby current or a passing object. In the short term, more than one pattern may be evident consistently. For instance, a couple may have one pattern of fierce arguments over disciplining their children and another of co-operation and tenderness in love-making that is not predictable from the intensity of their arguments. Over the long term, general patterns of consistency and adaptive variation can be recognized.

Dysfunctional couples get stuck doing the same ineffective thing over and over, following the *self-same pattern* of a limit-cycle attractor. Healthy couples, like healthy biological systems, move in and out of chaos in daily life, following the *self-similar patterns* of strange attractors—never exactly the same, but patterned enough to be recognizable as part of a dynamic system. Chaotic patterns eventually self-organize and so have an enhanced capacity to adapt to new circumstances and needs.

The strange attractor of the couple relationship

When two individuals form a couple, the patterns of each personality based on their histories behave as strange attractors, each of which interacts with the other and exerts a tuning force on it until the systems combine to form a new, overarching strange attractor, the pattern of the joint marital personality. When that couple has a child, the strange attractors of the two parents' personalities and of their overall relationship pattern exert tuning forces, which create basins of attraction that interact with the inherent personality patterns of the child, pulling the child's self towards this or that system of organization. When we compare each parent's strange attractor pattern, the joint marital personality, the developing personality of the child, and the overall family interaction patterns, we notice that they show fractal similarity to one another.

Patterns of a couple's life appear to attract partners into repetitions of actions, and the couple will often report that they cannot resist the pattern. Or they might report that going to visit a set of in-laws, or dreaming about their family of origin, exposes them to a force they cannot resist. This is to say that the closer they get to the extended family's basin of attraction, the more they get swept up in the family's pattern.

A baby is a living embodiment of a couple's interpenetration, and gives life to their partnership. The child arises from, and is a representative of, the sexual and emotional coupling of the parents. In addition, the child is a person in his or her own right, therefore a new object of affection, interest, and hate for the couple. At the same time, the child is also a reminder of the parents' original objects, their own parents, now grandparents, and the internal objects based on early experience with them. The parents respond to aspects of the grandparents that they imagine in the child, and evoke them in the child unconsciously through projective identification. Experience with the child is installed as a complex internal object that is both old and new, and that in turn restructures the parents' selves and their couple relationship. Just as the sea shapes the edge of the land and the land shapes the edge of the sea, parents and child sculpt one another's interaction and personality. This happens every day as they iterate their family equations, each new day offering a new starting point with sensitive dependence on the day's initial conditions, resulting in an infinitely complex interaction of strange attractors and basins of attraction, perturbations, tuning variables, and self-organization at every fractal level.

Chaos theory and therapeutic action

All this leads to the question of how we can promote change when couples seek help. By introducing perturbations into the operating system of the couple relationship, couple therapists disturb the relatively fixed, maladaptive, limit-cycle systems in which the couple is stuck. We use the tuning force of our own internal object relations organization honed by training, therapy, and supervision, to create a new basin of attraction, and to join with couples to structure a more flexible strange attractor system with better capacities for adaptation and self-organization.

According to the principle of fractal scaling and sensitive dependence on initial conditions, relatively small changes in therapy can have major effects. Theoretically, the flapping of a butterfly's wings in Brazil can create a hurricane in Texas (the so-called butterfly effect). Similarly, an interpretation of the transference in a single session can produce a thunderstorm's worth of change in the couple's state of mind and way of interacting with the world. Through the butterfly effect, a change in one partner can affect the couple or the whole family.

Couple therapy example: sessions 1 and 2

Lucien and Rachel are now in their forties and have been married for ten years. Both had been married previously to partners who betrayed and abandoned them, leaving them fearful of intimacy. They are slim, attractive, and in good shape, but they have no sex life. They have no children, a decision reached by mutual agreement and without later regret. They stay in touch with their families in an occasional way. They experience Lucien's mother as a domineering woman and his father as a retiring man, emasculated by her and by Lucien's grandfather. They find Rachel's mother to be a warm and friendly person, but her father is temperamental and not tuned in to Rachel's wavelength. Rachel initiates sexual interaction, but Lucien has no desire. His energy goes into fending off Rachel, delaying the moments when intimacy might occur, and in general avoiding sex. Rachel tends to pressure Lucien, despite the fact that this tends to drive him away. Lucien blames her for pressuring him, but he invokes it by his avoidance. If Lucien were to have sex wholeheartedly, he fears that Rachel would take control of him.

Prior individual and couple therapy having been ineffective in releasing Lucien's sexual desire, the couple sought therapy with Dr David Scharff. In marital and sex therapy with him, Lucien slowly became able to tolerate sex, find the idea exciting, and progress to pleasurable intercourse, but the couple still encountered a barrier in the approach phase of every exercise or encounter. Lucien repeatedly insisted that Rachel should not pressure him by scheduling times for sex. He wanted sex to occur spontaneously, but he did not allow it to happen, and thus fuelled her need to pressure him for a schedule. Despite improvement, their sexual interaction remained a totally predictable, repetitively frustrating pattern, governed by limit-cycle attractors.

In the first session of three that we will report, the therapist (DES) worked on a dream that Lucien had. He said,

"It was a dream of a man with salt and pepper hair, holding a dead baby in his lap. The man wasn't dressed as a physician, but he had eviscerated the baby, and was asking me to understand and accept that. I was horrified at the idea of what this man must have done. He wanted me to understand, but it wasn't my child, and I didn't have any feeling for it. I was just an observer."

Lucien associated to a business partner who might want to scuttle a new business venture that he refers to as "his baby", and to his aunt's late fourth husband, a gambler who wasted her money. Rachel thought that the baby might be Lucien's self. I thought that the dead baby with no parents was the couple's sexual life for which I (a grey-haired physician who, however, does not wear a white coat) was responsible. Lucien said I was nothing like the physician in the dream. When he added that it was a hollow baby, I commented that he might be watching the sex therapy project die. He said that he was trying not to, and Rachel objected that she had again been unable to persuade him to do a sex exercise.

Lucien's thoughts about the aunt's husband led to his feelings about his aunt. He said, "My aunt has come to be known as the 'black widow' because all her husbands have died. She tells my mother, who is quite overweight, that you can't be too thin or too rich. She is the horror show at our family Christmas. She dresses to kill and uses her money to lure men. She's not fit for society."

I said, "A lethal, predatory woman. Your association to your 'black widow aunt' tells me you feel at risk in this sex therapy project. The dead baby in the physician's lap represents the horror of what you might be doing right now, while acting as though you had no part in it. You cut yourself off from that feeling and put it into Rachel, and then get mad at her when she expresses the anxiety and longing for a lively sexual life on behalf of you as a couple. You then feel as if she is luring you into her web, and you stay away from her and from your own desire. It is your own desire that is the spider's web you fear."

Lucien said, "I recognize that I cut myself off. I enjoy the absence of pressure. Each week, I try to buy as much time before sex as possible [by not specifying when to do the exercises] because if we put down a marker [like a gambler], the clock starts ticking, and I get anxious. I want sex to be something that is just normal, not special, and I don't know how to get to normalcy."

Rachel said, "I think normalcy for you is not having sex, and we'd still be stuck with that."

The various elements of the dream and the couple's associations in the session (transference manifestations, family history, fantasies about women) reflect many facets of individual and couple organization. Each element is a fractal of the other, showing pattern similarity on different orders of scale.

> Shifting my focus from the transference to the fractal of Lucien's self and his object relations, I then commented that I now saw the grey-haired man as Lucien himself in the future, still unable to protect the baby (both himself as an infant and the sexual life with Rachel about which he was avoidant) and vulnerable to death at the hands of the black widow, which he sees in her but which is active in him, entrapping him and killing off his desire.

Lucien and Rachel have no children and take no pleasure in sexuality. Lucien's dream shows that their procreativity and capacity for pleasure is being pulled into a basin of attraction dominated by limit-cycle attractors governed by death anxiety and murderousness, in turn attributed to the destructive seductiveness of the sexual woman, from which both of them turn away to avoid the impact of their own desire.

> At their session the next week, Lucien reported that he had had another dream. This time I was more clearly in it, and it was set in my waiting room at the end of a session. Lucien said, "In the dream, Rachel left your office ahead of me. As I left, I reached what I thought was your front door until I realized that it was a beautiful, tall, gilded French armoire. When I opened it, I couldn't see anything inside. Next to it, a fourteen-year-old girl was admiring an iron sculpture of herself. You and your wife entered the vestibule. I admired the furniture, and your wife accepted the compliment. Then she showed me a spot on the lower right-hand corner of the armoire where the gilt had been rubbed off, and she repaired it with some gilt from the other side. It was like a magic armoire. You entered, reminded me that Rachel was waiting for me, and I scurried off."

> He continued, "You and your wife, you're keepers of the flame, healers. Gilt is like guilty. I might be guilty about my new business venture hurting my partner."

> I said, "That's quite an idealized image of my wife and me. What she does is put gold over the bare spot."

> He said, "Right, healed by copy and paste, healed by a new reservoir of golden objects."

I said, "The dream also shows us a young woman admiring her lifeless statue. Who could that be? Then you focus on my wife quietly patching things up. Both are different images of women than your mother or your wife."

He said, ignoring my reference to the image of the young woman, "I think of you and your wife as keepers of the image—restorative figures, completely different than my mother, who is a destructive force of nature. She captured too much of me."

I said, "So you developed armour for your amour, and covered it in guilt."

He said, "The gilt is a protective adornment."

The dream presents the couple as split in time and space, as Rachel goes ahead and Lucien gets lost in contemplating the magic armoire. Lucien's dominant image of a black widow in a deadly couple (a limited cycle attractor) has given way to the pull of new female objects (strange attractors), in the form of the young girl looking at her own statue and the therapist's wife who deals with his guilty conscience by "a cut and paste operation" that gilds it over. These new strange attractors draw Lucien and the couple away from the limited attractor functioning most often seen in their sessions. Their pattern loosens in relation to the appearance of new objects in foreground of the dreams—the young girl in a self-examining, possibly admiring pose, the magically reparative woman, and the idealized generative therapist couple—and in the context of the therapy, new strange attractors in the form of the therapeutic relationship and the therapist's technique. New images of women as objects and as parts of Lucien's own identity lead the internal organization of a more complex internal couple with restorative potential.

In the meeting of the unconscious organizations of Lucien and the therapist, both in his dreams and in the couple's analysis of them, the therapist's inner world acts as a tuning variable that causes a perturbation in Lucien's inner world, bringing to the surface latent, previously suppressed organizations that bring new possibilities for reworking the couple relationship. This is an example of a strange attractor in formation. In these two sessions, Lucien's part of the pattern is most apparent. We will show its fractal similarity to Rachel's, as the couple works on her dream in the third session, to which we will return after the next section on concepts regarding neurological development and complex attachment.

Integrating neuroscience, attachment, and affect regulation in couple therapy under the rubric of chaos theory

There is now ample evidence from brain imaging and developmental research that the infant's brain grows best when the infant is nurtured in a warm, reciprocally responsive relationship with a well-attuned mother or devoted care-givers (Schore, 1994). The right brain is built for the task of processing interaction with the mother quickly and repeatedly, and for receiving and reading the complex emotions of others. The left brain enables the development of linear and logical thinking, and fluid verbal communication. The baby's brain is organized by the mother's brain in a cycle of exchange determined by attractor patterns that move naturally from limit-cycle to strange attractor patterns as the infant matures (Schore, 2003a,b).

New brain studies reveal the presence of *mirror neurons*, which are activated when one monkey watches another monkey make movements (Cozolino, 2002; Modell, 2003). We now propose that there are similar mirror neurons in the parts of the human brain that record facial expressions and tone of voice, giving a neurological basis for the mental mechanisms of projective and introjective identification that convey emotional experience among intimate partners. In partnership, mother and infant read each other's minds at levels far below conscious awareness and far more quickly than two adults can understand one another's words.

The mother mirrors the newborn's expressions exactly, and the infant feels understood emotionally. This is called *contingent mark - ing* (Fonagy, Gergely, Jurist, & Target, 2002). Later, at about three months of age, infants want their mother's reaction to be nearly the same, but clearly not the same. This is called *non-contingent marking* (*ibid.*). The mother makes an expression similar enough to convey that she has received the message, but different enough to modify the original affect, for instance by tuning its volume up or down. Thus, she not only marks the affect, but also begins to regulate it.

Similarly, in the intense intimacy of couple interaction over time, each partner's mind structures and restructures the other through continuous non-random chaotic interaction.

At birth, the baby's brain is already rich in neurons, but not in the rich connective networks that experience builds. Attachment research has shown that secure attachment fosters the growth of connectedness between neurons and sub-units of the brain (Ainsworth, Blehar, Waters, & Wall, 1978; Fonagy, 2001). Brain scan studies show that the brains of those who suffered severe neglect and trauma show more rigid, limit-cycle patterns of brain function, less overall right brain growth, accentuation of fear centres, and less neural network interconnectivity (Cozolino, 2002; Siegel, 1998; Schore, 2003a,b).

In each member of a couple, their right orbito-frontal cortexes process reciprocal emotional interactions through projective and introjective communications in a continuous unconscious communication (Schore, 2003a,b; Scharff, 1992; Scharff & Scharff, 1991). In chaos theory terms, each individual intrapsychic organization exerts a tuning force on the other. In couple interaction over time, each partner's mind structures and restructures the other through continuous non-random chaotic interaction.

The principal evolutionary importance of the mother–infant attachment relationship is to provide the platform from which to teach the infant to regulate affects and states of mind, thereby establishing both an autonomous self and a self-in-relation to others (Sutherland, 1980). Autonomous people form healthy couples. In the process of forming their relationship, each couple forms a *complex attachment* in which partners depend on and support each other (Clulow, 2001a, 2006; Fisher & Crandall, 1997, 2001). Healthy couples use their relationship to regulate affect, to support healthy, individuated selves, and to enjoy the vitality of intimacy through multi-channel communication—verbally, affectively, sexually, as parents, lovers, or friends. Their patterns of interaction, both on the large scale and moment-to-moment, have mainly a reassuring self-similarity in which patterns of reliable, accurate attunement are combined with small but crucial variations in response.

Couples come together in an infinite variety of combinations reflecting the complexity of two brains in interaction with multiple influences in childhood (Morrison, Urquiza, & Goodlin-Jones,

1997a,b). Secure partners, whose relationship is organized by strange attractors, enjoy reciprocity and flexibility in role differentiation, equality, and respect. Insecure partners take up rigid roles, defensive positions, and interact by limited attractors, such as patterns of domination and submission. Traumatized partners have the most limited patterns, governed by fear and reactivity (Scharff & Scharff, 1994).

Trauma and deprivation limit maturation at every level, narrowing the brain's and mind's repertoire of responses to those most basic for survival, and depriving an individual and couple of the quality of vitality that depends on freer ranging interactions. The right amygdala is the seat of the first alarm response to new experience, when fear and avoidance of danger may be the safest option. Trauma and deprivation leave the developing child with a propensity to insecure attachments and limited reaction patterns. Mutually persistently fearful couples like Lucien and Rachel are haunted by ingrained, amygdala-driven limit cycle responses (Schore, 2003a,b).

Couple therapy example: session 3

At the next session, Rachel described a dream of her own. She said, "I only remember the end, and I awakened screaming. We were in Paris, my favourite place in the world, looking for a selection of good cheeses, and we got separated by crowds. When I saw Lucien again he was on an old street, carrying a thin, young French woman who was feeding Lucien his favourite cheese. I started yelling at him that he'd been lying and that some other woman did make a difference."

Rachel said that the dream relieved her guilt about the sexual relationship going wrong. It showed her Lucien's attachment to another woman, his carrying her and receiving nurturance from her the way Rachel would like him to carry their sexual life and its repair and to receive nurture from her in sex. Lucien asked whether the French woman could be his mother, who had been thin before his birth.

Both dreamers referred to guilt, and to a thin young woman. Lucien had ignored the image of the thin, young, self-absorbed woman in his dream, and now Rachel was picking it up, feeling anguish at being excluded by Lucien's pleasure in being fed by the young woman. Rachel's dream was marking Lucien's concern, but doing so non-contingently, up-regulating the volume of distress with an infusion of her own alarm. The limit-cycle attractors of their paired amygdala-driven fears magnify the dread of their relationship.

> I talked about the overlap in the two dreams. In Rachel's dream, Lucien is searching for something, and he finds it with a thin woman in his arms, feeding him. In Lucien's dream, a thin woman was self-involved. Lucien was opening the door looking for something, not seeing anything, and closing it again. Then, another woman connected to me marks the gilt/guilt on the armoire/armour in a contingent way and down-regulates it by magic repair, the way that a mother's kiss can make it better. What did this mean for them as a couple?
>
> Lucien said, "She fixed it so easily. I wanted to look inside, but it was blank."
>
> Rachel said, "I see you caught up in the emptiness of your relationship to your mother and the damage it does to us."
>
> Lucien's mother is quite overweight, but Rachel is thin. Rachel had seen a thin woman in his arms. Yet when Rachel asks for sexual intimacy, Lucien sees her as the intrusive, enveloping mother that he must fend off. Lucien is afraid of searching for her in case he finds nothing inside. Rachel is sad that she cannot compete with Lucien's fantasy of a nurturing mother and cannot dispel the image of one who will overpower him.
>
> Now I said to Rachel, "You have an image of a woman who has captured Lucien by feeding him his favourite food in your favourite place—that is, your sexual life—and frequently, you're furious at his mother."
>
> Rachel agreed, "Yes, I feel she is a rival for his affection even now."
>
> I said, "Lucien carries inside a black widow mother who seduces his attention from you. But this is your dream. Who is the woman inside *you* who seduces the man you yearn for and keeps him from you?"
>
> Rachel said, "I love my mother. She's great. She keeps herself in great shape. We're good friends. My father was the difficult one for me. He wasn't as bad as Lucien's mother, and he really loved me, but he was temperamental and difficult, and arrived at some terrible misunderstandings of me. My mother put up with him, and she got the best of

him. She kind of seduced him into a relationship that was much more loving than ever I could manage with him."

I said, "So although your father cared for you, there is a part of him you could never have, but your mother could. This is the thin, seductive mother that you see inside Lucien winning him over. His attachment to his black widow overlaps with your thin, attractive mother. And inside his overweight mother hides a thin attractive fourteen-year-old who could be self involved or who could seduce him with food. Both of your mothers seduced men: Rachel, your mother seduced your father and left you out; Lucien, your mother seduced you into her web and left your father to die emotionally, and that also leaves you feeling left."

Rachel's dream shows up the area of overlap in painful internal objects, which are psychic strange attractors. Both have organizations that trigger overlapping, amygdalae-driven fear responses. They have mirror neuron responses that reinforce fear and rejection in each other. The result is the development and reinforcement of a limit-cycle attractor in each of them individually and in their interactions that colours their joint marital personality.

In this session, Rachel follows Lucien in sharing a dream. The dreams are close together, resonate with the same theme, and move the work forward. The swirl of the attractor patterns in therapy both brings the image of a couple closer and shows that the block to Rachel and Lucien establishing a sexual couple is their longing for a feeding couple and fear of emptiness. The strange attractor of the therapist's mind exerts a destabilizing tuning force that continues to bring previously hidden patterns to the surface, and then works to increase the range of motion in a new, interactional strange attractor.

Concluding remarks

A therapist's main influence comes through unconscious communication—right brain to right brain. The strange attractor of the therapist's endopsychic system exerts a tuning force on the couple relationship. The complex co-regulation of affect between couple and therapist leads to new self-regulation and self-growth. The couple therapist's verbal understanding helps the left frontal cortex to develop a capacity for self-reflection in each individual, and therefore in the couple, which reinforces right brain reflective function. The couple can learn to expand the use of mirroring from simply appraising the danger of the other to the complex function of actually understanding the other's interior experience.

Attachment theory, neuroscience, understanding of the limitations imposed by trauma and deprivation, all change the way we listen to couples, and how we interpret the transference. We listen for inconsistencies and breaks in the flow of the couple's narrative. We notice whether their memories are described in words, conveyed in images, recreated in the transference, or experienced in the countertransference. Couple therapy functions as a secure base (Bowlby, 1969, 1980) from which couples can embark on exploration of trauma and loss and reach toward growth (Bowlby, 1973, 1980). In reactive couples, we see automatic, brain-driven responses rather than the more flexible mentalizing of matured minds (Cozolino, 2003; Fonagy, Gergely, Jurist, & Target, 2002). Like a secure parent caring for a child, the couple therapist mentalizes, senses, imagines, and understands the couple's experience. All of these functions form the tuning force we bring to couple therapy. We hope—but cannot predict for sure—that our tuning force will introduce perturbations in the most limited of the couple's attractor patterns, throwing them into destabilized, chaotic, and confused states, and that from this edge of non-random chaos, new, more flexible strange attractor patterns will take over and bring a capacity for vitality to the newly autonomous self-organizing couple relationship.

References

Ainsworth, M. D. S., Blehar, M. C., Waters, E., & Wall, S. (1978). *Patterns of Attachment: A Psychological Study of the Strange Situation.* Hillsdale, NJ: Lawrence Erlbaum.

Bowlby, J. (1973). *Attachment and Loss: Volume 2, Separation Anxiety and Anger.* New York: Basic Books.

Bowlby, J. (1980). *Attachment and Loss: Loss, Sadness, and Depression* (Vol. III). New York: Basic Books.

Clulow, C. (2001a). *Adult Attachment and Couple Psychotherapy.* London: Brunner-Routledge.

Clulow, C. (2006). Couple psychotherapy and attachment theory. In: J. Savege Scharff & D. Scharff (Eds.), *New Paradigms for Treating Relationships* (pp. 253–266). Lanham, MD: Jason Aronson.

Cozolino, L. (2002). *The Neuroscience of Psychotherapy*. New York: Norton.

Fisher, J. V., & Crandall, L. (1997). Complex attachment: patterns of relating in the couple. *Sexual and Marital Therapy, 2*(3): 211–223.

Fisher, J. V., & Crandall, L. (2001). Patterns of relating in the couple. In: C. Clulow (Ed.), *Adult Attachment and Couple Psychotherapy* (pp. 15–27). London: Brunner-Routledge.

Fonagy, P. (2001). *Attachment Theory and Psychoanalysis*. New York: Other Press.

Fonagy, P., Gergely, B., Jurist, E. L., & Target, M. (2002). *Affect Regulation, Mentalization, and the Development of the Self*. New York: Other Press.

Galatzer-Levy, R. (1995). Psychoanalysis and chaos theory. *Journal of the American Psychoanalytic Association, 43*: 1095–1113.

Modell, A. H. (2003). *Imagination and the Meaningful Brain*. Cambridge, MA: MIT Press.

Morrison, T., Urquiza, A. J., & Goodlin-Jones, B. (1997a). Attachment and the representation of intimate relationships in adulthood. *Journal of Psychology, 131*: 57–71.

Morrison, T., Urquiza, A. J., & Goodlin-Jones, B. (1997b). Attachment, perceptions of interaction, and relationship adjustment. *Journal of Social and Personal Relationships, 14*: 627–642.

Quinodoz, J.-M. (1997). Transitions in psychic structure in the light of chaos theory. *International Journal of Psycho-Analysis, 87*(4): 699–718.

Scharff, D., & Scharff, J. (1991). *Object Relations Couple Therapy*. Northvale, NJ: Jason Aronson.

Scharff, J. (1992). The influence on individual development of projective and introjective identification in the family. In: *Projective and Introjective Identification and the Use of the Therapist's Self* (pp. 99–132). Northvale, NJ: Jason Aronson.

Scharff, J., & Scharff, D. (1994). *Object Relations Therapy of Physical and Sexual Trauma*. Northvale, NJ: Jason Aronson.

Scharff, J., & Scharff, D. (1998). Chaos theory and fractals in development, self and object relations, and transference. In: *Object Relations Individual Therapy* (pp. 153–182). Northvale, NJ: Jason Aronson.

Schore, A. (1994). *Affect Regulation and the Origin of the Self: The Neurobiology of Emotional Development*. Hillsdale, NJ: Lawrence Erlbaum.

Schore, A. (2003a). *Affect Regulation and the Repair of the Self*. New York: Norton.

Schore, A. (2003b). *Affect Dysregulation and Disorders of the Self.* New York: Norton.

Siegel, D. (1998). *The Developing Mind: How Relationships and the Brain Interact to Shape Who We Are.* New York: Guilford.

Sutherland, J. D. (1980). The autonomous self. In: J. S. Scharff, (Ed.), *The Autonomous Self: The Writings of J. D. Sutherland* (pp. 303–330). Northvale, NJ: Jason Aronson, 1984.

CHAPTER FOURTEEN

Can attachment theory help define what is mutative in couple psychoanalytic psychotherapy?

Christopher Clulow

Introduction

P sychoanalysis places interpretation, and especially interpretation of the transference, as the foremost agent of therapeutic change. From Strachey's (1934) paper onwards, the quest for the "mutative" interpretation has featured in the development of psychoanalytic thinking and practice. If the literature has sometimes suggested that the key to change lies in the cognitive competence of the therapist, this has belied a therapeutic tradition that sees affective engagement and mutual learning between patient and therapist as the road to change. What has come to be known as the relational model of psychoanalysis is rooted in this therapeutic tradition.

For Bowlby (1969), the architect of attachment theory, "attachment" had a precise meaning that related to an innate behavioural system evidenced by four types of behaviour displayed in relation to a specific other: seeking proximity, displaying distress at separation, retreating to a safe haven when threatened, and exploring from a base that is felt to be secure. With time, "felt security" (Sroufe & Waters, 1997) could be achieved without actual physical proximity, but as a result of a growing confidence that attachment figures were accessible and responsive. There is an ongoing debate about whether and how adult partnerships are "attachments" in the sense that Bowlby defined from observing relationships between mothers and infants, but an acknowledgement that the similarities are sufficient for the term to be useful for practitioners and researchers in their work with adult couples (Hazan, Campa, & Gur-Yaish, 2006). So, if we accept that attachment is a useful concept to apply to adults, in what ways might attachment theory be useful for clinical practice with couples?

Some years ago I extrapolated to couple psychotherapy some of the therapeutic applications of attachment theory that Bowlby (1988) had pulled together late in his publishing lifetime. I suggested six processes for establishing and using the therapeutic frame (Clulow, 2001b):

- focusing on the "secure base" potential of the couple;
- establishing a secure therapeutic base;
- elucidating shared internal working models;
- encouraging play and exploration;
- recovering and reliving trauma;
- accessing and reprocessing feelings.

Correspondence with an American psychoanalyst, in connection with a paper she presented at a TCCR conference on couple therapy and attachment theory (Petith, 2006), focused my attention on the sixth of these processes. She cited the work of Johnson (2004), an English-born and Canadian-trained couple therapist who has developed a form of intervention known as Emotionally Focused Therapy (EFT). She commented that analytic approaches to couple therapy focused on the mutative relationship of the partners and the couple with the therapist, but neglected the mutative relationship between the partners themselves. In short, her argument was:

- in individual treatment there was only one mutative relationship—analyst and patient;
- in couple therapy there were three possible mutative relationships—analyst and each partner; analyst and couple; partner–partner;

- in the first two there was no problem with analysts working in the transference with the emotional experience that occurred in the moment;
- in the last, analysts might try to understand what was happening between the couple, and in transference terms, but they did not facilitate the partners living it with each other in the moment.

In other words, in terms of the relationship between the partners themselves, analytic couple therapists relied almost exclusively on the mutative power of understanding or interpretation, not on the reprocessing of affect. This was in marked contrast with Susan Johnson's approach, which, informed by attachment theory, worked to encourage emotional connection and the expression of feelings between partners as the centrepiece of her work, leaving the relationship to do the rest.

This challenged me to think about my own practice, and whether and how it had been affected by my understanding of attachment theory. This chapter marks the point I have reached so far in responding to the challenge.

Mirroring

A process that I think is central to therapeutic change is what Winnicott (1974) described as "mirroring". The accessing and reprocessing of emotional experience that he describes within the mother–infant relationship can be seen as a prototype for therapeutic change. The significance of affect for couple work is not in doubt. Couple relationships flourish or founder on the quality of the emotional connection between the partners. Powerful feelings affect the capacity to think and the coherence of thought. Relationship difficulties can be rooted in inflexible thinking, as if a train of thought has become stuck in a repetitive groove and impermeable to attempts to move things on. Or they may be rooted in confused and tenuous thinking, as if taking up a position is just too difficult, leaving partners vulnerable to the intrusion of other people's thoughts and feelings. Either way, emotional conflicts can shatter the coherence of thought.

As therapists we know that solutions to problematic emotional and mental states may be pursued through relationships: we may subject others to things we have difficulty knowing about in ourselves, or we may absorb, as our own, the states of mind that others have difficulty tolerating in themselves. Such intersubjective linking of experience reconfigures the way we think, the reconfiguration occurring through processes of projective identification, both the attributive kind: the "you are me" process, by which we colonize others and the acquisitive kind: the "I am you" process, by which we allow ourselves to be colonized by others. These processes can be regarded not only as defences against anxiety and forms of communication, but also as a means of regulating emotion. Developmental research has adopted two methods of capturing patterns of relating: observing behaviour and representing experience. Each approach provides a means of accessing the processes that have shaped the ways we regulate our emotions and states of mind from infancy onwards. For therapists, they provide a perspective from which to view adult couple relationships and the processes operating between therapists and couples in the consulting room.

Non-verbal processes: observing behaviour

Ainsworth and colleagues' landmark classifications of attachment security was drawn from observing how young infants (between twelve and eighteen months) responded to being separated from and reunited with their mothers (Ainsworth, Blehar, Waters, & Wall, 1978). The Strange Situation Test (SST) that she and her colleagues devised was designed to activate attachment behaviour by exposing infants to the moderately stressful situation of being temporarily separated from a parent. Close examination of the behaviour of infants in SSTs show how linked are their responses to the behaviour of their parents. What is being observed in the SST is a relationship. The same infant may behave differently in different relationships—for example, when with father instead of mother. It is as if, from the outset, infants are using their attachment figures to regulate their own emotional states and determining how best to do this through figuring out the emotional states of their parents and responding accordingly. With repeated encounters, such patterns can become embedded in children, and later in adults, constituting their default mode of operating in close relationships when feeling anxious. What may also become embedded is the degree of freedom they feel themselves to have in exploring and evaluating situations for themselves, and the extent to which others are discarded, colonized or engaged with in managing perceived threats and danger.

I have written elsewhere about how the rhythm of separations and reunions endemic to the psychotherapeutic process lends it some of the qualities of a SST for adults, with breaks and restarts often highlighting characteristic strategies for managing anxiety (Clulow, 2006). Couples are often anxious when they see their therapist for the first time, as they may be in the lead-up to breaks, returns, and endings in therapy, and at these times habitual strategies for managing anxiety (defences) may be particularly in evidence. This has implications for how free couples feel to explore their situation with a therapist at these threshold periods.

It is not simply the presence of a therapist or parent figure that regulates attachment anxiety. Following the critique of proximity as the arbiter of attachment security (Rutter, 1981), Bowlby subsequently made clear his views that in therapy, as in parenting, it was the quality of the care-giver's response that was crucial (Bowlby, 1988). Stern (1985) described this quality of responsiveness in relation to children as "attunement", Trevarthen and Aitken (2001) as "primary intersubjectivity". Infant research has shown that attunement is not a one-way affair, but that mothers and infants engage each other in a reciprocal process, modifying their responses in accordance with the feedback they receive from each other. The important conclusion that follows is that there is an intimate connection between the regulation of relationships and that of internal states. Mothers and infants can stimulate and damp down affect in their relationship. So, the capacity of children and, by extension, adults, to regulate their own emotions follows from the emotional availability of those who care for them. Child observation studies have showed how that availability is conveyed by facial expression (Tronick, Als, Adamson, Wise, & Brazelton, 1978), tone and modulation of voice (Jaffe, Beebe, Feldstein, Crown, & Jasnow, 2001), and timing of response (Murray & Trevarthen, 1986).

We are now well into the conceptual territory of "mirroring", the interpersonal process through which infants begin to discover a sense of agency, and of who they are in the world. Winnicott's concept of maternal mirroring was that infants see themselves in their mother's face, because what she looks like is related to what she sees in her infant's face (Winnicott, 1974). Mirroring is a less than perfect term for what goes on in this process except, perhaps, in its pathological form. It captures insufficiently the two-way co-construction of the mirroring process, and implies an exact, if reverse, perfect reflection. What the mother does, in the best of all worlds, is to read accurately the cues of her baby and to respond in a way that is in tune with the baby's internal state, but not in a way that replicates it. When her responses are in tune with the infant's gestures they are said to be *contingent*. But what she also does is *mark* her responses, so that a distinction is drawn between what belongs to her and what belongs to her baby (Gergely & Watson, 1996). So, if the baby coos and smiles the mother may respond with exaggerated delight, encouraging more smiles from the baby, who sees his own delight in the mother's face and gains satisfaction from experiencing a sense of agency—he can trigger a response that is contingent with his own internal state. Likewise, if the baby is grizzly and upset, his mother will not grizzle back (as a mirror might), but may reflect her recognition of his discomfort with a long drawn out "ahh", perhaps making sympathetic noises about teething if she sees the dribbling of saliva that connects with the crying.

So the mother produces a different, perhaps exaggerated, version of her baby's experience that has an "as if" quality that lets the baby know that she is not having the same experience as him, but is in tune with his experience. This decoupling of the mother's experience allows the infant to recognize the experience as his own, and not that of his mother. In this way the mirroring environment provides for homeostatic regulation of the infant's affective state. Through the attachment relationship the infant can internalize a secondary representation of his experience, secondary in the sense that it is one that has been processed by the mother from the infant's primary affective experience. Attachment and affect mirroring constitute the process by which the self is constituted through inter-actions with others; the capacity for self-regulation develops from the experience of co-regulation in relationships with others. What is seen in the face names emotional experience, and neuroscientists would argue that it simultaneously patterns developments in the brain—emotional connections firing synaptic connections (Schore, 1994).

Verbal processes: language, symbolism and representation

Main and colleagues' measure of attachment security, the Adult Attachment Interview (AAI), seeks to do with adults what the SST did with infants, but by studying representations of family experiences rather than observing behaviour. Their analysis focuses on the structure of discourse, not its content or its meaning (George, Kaplan, & Main, 1985). Secure narratives tell stories that are "truthful" in the sense that they have cohesion, that there is evidence for images provided at a semantic level, and that the teller is open to reviewing and reconstructing their stories in the process of telling them. They convey emotional rather than factual or historical truth, and are convincing to the listener. Insecure narratives breach one or more index of coherence in discourse style:

- quality—be truthful and have evidence for what you say;
- quantity—be succinct and yet complete;
- relation—be relevant and co-operative in presenting what has to be said;
- manner—be clear and orderly.

Dismissing narratives attempt to limit the influence of attachment relationships and experiences in their representations of past family relationships. Idealization, lack of recall, abstraction, and sometimes denigration, serve to keep attachment systems deactivated. They breach the indices of quality and quantity—internal contradictions and brevity undermine their truthfulness. Preoccupied narratives are confused, lacking in objectivity, passive, vague, unconvincingly analytical, angrily conflicted, and sometimes fearful—breaching the indices of relation and manner. Unresolved/disorganized states of mind betray themselves through temporary blips in what might otherwise be judged as either secure or insecure narratives.

Fonagy and colleagues have argued that attachment is not an end in itself, but that its importance lies in creating the relationship framework within which children and adults can discover their own mind, a mind that can both reflect on its own intentional stance and "know" the minds of others (Fonagy, Gergely, Jurist & Target, 2002). This, it is argued, has an evolutionary function by equipping humans with emotional as well as cognitive intelligence, which confers distinct advantages through allowing social situations to be read and predicted accurately. Such "mentalization" is crucial to the unfolding sense of agency and self. Fonagy argues that rather than seeing early relationships as setting the internal template for later ones, we should regard these relationships as determining the depth to which later experiences in the social environment can be processed. Taking this approach, we might assess the mutativity of therapeutic interventions with couples in terms of their capacity to increase the depth to which the partners can process their experiences together.

Case illustration

The context for the session described below is that the husband has just returned from working abroad following a very difficult time in the relationship when the wife had withdrawn from him after her mother's death.

> She begins by saying that since his return home her husband has been a brooding presence. While she had tried to avoid getting into arguments with him, as she recognizes his work situation is difficult, they had an argument the previous day when she lost her temper. He does not respond to this. The therapist resists asking about the argument, and instead comments on the cloud that seems to be hanging over them both. She waits for him to respond and he says nothing, but his uncommunicative state seems angry. The therapist's image is of a child that wants to be rescued from himself, but who also fights against attempts to do this by removing himself and waiting to be found. He comments on the possibility that the husband is longing for someone to make it all better by being available and offering support, and in the absence of this is feeling quite isolated and despondent on his own.

The husband says they do better when they are apart, that they proba-bly both feel that way, and returning to the family and therapy was deeply depressing, like going back to all the problems they had been facing before. Since returning home he had not been able to settle to any project. He resented the fact that the family was financially depen-dent on him and thought that without this burden he would have more freedom to pursue what he wanted in his career. He was filled up with despair about not achieving what he was capable of at work. He did not know what he wanted or where he was going, was losing confi-dence in himself, and all this made it worse. The therapist comments on how difficult this is for them both. The husband continues in a vein that conveys his sense of having no choice or control over his life because of all the appointments and commitments he has to cope with. The therapist makes a light-hearted remark that he can understand the wish not to come to therapy when it makes things so bad for them. She laughs and he grins ruefully.

She says they had quite a good weekend, and while he had not attended a ceremony scattering her mother's ashes on the previous Friday, something she had been cross with him about at the previous session, she had been touched that he had left her a considerate message. He overrides this, saying she does things to upset him, as with the argument that had blown up between them the previous day. He begins to describe what had happened, saying that the argument was about her having left their teenage daughter in their car unat-tended for a few minutes when collecting her from school, so that she was exposed to a potential threat from a passing man, and begins to warm to his complaint. She gets angry as he becomes more critical of her, and mounts an eloquent defence of her position: that their daugh-ter was a teenager, not a toddler, he was always going on about her being over-protective, she had not been away from the car long, their daughter was exploiting a rift between them because she had had a go at her for not coming out of school on time, and so on.

Rather than go into the details of this incident, the therapist comments on how a good experience between them had quickly been turned bad, both at home and in the session. The husband says something muted about needing things to be negative between them to shore themselves up against being taken over. The therapist pursues this idea, asking him what he means, and he launches into a description of his wife's childhood problems and how she was always at odds with other family members and fought her way out of difficulties, tailing off into a muted remark about how that might also apply to him and his mother.

His wife swoops on this, and in a pointed and somewhat aggressive way, tells him that his problem is that he's never sorted out his feelings about his mother and the awful way she treated him. She makes the transference interpretation that she has been made to pay over the years for things he never resolved with his mother, and the accusations of control, rejection, and lack of support are things that should be laid at his mother's door, not hers. He responds by leaping to his mother's defence, retaliating with details from her family history.

The therapist winds back, reminding him that he started off this really interesting thought that he might need to ward off a fear that he might get lost in relationships, that perhaps he longed for as well as feared this happening, and that this might be something that applied to them both and affected how they operated together as a couple. He remains fixed on how she never got on with her family. The therapist wonders aloud if thinking about this idea, which he started, was difficult because it spoilt a positive recollection of his mother that he wanted to preserve. Perhaps it seemed better to have all the negatives in the marriage and thereby preserve a notion of his family in very positive terms.

She agrees with this and says he never looks at his own family problems and that is half the problem between them. The therapist says that she sounds quite angry with him, as if he should know more about this and have taken things up with his mother. She says, no, that was not how she felt. There were things she held members of her own family accountable for, and she did think he could do with reflecting more on his experience, but she didn't blame him for what had happened in his family. She mentioned a press article where an abuse scandal had been reported at his old school, adding how he had often spoken to her of an incident in which he thought he had been abused at school and his mother had never believed him. She thought that was terrible, and showed how little support he had received from her. He relaxes and becomes less angry, although remaining guarded about his mother. The therapist comments on how important their parents are in the marriage, despite their physical absence, and maybe that was part of the cloud that kept gathering over them.

Comment

In this fragment of a session there are plenty of attachment themes— reunions after a break, defensive patterns of relating that keep the prospect of intimacy at bay, the absence of "marking" when the problem is attributed to one or other of them, the idealization of parent figures against feelings of anger about disappointment and neglect, the repercussions of bereavement, and abuse as an indicator of what goes unnoticed in "non-contingent" mirroring. In terms of therapeutic intention, the emphasis is less on interpreting what is going on than on trying to achieve a degree of "contingency" in the mirroring process, accessing what they might be feeling (especially him), and paying less attention to "marking" except in relation to aspects of experience that get located and attacked in each other. The meaning, in terms of interpretation, comes from them in the context of the therapist trying to stay with the affect.

What the therapist is not doing, as Susan Johnson might do, is positioning himself to orchestrate the partners speaking directly to each other about how they are feeling, although some of this does happen spontaneously. Instead, he tries to engage with and explore the emotional climate in the room, a climate that involves himself and the couple, and from this makes some muted transference observations both in relation to himself as well as to the relationship between them.

Summary

Attachment, theory-informed, couple psychotherapy aims to enhance the opportunities for partners to discover themselves and each other as feeling, thinking, and intentional beings through fostering an interpersonal environment in which it is safe to embark upon this developmental quest. Safety involves establishing a secure base from which partners and therapists create the freedom to "play", or "play along", with each other's reality, being connected with the experience of the other (contingency) while countering pressures to equate inner states with outer realities (marking), thereby relieving the fear that to have a thought makes it true.

Transference and countertransference enactments may act as a guide for therapeutic technique. The enmeshed relationships and borderline states of partners, who are likely to be rated preoccupied or unresolved with respect to trauma or abuse, make the "marking" role of the therapist crucial, and boundaries may become the primary object of the work to counter psychic equivalence modes of relating. Dismissing/avoidant partners may require something different from the therapist in terms of having to believe what partners have difficulty believing—that they are important enough, and the risk of rejection is sufficiently manageable, for attachments to be valued. Contingency is important here, and there may be a need to step out of the frame; for example, by reminding forgetful couples by letter or phone in advance about their imminent appointments. There may also be indications for modulating the frequency of meetings, or accommodating difficulties in meeting appointment times, in order to foster engagement.

The modulation of posture, gaze, timing, and tone of voice may be important in matching the affective state of the couple, building on the language and metaphors that they use, and offering something back that is both similar but noticeably different, in order that what they have offered might be thought about differently. Therapists might also think about how closely they feel they have to monitor what is going on in terms of how they respond, and how this might link with attachment security. Special attention may need to be paid to fleeting "moments of meeting" between partners, or with their therapists, so that what happens can be thought about and understood—and remembered as part of the history of the therapeutic process. These are the moments most likely to be associated with change. Interpretations may be as much about giving a name to experience as to understanding the whys and wherefores. For example, in so far as bodily symptoms, illness, or sexual functioning can be channels for expressing unprocessed affective states, attention may be drawn to these possibilities. In the absence of reflective capacities, supportive work may be what is mutative, especially early on.

Then there is the attachment status of the therapist. If change arises from the co-construction of experience and the mirroring role of the therapist, his/her own lacunae will have a significant effect upon what can and cannot be managed. Mirroring involves thinking about emotional states, which, in turn, presupposes the capacity to experience, withstand, and reprocess affective states through reflecting on them. All of us suffer from limitations in areas that are particular to each of us, and it is often those who are seeking help from us who make us aware of what we most lack in ourselves.

References

Ainsworth, M. D. S., Blehar, M. C., Waters, E., & Wall, S. (1978). *Patterns of Attachment: A Psychological Study of the Strange Situation.* Hillsdale, NJ: Lawrence Erlbaum.
Bowlby, J. (1969). *Attachment and Loss: Volume 1.* London: Hogarth.
Bowlby, J. (1988). *A Secure Base: Clinical Applications of Attachment Theory.* London: Routledge.
Clulow, C. (2001a). *Adult Attachment and Couple Psychotherapy.* London: Brunner-Routledge.
Clulow, C. (2006). Couple psychotherapy and attachment theory. In: J. Savege Scharff & D. Scharff (Eds.), *New Paradigms for Treating Relationships* (pp. 253–266). Lanham, MD: Jason Aronson.
Fonagy, P., Gergely, G., Jurist, E. L., & Target, M. (2002). *Affect Regulation, Mentalization and the Development of the Self.* New York: Other Press.
George, C., Kaplan, N., & Main, M. (1985). The adult attachment interview. Unpublished manuscript, University of California at Berkeley.
Gergely, G., & Watson, J. (1996). The social bio-feedback theory of parental affect-mirroring. *International Journal of Psycho-Analysis, 77*: 181–212.
Hazan, C., Campa, M., & Gur-Yaish, N. (2006). What is adult attachment? In: M. Mikulincer & G. Goodman (Eds.), *Dynamics of Romantic Love: Attachment, Caregiving, and Sex.* New York: Guilford Press.
Jaffe, J., Beebe, B., Feldstein, S., Crown, C., & Jasnow, M. D. (2001). *Monographs of the Society for Research in Child Development, 66*(2): vii–132.
Johnson, S. (2004). *The Practice of Emotionally Focused Couple Therapy. Creating Connection* (2nd edn). New York: Brunner-Routledge.
Murray, L., & Trevarthen, C., (1986). The infant's role in mother–infant communication. *Journal of Child Language, 13*: 15–29.
Petith, M. (2006). Enactments: the therapy within the therapy. Paper given at a conference on Couple Therapy and Attachment Theory at the Tavistock Centre for Couple Relationships, London, 20 May.
Rutter, M. (1981). *Maternal Deprivation Reassessed* (2nd edn). Harmondsworth: Penguin.
Schore, A. (1994). *Affect Regulation and the Origin of the Self: The Neurobiology of Emotional Development.* Hillsdale, NJ: Lawrence Erlbaum Associates.

Sroufe, L., & Waters, E. (1977). Attachment as an organisational construct. *Child Development, 48*: 1184–1199.

Stern, D. (1985). *The Interpersonal World of the Infant*. New York: Basic Books.

Strachey, J. (1934). The nature of the therapeutic action of psychoanalysis. *International Journal of Psycho-Analysis, 15*: 127–159.

Trevarthen, C., & Aitken, K. (2001). Infant intersubjectivity: research, theory and clinical applications. *Journal of Child Psychology and Psychiatry, 42*: 3–48.

Tronick, E. Z., Als, H., Adamson, L., Wise, S., & Brazelton, T. (1978). The infant's response to entrapment between contradictory messages in face to face interaction. *Journal of the American Academy of Child and Adolescent Psychiatry, 17*: 1–13.

Winnicott, D. W. (1974). Mirror-role of mother and family in child development. In: D. W. Winnicott (Ed.), *Playing and Reality*. Harmondsworth: Penguin.

CHAPTER FIFTEEN

Attachment therapy with couples: affect regulation and dysregulation in couple relationships; effective and ineffective responses to painful states by therapists and partners

Una McCluskey

Introduction

This chapter explores the importance of effective care-giving within adult couple relations from the perspective of the *theory* introduced by Heard and Lake (1997) and the practice, *attachment therapy* by Heard, Lake, and McCluskey (2008). Effective care-giving enables couples to regulate each other's emotional states. To manage the stresses and strains of life couples need to be able to relate empathically to one another when under stress. The capacity to sustain an empathic stance towards another is more easily available to people who have had experience in early relationships which has helped them both to be in touch with their own feelings and to consider the feelings of others. People who have not had this experience as young children are more inclined towards self-defence if their initial show of empathy is rebuffed or avoided. Such a situation leaves the person who is care-seeking in the relationship in a state of distress and leaves the person who is trying to provide care in a state of frustration and incompetence.

Couples who cannot negotiate effectively the dynamics of care-seeking and care-giving as these get aroused between them are vulnerable to crises every time one of them is in a panic. This chapter explores the idea that effective care-giving is as important in adult relationships as it is in parent–infant relationships. Without true other directed, effective care-giving between partners, their capacity for interest sharing with each other or others will be inhibited and their expression of affectionate sexuality may be infiltrated with defence.

Recent research (Gottman, Murray, Swanson, Tyson, & Swanson, 2005) shows that an indicator of whether a couple is likely to stay together or separate is the proportion of negative comments they make as an overall percentage of their total verbal communication. Relationships that have become patterned with negative judgements and attributions are clearly painful to the parties themselves, their children, and to friends and onlookers.

The chapter begins with a brief account of early development and the importance of accurate affect identification and attunement as a basis for security in self–other relations. It looks at the ways in which early experience of misattunement and affect dysregulation permeates the way in which people seek and respond to care in early childhood and colours how they relate to intimate others in adult life. I conclude with an example of dysregulation within a couple relationship in the context of a consultation with a couple psychotherapist.

Attunement, misattunement, and regulation in the early interactive experience between infant and "mother"

We have known for many years (Ainsworth, Blehar, Waters, & Wall, 1978; Cohn, Matias, Tronick, Connell, & Lions-Ruth, 1986; Meltzoff, 1983; Murray & Trevarthen, 1985, 1986; Papousek & Papousek, 1979; Tronick, 1989; Tronick & Cohn, 1989) that infants cannot regulate their own autonomic systems and that they require the actual physical holding of another human being to maintain their physiological state in equilibrium. We know from Tronick's work that infants have some capacity for self-regulation when this is not forthcoming within the context of a relationship. The behaviours that infants use are (a) self-comforting orally, (b) turning their heads away, (c) rocking, and (d) self-stimulating, and that when infants chronically experience a lack of interaction with adults, they lose postural control and have dull-looking eyes. In other words, infants and small children literally come alive and develop in the context of a relationship and, in its absence, they lose crucial capacities for understanding themselves and others in relationships. Schore's work (1994, 2003a,b) shows that interaction with another human being is crucial for the development of the infant's brain and for their later capacity to process emotion

Ainsworth and Wittig (1969) were the first to notice that the speed with which mothers responded to their crying infants and managed successfully to soothe them was positively correlated with security at one year of age. Later Ainsworth and colleagues (1991) devised what has become known as the Strange Situation Test, which has been used reliably to classify the attachment status of young children into, first, three groups, and then, after further analysis by Carol George and Mary Main and colleagues (George, Kaplan, & Main, 1985; Main & Hess, 1990; Main, Kaplan, & Cassidy, 1985), into four groups (Cassidy & Shaver, 1999). These four groups are: secure, insecure ambivalent–resistant, insecure avoidant, and disorganized. Children classified as disorganized do not have a strategy for responding to their care-giver when their care-seeking system is aroused and are likely to become completely emotionally, cognitively, and behaviourally disorganized. Care-seekers who feel secure have generally experienced attuned, accurate and sensitive responses from readily available care-givers and, as a consequence, accurately identify their own and others' affect and are direct and coherent in asking for help (Bretherton, 1990; Grossmann & Grossmann, 1991a,b). Insecure ambivalent–resistant care-seekers have generally experienced a mix of responses. The insecure avoidant pattern tends to occur in response to both insensitive intrusiveness on the part of the care-giver and also the experience of care-seeking being rebuffed, overridden, and dismissed. The avoidant person learns to rely on themselves and manage on their own, in spite of being highly aroused and in a state of stress.

Affect regulation in couple relationships

Bowlby (1973) suggested the attachment system remains active throughout our lives. Hazan & Shaver's (1987) research provided some evidence that early attachment styles correlated with the choice of partner in adult life. Heard & Lake (1986) extended Bowlby's ideas to include the instinctive goal-corrected systems of interest sharing, sexuality and self-defence and postulated how these worked as one process to maintain well-being. Using these ideas, this chapter considers how we can understand interaction between adults from the perspective of attachment theory, as it has been developed by Heard & Lake (1986, 1997 and Heard, Lake & McCluskey (2008)).

Within adult partnerships, when care-seeking is aroused, people will look to each other to assuage and regulate that aspect of the self. If one or other of the partners has had early experience of being extremely frightened by their care-giver, then when *their* care-seeking system is aroused, they are also likely to have to deal with the arousal of their fear system. The fear system is likely to overwhelm them both cognitively and emotionally.

While conducting research in attunement in adult psychotherapy (McCluskey, 2005; McCluskey, Hooper, & Bingley Miller, 1999; McCluskey, Roger, & Nash, 1997), I identified five typical care-seeking behaviours and five typical care-seeking responses that together yield nine patterns of interaction. Three of these patterns are effective and six are ineffective in regulating affect and assuaging care-seeking. I suggest that the same patterns may be present in couple relationships. For the purposes of this chapter, I will introduce two of these patterns of interaction, Patterns one and four, as set out in McCluskey (2005). The first pattern is effective in regulating emotion, while the second one is ineffective.

Pattern one

> Careseeker produces source of worry; care-giver responds to the affect and the thoughts and orients to context; careseeker carries on presenting issues; caregiver responds to affect and concerns; careseeker and caregiver are mutually responsive. [McCluskey, 2005, p. 221]

I classify this pattern of interaction as being "attuned to goals of careseeker using the process of goal-corrected empathic attunement". It involves effective purposeful misattunement to affect, which regulates, contains, and attends to care-seekers goals. By "effective misattunement", I mean that the care-giver will either amplify the affect of the care-seeker or down-regulate it in such a way that the other person is better able to have access to their own emotions, to contain them and express them coherently.

Pattern four

> Careseeker is demanding; caregiver's responses are cognitive and fail to regulate affect; careseeker becomes more demanding; caregiver continues engaging cognitively; careseeker becomes more aroused; caregiver, careseeker or both, attack or withdraw. [*ibid.*, p. 222]

I classify this care-giving response as "not attuning to careseeker affect, avoidance of engagement with it and their capacity for affect regulation disabled". The care-giver is not attuned to affect and their own care-giving system is infiltrated by self-defence and they become disorganized. "Pattern four" describes a mode of interaction between adult partners that we may all recognize, when one partner fails to address the other's emotion and instead offers cognitive solutions.

The concept of goal-corrected empathic attunement refers to the results of earlier research (McCluskey, Hooper, & Bingley Miller, 1999) where we noted that in adult psychotherapy the offer to help aroused the dynamics of care-seeking, and that until the therapist assuaged the care-seeking of the client, exploratory behaviour was inhibited. What is important for us to grasp from this research is that if the care-seeking system is activated in situations of professional care-giving, the care-giver has to be very alert to defensive forms of care-seeking and respond undefensively themselves, remaining actively explorative, until they have ascertained what the care-seeker needs and can give it to them. This requires a capacity for sustained empathy on the part of the care-giver, often in the face of attack, withdrawal, entanglement, or incoherent expression of need. I am suggesting that in the absence of being able to offer this type of response within adult couple relationships, the parties are vulnerable to distress and unable to function to their full potential.

Case illustration

The following is an excerpt from a verbatim transcription of a videoed clinical session where two people agreed to seek help from a marital consultant and to the session being taped and video recorded for research purposes. (Some of the dialogue is omitted to protect confidentiality.)

It offers an example of dysregulation within the couple relationship, where neither party is able to regulate the other, and both resort to defensive behaviour and self-comforting. While this does not show attachment therapy with a couple, as such practice is only beginning to be developed, there is a critique of the therapist's response from the perspective of attachment therapy for adults, (Heard, Lake, & McCluskey, 2008). The couple have told the therapist about a row they had while on holiday. The husband is extremely heated, raising his voice and waving his arms about, and often putting out his hand with force, right up against his wife's face. She sits with her legs very close together in front of her, her arms crossed and wrapped around her and her head slightly to one side. In other words, she has adopted a very still, submissive posture, while he is very mobile and flaying around. He describes a sequence of events culminating in hitting his wife: she locking him out of the bedroom, he getting frantic and thinking she may have returned home and then being completely irate when she let him in, but wouldn't explain why she'd locked him out.

> Stephen: "Well, I thought you were on a plane going home, I didn't know where you were, that thing aggravates me as well, beyond the irrational feelings, I found that totally irrational. Just up and cleared off, without saying where she's going, I'm stuck in the middle of Morocco not knowing where she's gone, driven to the airport."

This speech shows that Stephen is irate. We might deduce that his fear system is active because he is seeking to dominate his partner and make her submit.

> Lynne: "You'd just been violent, I was in the middle of Morocco."

We see that Lynne stands up to Stephen, even though speaking in a very low voice that it was almost impossible to hear. Her soft voice made me wonder whether this was her attempt to regulate and contain Stephen, by not fanning the flames any further, while at the same time being assertive and clear about her position. One is left wondering whether Stephen needs somebody to give in completely to his perception of events and that only then will he calm down. This bears out how dominant–submissive interactive patterns work. The relationship is only temporarily regulated by the partner who has been made to submit, actually submitting.

Stephen: "Yeah, you were violent back, Lynne."

Stephen's tone was extremely loud and self-assured, but slightly high-pitched, indicating to me that he was in self-defence. His accusation to Lynne underlines the dominant submissive dynamic. He cannot tolerate Lynne asserting herself.

Lynne: "Not to you."

It must have been around this point in the quarrel they are recalling that Stephen hit her, which means that the row had been escalating, there was no containment and regulation. In the absence of submission by Lynne, Stephen escalates his dominance over her.

Stephen: "Well, when somebody is grabbing a newspaper off you like that when saying, 'please leave me alone'. It takes a lot of self-control and I haven't got that much self-control, I admit it."

This was said with a lot of force while pushing his arm at Lynne and demonstrating in a sawing motion, backwards and forwards, what he meant by "grabbing . . . like that".

Lynne: "That was an incident, I think, at the end of a strained relationship."

Lynne's relatively overarching view of the interaction might mean that she is not controlled by her own fear system and can think about how to react and interact.

Stephen: "No, you're saying that, that's news to me. I thought we were having a great time—Lynne, you're painting a black picture here and it's not true. We were going out every day, we were going out for meals, you didn't cook one thing—we'd go . . . we were having a great time, I thought, this is news to me, bloody news to me."

In spite of making several attempts to be seen, recognized and assuaged by the other, neither can empathize with the other; both are in self-defence. Having shown video clips of this session at workshops to demonstrate affect regulation and dysregulation in couples, I have asked the audience to identify the tone of voice being used. Invariably people say that the man is attacking; that he has a whine in his voice indicating that he is both self-centred and aggrieved, while the woman is holding herself together, being very still and displaying a mixture of sad, angry, and resigned.

In the absence of empathy for each other's state by the couple themselves, the therapist interjects in a way that keeps both of them in mind:

> *Therapist*: "But supposing you thought you were having a good time and Lynne was less sure about that. Supposing you'd got rather different experiences of the same event, how do these get . . . broached between the two of you? Because it feels as if at the moment this situation could only be defined in one of two ways—it was either a great holiday, or it wasn't a great holiday, and those are the only two positions that are possible. Whereas I think you're saying you've had . . . two different experiences."

The therapist's empathy for them both invites them to think about how they manage separate realities. Stephen responds by saying, "Yeah", which the therapist follows up saying

> *Therapist*: "What is very frustrating is that you come up against each other's experience and you don't agree."

Again the therapist shows empathy for both and elicits from Stephen more of his grievances. One might expect this from the perspective of attachment theory, because when the person feels met and understood, they perceive the care-giver as reliable; the care-seeker then shows more of their distress. Nevertheless, we note that the therapist's empathic comment, directed at each partner, is received personally by Stephen, who is not able to see that Lynne might have her own response to this.

> *Stephen*: "Well, for me, except for the drive back . . . which was a foul up . . . we were so angry . . . Lynne shouting at me, I'm shouting at her, so I said we'll drive back, so we drove back . . . I thought it was a great holiday."

The therapist responds to this outburst by not referring to the content directly, but going back to something said earlier about the drive being a distance of 150 miles and conducted in silence. By so doing, he manages not to get entangled with the particular perception of one partner (i.e., Stephen), but restores a focus on their joint experience.

> *Therapist*: "Your withdrawal seems to be that actually this is the fight going on. It's going on in silence, but you're both actually very angry with each other."

Again, Stephen remains in self-defence, unable to pick up the cue from the therapist that Lynne may be sharing a similar experience.

> *Stephen*: "Yeah, I was furious, because I said we can't ruddy stop here—there's a reason we can't go through the gate. In the end Lynne insisted, she had her own way . . ."

Using an attachment perspective, a therapist would consider what system is aroused in Stephen now or at the point in the quarrel being described. If the conclusion was that the fear system was operating, one might ask the couple what they thought might have happened if the other did not give in to them. What was their fear about? The dialogue, however, proceeded as follows:

> *Lynne*: "I was driving, Stephen, it was difficult when you're driving, so I went through but I mean that's just . . ."
>
> *Stephen*: "But you knew it, you wouldn't have it."

(The place they wanted to visit was shut, but they could have stayed overnight.)

> *Lynne*: "The rational thing would have been to say—oh, it's a shame isn't it, we've got our things here . . . let's find a hotel.
>
> *Stephen*: "Lynne, you were *just* as livid, now *come* on, in the end you said, *I don't want to come here again.*"
>
> *Lynne*: "Yeah, no, no, I said 'if we leave . . . now, I'm not coming back—I'm not driving 150 miles back again, but we could have stayed . . ."
>
> *Stephen*: "No Lynne, by then you know it had lost its charm."

We can see that the row is getting into full swing again, with each seeking to convince the therapist of the rationality of their position. They do not explore their level of arousal, their pain, and their attempts to get the other to alleviate it. They are not exploring what it was all about and why they were failing with each other so miserably. In effect, both of their care-seeking systems are active and infiltrated by self-defence. Their capacity for care-giving and exploratory interest sharing is overridden. An attachment therapist might raise with them what aspects of themselves were aroused and remained unregulated in their relationship, their history of this, and whether there were times and circumstances when they managed this better.

The therapist intervenes again with empathy for both:

Therapist: "It is interesting because in both these situations . . . you're both in a sense starting out on the same side. You're both angry about the way your son's behaving, you're both angry about the frustration of not being able to sightsee . . . but something happens that doesn't allow you to be on the same side and to share the disappointment and the distress in what's happened, but to fight each other . . ."

Stephen can apparently see what the therapist is saying and comments, "You're right", followed by an immediate response from the therapist. We don't know, if the therapist had left a gap, whether Lynne might have said something. She seems to murmur. There seems enough indication from both that their care-seeking has been assuaged in the interaction with the therapist and that they can access the exploratory part of themselves.

Therapist: "It's puzzling, isn't it, because actually you're talking about an experience where you might have expected to have become allies . . . to feel very annoyed together about something."

Stephen clearly feels met and understood by this, referring directly to something he had talked about earlier in the session.

Stephen: "Well, I felt that way to start with and I felt that way about my son. And the next thing, no. No, I shouldn't have done that. I shouldn't have banged the chair—well I was on Lynne's side against the son you see, but now it's not. No, no of course not, I should never lose my temper, but *I do*."

At this point the therapist intervenes again, not about what Stephen has just said, but to address the underlying dynamic between the couple, again showing empathy for both. I deduce that the therapist's own care-giving is active and he is in exploratory mode; he is trying to figure out what is going on and coming in empathically. He is not in self-defence.

> *Therapist*: "I think you were talking about something that is quite uncontrollable about the experience. It sort of spirals between the two of you so that when you get angry, instead of feeling that you have got some way of damping things down, it just aggravates the situation. So if either of you are angry the response to the other one is going to jack [it] up, it's not going to help alleviate that until something blows."

Again, Stephen responds very quickly, as if he feels met and understood, but he doesn't seem able to appreciate or take in that the therapist is talking about a dynamic between them; rather he takes what is being said as affirmation of his own position. I suggest that Stephen is still in self-defence and that his exploratory system is still overridden. In other words, his care-seeking has not yet been assuaged.

> *Stephen*: "That's right. No, you're dead right. So I said that I would leave, I would go out—it so frightened me this time, I said I'm not going to get in a situation any more. I'm not going to stay and argue, but that's not my way to walk out away from something."

We now l see that the therapist ignores Stephen's focus on himself and returns to the couple, inviting them to take an over-view of the dynamic between them and to think about it. He suggests that there may be transference on to each other from early life experiences. When they are in a state, they stop seeing each other as themselves, but as reminders of people from the past.

> *Therapist*: "But you become something other to each other when this happens I imagine. I am just wondering whether you think yourself back into that situation, because it is as if when it flips and you're really angry with each other, I'm wondering . . . who it is that you're angry with, because something changes very quickly . . . and you see something in each other then which becomes the target. What is it that happens? What is it that you see in each other? What is it that you are responding to?'

Lynne seems to grasp the therapist's meaning though she doesn't use the opportunity to explore how she sees Stephen, or how Stephen sees her, but to concentrate on Stephen's behaviour, indicating that she too is in self-defence.

Lynne: "Stephen controls the situation . . ."

The therapist shifts the focus slightly from Lynne defining Stephen, to reframing it as her experience of Stephen, and says,

Therapist: "So he becomes very controlling in your eyes?"

Lynne: "Yes . . ."

Therapist: "Is it then that you feel a bit robbed of your experience, because you're more angry, whether it's about your son or sightseeing. If Stephen then comes in to take over the situation, you can't be angry any more. You somehow then have a different problem to deal with?"

The therapist's comment is interesting, focusing on Lynne's experience as a person and what is happening to her in the interaction—that her self-identity is being threatened. This is empathy at a very deep level and Lynne responds immediately.

Lynne: "Yeah."

The therapist turns to Stephen to explore with him at the same level:

Therapist: "I'm just trying to think about what your experience is here. I'm wondering what happens to you, Stephen, because obviously something important is happening to you, because Lynne's getting angry as in these two situations. I don't know if you see it in the same way in terms of your response. What happens for you?"

Stephen, however, is unable to retain an interpersonal focus and comes back again to himself. He is unable to explore what is going on between them as a couple as having a dynamic of its own, only seeing it from his point of view. As suggested earlier, Stephen is still relating from a dominant–submissive position and will only calm down (temporarily) when the therapist and his wife agree with him.

Stephen: "The wrong thing was happening; that's why I got angry . . ."

Therapist: "The wrong thing?"

Stephen returns to the row about Lynne wanting to park beside the museum even though it was closed.

Stephen: "It's closed—it says so on the gate . . ."

The therapist invites Stephen to explore his feelings about being shut out and unable to do what he wanted to do:

Therapist: "So what were your feelings abut the gate being shut and not being able to get . . ."

Stephen: "That's the way museums are, it was irritating . . ."

Therapist: "Were you bothered about it?"

Stephen shows that his anger was not with the situation itself, but that he was focusing it on Lynne.

Stephen: "The fact she insisted on going into the car park . . ."

The therapist does not lift this comment as an example of how Stephen targets Lynne when he is frustrated, rather than joining her in their shared frustration. He focuses on why Lynne's response provoked Stephen. Technically, I think the therapist lost an opportunity to keep the couple focused on exploring their interactional dynamics.

Therapist: "So what was it about Lynne's response that got inside you?

Stephen: "Well . . . she wouldn't listen to me . . . and I could see I was right."

So we see that Stephen really wanted Lynne to agree with him. He remains in self-defence with his exploratory system overridden and unable to accept the therapist's thought that they could have handled this situation otherwise. They were both disappointed by their long and abortive journey and they might have mutually supported each other, rather than attacking each other in a way that escalated into violence.

The couple therapist did not use extended attachment theory to formulate their interaction and to determine what interventions might enable them to become more exploratory about their situation. The therapist's care-giving was active and he remained in exploratory mode. He demonstrated empathy for both parties and invited them to step back to see that there was more that joined than separated them in their quarrels. Neither party could see the other's perspective while still relating at the level of a dominant/submissive position. To free the couple to develop mutual empathy, the therapist needed to help them explore why empathic relating was important and what level of fear they hoped to address and contain by behaving as they did.

An attachment therapist might focus their failure to regulate each other's anxieties and might explore what they knew about how and whether that situation could be retrieved. Each partner brings a well-embedded history of how their care-seeking has been regulated and met and has a long experience of trying to re-enact those dynamics within the couple relationship. With this couple, a therapist might focus on the fear system rather than on care-seeking. Questions that an attachment therapist could raise with them as a couple might be about: what arouses their care-seeking; what arouses their impulse to dominate or submit; how do they enact these behaviours within the relationship, how effective or ineffective are they, and what can they do as a couple to shift their pattern of interaction so that it becomes mutually more satisfying.

Working from an attachment perspective allows one to monitor whether one's own care-giving is being infiltrated with defence or whether one is remaining open and exploratory with the couple. One can also track which system is active within each person (i.e., care-seeking) and which systems are being overridden, (i.e., interest-sharing), as well as whether the couple actually move out of care-seeking into exploratory interest-sharing and how that might be facilitated.

Conclusion

This chapter presents the way in which adults require emotional regulation, especially within their close intimate relationships, when their care-seeking systems or their fear systems have been activated. Extracts from the couple consultation illustrate how a particular couple failed completely to meet or regulate each other's care-seeking needs and used primarily dominance–submission as a form of regulation. My commentary on the transcript indicates from the perspective of extended attachment theory which systems I consider to be active in the couple and suggests how an attachment therapist might have intervened. I hope the reader is sufficiently interested to take these ideas further for themselves.

References

Ainsworth, M. D. S. (1991). Attachments and other affectional bonds across the life cycle. In: C. M. Parkes, J. Stevenson-Hinde, & P. Marris (Eds.), *Attachment Across Life Cycle* (pp. 33–51). London: Routledge.

Ainsworth, M. D. S., & Wittig, B. A. (1969). Attachment and the exploratory behaviour of one-year-olds in a strange situation. In: B. M. Foss (Ed.), *Determinants of Infant Behaviour, Volume 4* (pp. 113–136). London: Methuen.

Ainsworth, M. D. S., Blehar, M. C., Waters, E., & Wall, S. (1978). *Patterns of Attachment: A Psychological Study of the Strange Situation.* Hillsdale, NJ: Lawrence Erlbaum.

Bowlby, J. (1973). *Attachment and Loss: Volume 2. Separation: Anxiety and Anger.* London: Hogarth.

Bretherton, I. (1990). Communication patterns, internal working models, and the intergenerational transmission of attachment relationships. *Infant Mental Health Journal, 11*: 237–252.

Cassidy, J., & Shaver, P. R. (Eds.) (1999). *Handbook of Attachment.* New York: Guilford.

Cohn, J. F., Matias, R., Tronick, E. Z., Connell, D., & Lions-Ruth, K. (1986). Face-to-face interaction of depressed mothers and their infants. In: E. Z. Tronick & T. Field (Eds.), *Maternal Depression and Infant Disturbance* (pp. 31–45). San Francisco, CA: Jossey-Bass.

George, C., Kaplan, N., & Main, M. (1985). The adult attachment interview. Unpublished manuscript, University of California at Berkeley.

Gottman, J. M., Murray, J. D., Swanson, C., Tyson, R., & Swanson, K. R. (2005). *The Mathematics of Marriage: Dynamic Non Linear Model.* Boston: Bradford Books, MIT Press.

Grossmann, K., & Grossmann, K. E. (1991a). Newborn behaviour, early parenting quality and later toddler–parent relationships in a group of German infants. In: J. Nugent, K. Lester, B. M. Lester, & T. B. Brazelton (Eds.), *The Cultural Context of Infancy (Vol. 2)*. Norwood, NJ: Ablex.

Grossmann, K., & Grossmann, K. E. (1991b). Attachment quality as an organiser of emotional and behavioural responses in a longitudinal perspective. In: C. M. Parkes, J. Stevenson-Hinde, & P. Marris (Eds.), *Attachment Across the Life Cycle* (pp. 93–114). London: Routledge.

Hazan, C., & Shaver, P. R. (1987). Romantic love conceptualised as an attachment process. *Journal of Personality and Social Psychology, 52*: 511–524.

Heard, D., & Lake, B. (1986). The attachment dynamic in adult life. *British Journal of Psychiatry, 149*: 430–439.

Heard, D., & Lake, B. (1997). *The Challenge of Attachment for Caregiving*. London: Routledge.

Heard, D., Lake, B., & McCluskey, U. (2008). *Attachment Therapy for Adults and Adolescents: Theory and Practice post Bowlby*. London: Karnac.

Main, M., & Hess, E. (1990). Parents' unresolved traumatic experiences are related to infant disorganised attachment status: is frightened and/or frightening parental behavior the linking mechanism? In: M. Greenberg, D. Cicchetti, & E. M. Cummings (Eds.), *Attachment in the Preschool Years: Theory, Research and Intervention* (pp. 161–182). Chicago, IL: University of Chicago Press.

Main, M., Kaplan, N., & Cassidy, J. (1985). Security in infancy, childhood and adulthood: a move to the level of representation. In: I. Bretherton & E. Waters (Eds.), *Growing Points of Attachment Theory and Research* (pp. 66–104). Chicago, IL: University of Chicago Press.

McCluskey, U. (2005). *To Be Met as a Person: The Dynamics of Attachment in Professional Encounters*. London: Karnac.

McCluskey, U., Hooper, C., & Bingley Miller, L. (1999). Goal-corrected empathic attunement, developing and rating the concept. *Psychotherapy, Theory, Research, Training and Practice, 36*: 80–90.

McCluskey, U., Roger, D., & Nash, P. (1997). A preliminary study of the role of attunement in adult psychotherapy. *Human Relations, 50*: 1261–1273.

Meltzoff, A. (1983). Newborn infants imitate adult facial gestures. *Child Development, 54*: 702–709.

Murray, L., & Trevarthen, C. (1985). Emotional regulation of interactions between two month olds and their mothers. In: T. M. Field & N. A. Fox (Eds.), *Social Perception in Infants*. New Jersey: Norwood.

Murray, L., & Trevarthen, C. (1986). The infant's role in mother–infant communications. *Journal of Child Language, 13*: 15–29.

Papousek, H., & Papousek, M. (1979). Early ontogeny of human social interaction: its biological roots and social dimensions. In: M. V. Cranach (Ed.), *Human Ethology* (pp. 456–478). Cambridge: Cambridge University Press.

Schore, A. (1994). *Affect Regulation and the Origin of the Self: The Neurobiology of Emotional Development*. Hillsdale, NJ: Lawrence Erlbaum Associates.

Schore, A. (2003a). *Affect Regulation and the Repair of the Self*. New York: Norton.

Schore, A. (2003b). *Affect Dysregulation and Disorders of the Self*. New York: Norton.

Tronick, E. Z. (1989). Emotions and emotional communication in infants. *American Psychologist, 44*: 112–119.

Tronick, E. Z. & Cohn, J. F. (1989). Infant mother face-to-face interaction. Age and gender differences in coordination and miscoordination. *Child Development, 59*: 85–92.

CHAPTER SIXTEEN

Psychopathology and therapeutic style: integrating object relations and attachment theory in working with borderline families

Timothy Keogh, Maria Kourt, Charles Enfield, and Sylvia Enfield

> "I don't remember parents being children very much. I don't remember smooth brows forming innocence of afternoon, allowing raindrops to be listless in a row"
>
> (Murphy, 2004)

Introduction

This chapter focuses on the application of Object Relations Theory, coupled with Attachment Theory, to psychotherapeutic work with families. It specifically examines the issue of matching therapeutic style to family psychopathology. In particular, an argument is made for an object relations approach to family therapy with a borderline family, in which the approach focuses on the relationship aspects of the therapy, and where countertransference is used as the guide to the direction of the therapy.

This post Kleinian approach distinguishes itself from that of the American Relational School (Frank, 1998) by its focus on the use of the countertransference and the unconscious phantasies operating in families. The case example discussed illustrates how therapists

239

use their countertransference to guide their therapeutic approach to the projection and splitting in the family's relationship with each other and to the therapists. The aim of this approach to therapy is to facilitate integration in a family whose borderline pathology is seen to have its roots in disorganized attachment.

A clinical approach that utilizes a psychoanalytic (object relations) approach to working with couples and families, informed by attachment theory, owes much to the significant theoretical developments in psychoanalytic theory that have taken place in the last 100 years. Freud (1917e) made an embryonic reference to the idea of object relations as a cogent aspect of the internal world. His metapsychological writings set the stage for theoretical developments in an understanding of human behaviour in which the importance of internalized representations of relationships of the self with significant others in the development of the mind were emphasized.

Klein (1946) built on what Freud had proposed and stressed "object seeking" as a prime motivator in human behaviour, while still acknowledging the importance of instincts and drives. Klein suggested that "object relations exist from the beginning of life, the first object being the mother's breast which for the child becomes split into a good (gratifying) and bad (frustrating) breast, which results in a severance of love and hate" (ibid., p. 2), and that "early object relations are moulded by an interaction between introjections and projections between internal and external objects and situations" (ibid.).

Klein saw early development as dominated by the psychological mechanisms of splitting, projection, and projective identification. These mechanisms are part of what she referred to as the "paranoid–schizoid position" and help to ensure that the severance of love and hate is maintained until the child can progress to a later phase of development where they can be integrated. In normal development this involves a greater mylenation of the nervous system. This greater synthesis of love and hate also allows for the development of a capacity to acknowledge separateness and otherness (the "depressive position").

Recognizing separateness also introduces the concept of triangulation or oedipality. This has important implications for the capacity to form mutually reciprocal adult relationships rather than limiting narcissistic object relations. Britton (1989) notes that, "A third position comes into existence (in the oedipal situation) from which other relationships can be observed. Given this, we can also envisage *being* observed . . . reflecting on ourselves whilst being ourselves" (*ibid.*, p. 87).

Fairbairn (1944) was more fully liberated from the vestiges of instincts and drive theory than Klein, in developing a psychoanalytic theory wholly based on the notion that human beings are motivated by the need for relationship. Fairbairn felt that "the great limitation of (the present) libido theory as an explanatory system resides in the fact that it confers the status of libidinal attitudes upon various manifestations which turn out to be merely techniques for regulating the object relationships of the ego" (*ibid.*, p. 252).

Notwithstanding such theoretical differences, all object relations theorists have emphasized the role of unconscious phantasy in psychic life. Bowlby (1969), who introduced Attachment Theory, stressed how internalized experiences are built up on "actual experiences", which become a blueprint for expectations about the external world. These he referred to as "internal working models".

Attachment theory has provided a language for many practitioners who have felt uncomfortable with the lack of commonly held criteria of natural science seen to be inherent in psychoanalytic approaches to therapy. Recently, theorists such as Fonagy (2001) have emphasized the close relationship between psychoanalysis and attachment theory and demonstrated how insecure attachment (and its related psychodynamics) can predict individual psychopathology. Empirical findings concerning the nature of insecure attachment have also supported the original theoretical tenets of attachment theory (Keogh, 2002).

Using Bowlby's attachment theory, such studies have shown that children are either securely attached or insecurely attached. If insecurely attached, their attachment is either avoidant, ambivalent, or disorganized. Findings concerning attachment in childhood (Ainsworth, Blehar, Waters, & Wall, 1978; Main, Kaplan & Cassidy, 1985) also spawned categories of attachment behaviours in adults. These revealed four parallel attachment categories: secure, preoccupied, dismissing, and fearful (Bartholomew, 1990). Sub-categories of these basic categories have also been derived and have set the stage for a deeper investigation into the attachment style of adults.

Sperling and Berman (1994) have defined adult attachment as

the stable tendency of an individual to make substantial efforts to
seek and maintain proximity to and contact with one of a few
specific individuals who provide the subjective potential for physical and psychological safety and security. [*ibid.*, p. 8]

Research has shown that individuals with particular types of
attachment difficulties and associated psychopathology may
respond more favourably to specific types of therapeutic intervention. For example, Blatt and Shahar (2004), referring to Classical
versus American Relational analytic approaches, have suggested
that anaclitic (borderline) patient types respond better to the relational aspects of therapy, while introjective (narcissistic) patient
types respond best to interpretive approaches.

Clulow (2001a) has also proposed this differential therapeutic
approach to couples work, on the basis of their attachment status.
Such ideas are at the frontiers of clinical theory in working with
couples.

The current case material and discussion represent an attempt to
expand the thinking on the above-mentioned issues *as they relate to
families*. This is explicated by considering how the attachment styles
(predominantly disorganized/fearful) in a family and their associated object relations, have affected family functioning in a family
that has been susceptible to intra-familial sexual abuse.

It is proposed that the attachment styles of individuals represent
positions and are rather like Klein's paranoid–schizoid and depressive positions, in which a predominant attachment style can, under
certain conditions, regress to a more primitive one. Relative shifts
in certain attachment dyads seem to occur in order to maintain a
complementarity of psychopathology. The stability of insecure
attachment dyads appears to be maintained by the mechanisms of
splitting, projection, and projective identification.

As categories of attachment have associated psychic representations and object relations, they denote varying levels of capacity for
mature reciprocal adult relationships. It is therefore proposed that
working within an object relations model, which articulates the
attachment styles of the couple/family members, provides a means
of evaluating progress with couples and family work. It also

enhances the richness of object relations theory's capacity for conceptualizing the dynamics of couples and families, especially its ability to assist the focus on the *moment to moment relational aspects of therapy*.

Such an approach to family therapy, which links attachment theory and object relations theory and which focuses on the relational aspects of the therapy and encompasses an exploration of unconscious phantasies, seems particularly helpful with borderline families. An approach to family therapy that focuses on the unconscious and conscious relational aspects of therapy (and the associated phantasies) with families is referred to as an r^{ph} approach to family therapy.

Clinical case study

A large family with four children was referred by a government agency for assistance with the emotional sequelae of intra-familial sexual abuse. The family comprised Edward, aged twenty-one years, Patrick, aged sixteen years, Max, aged thirteen years, and Chantal, aged nine years.

In the referral documentation we were advised that the mother, Ann, had an extensive background of childhood sexual abuse in an indigenous community. We understood that the father, Bob, came from a socially disadvantaged urban settlement in the Northern Territory and his background was characterized by physical and emotional deprivation.

The referral information also revealed that, in the context of increasing marital discord and family tensions, the parents had moved to another rural community, where they both found jobs and left their children in the care of a couple who were temporary residents there for seasonal work. During this time, the husband in the couple groomed the boys and engaged in sexually abusing them. The boys felt unable to disclose to their parents what had happened. Subsequently, the boys started having sex with each other.

The family was seen on a weekly basis over a period of thirty-two months. The period reported on is the first eighteen months of therapy.

The initial meeting

When the family arrived for their first session, they presented with an impoverished and deprived feel about them. Each of them appeared depressed and carried a sense of low self-esteem. The couple appeared disconnected and out of touch with each other. There seemed to be a strong sense of a persecutory object in the room. Ann appeared to become easily overwhelmed. We acknowledged that the family was in need of support as a result of what had happened to them.

Everyone in the family seemed to say the same thing, giving the impression of a high degree of enmeshment. The boys withdrew very easily into their own worlds and engaged in autistic type behaviours such as repetitively playing computer games and endlessly examining mobile phone text messages.

Initially, the family indicated that they felt very criticized and judged by their experience of the sexual abuse investigation. We commented that it seemed that they might see us as critical and judging of them, rather than that we were there to help them.

The interpretation, focusing on the relational aspect of the therapeutic relationship, seemed to modify to some extent the feeling of persecution in the room. It facilitated the family talking about the sexual abuse. Ann then went on to say she did not know if we knew that Patrick had been sexually abused by the husband of the babysitter some years ago. She said that nobody knew this was happening at the time and the family never got help. She said they subsequently discovered that Max had been abused by the same person.

There was great discomfort in talking about the sexual behaviour and *we felt pressured* not to talk about it. By reference to our own countertransference experience, we commented on how difficult it seemed to be to talk about the sexual abuse; this allowed an opening up of more of this family secret.

At the end of our first assessment session we felt that the family appeared to be imbued with anxieties that seemed to oscillate between those associated with autistic–contiguous and paranoid–schizoid positions.

The second session

In the second session we were told that Patrick was very angry after the initial session because we had dredged up all the issues about what had happened between the boys and his role in it. He had apparently told his mother he did not want to come back because it stressed him. Ann said this to us in such a way as to suggest we wanted to torture them and make them suffer.

Speaking directly from our countertransference once again, we said that there seemed to be a feeling that we wanted to make the family feel badly and ashamed and that we were not seeking to understand and help them. We suggested that it might be possible that we could find a way of talking about things that might help and that, in this way, we could start to understand what had happened in the family and start to address this.

We also suggested that perhaps Patrick was not the only person who felt upset during the last session. Ann said this was true, and that Edward had felt very angry and felt as though he could have exploded. We asked him about this, but he could not say why he was angry. We suggested that he felt the family was being bullied and criticized in some way by us. He agreed that this was true and then seemed to relax more. This then opened up the opportunity for Ann to talk about her depressive breakdown some years ago.

The couple told us that they felt that their marriage had died by the year the last child was born. It was at this time that Ann became quite depressed and said that she was barely able to cope with the demands of parenting. The couple reported that disappointments with the outcome of their relocation and financial pressures were the final stressors that affected their marriage. Bob reported that he had to take a large share in the parental responsibility, as his wife was taken up with long hours of work.

Ann acknowledged that she entered into the marriage with significant (unresolved) sexual abuse issues. It appeared that she hoped that these would resolve in the marriage, which she had viewed originally in an idealized way. She talked in a way that suggested that she felt very guilty about not being emotionally available to the children at that time. She became very tearful about this.

At the end of our assessment sessions, we formulated that the family as a whole presented with borderline features and, as such, had generated substantial reactions from a number of agencies. The individuals all had a personal history of trauma, although this was vicarious in the case of Chantal. The parents' history, especially

Ann's sexual abuse, was still unmetabolized and therefore enacted in the family relationships. There had also been a disruption to the child protection capacity in the parents as a result of their histories. The borderline features of the family accounted for the strong affect in the family and the extreme splitting that accompanied their perceptions of each other, outside agencies, and of us as therapists.

In the couple, unconscious idealized phantasies were being projected into each other. These projections concerned longed-for relationships that were never realized with their primary attachment figures. It appeared that neither of the couple was able to work through taking back idealized projections into each other. Instead, each began to feel persecuted, experiencing what Dicks (1967) has described as "the glove turning inside out", that is, the unmet needs inherent in these projections had been expelled by each of them.

The crisis point in the marriage was when the children became vulnerable to being sexually abused. The aberrant sexual behaviour between the boys became the only means of emotional communication within the context of severe marital discord and associated lack of maternal or paternal emotional containment.

Working through

During the working through phase of the therapy, significant work had to be done on the family's severe splitting and projection. As a consequence, the family members were gradually able to digest emotional experience with a resultant decrease in acting out.

One session into this phase of therapy illustrates these processes. Max arrived saying that Patrick had given him a new game called "Witches and Monsters", which we were told by Patrick was a game that involves goodies and baddies. He said that it was not always possible to know who the goodies and who the baddies are. We asked if everyone knew about this game. Ann said, "Yes, they all love it!"

Max said that if you take your eyes off the game even for a minute, the enemy encroaches on you. If the invaders get in, they kill the goodies and ultimately strike at their heart. When this happens, the castle where the goodies live can crash in on itself. We asked if this had ever happened. Edward said yes, and that if it happens three times the whole game collapses and the game is up. Max said that this has happened twice. We said, "It seems hard to know who is a goodie and who is a baddie in this game?" Max said, "You have to be a baddie and evil to win."

We noted that for Max perhaps it has felt like this for him. We suggested that one can end up not knowing whom to trust and discover that people one has trusted can turn out to be baddies. We also suggested that when someone does something wrong to him, like interfere with him sexually, then it is like the game master; he is made to feel like he is the bad one. He agreed. We then commented, "As you said, it feels like in the end you have to become a baddie yourself in order to survive?"

Ann acknowledged that she was well aware of this and strongly identified with her son. She looked sad for a moment and then suddenly turned and attacked her husband and said, "If you had not left Max alone, this would not have happened!" We noted that there is something very painful about what happened to Max and to others in the family and that it is important to acknowledge that the heart of the family has been under attack. We noted that at times there seem to be such a lot of bad feelings to deal with and that it can become overwhelming.

At this moment we noticed that Chantal was busy drawing a picture of a haunted house. We asked about the house and she told us that it is a very scary house and that there are lots of skeletons lying around the house that can come to life. She said that the skeletons can "turn into ghosts that can get you."

We said that it seems as if the family are coming into contact with some very scary feelings about what has happened to them, and what seems to be currently happening is that their ghosts are coming to life.

This session and subsequent material marked a shift in the family's tolerance for labelling states of mind and their ability to link these to their behaviours and modes of relating to each other. It also resulted in a reduction in the level of acting out and paved the way for the beginnings of more depressive states of mind and a greater sense of separateness among individuals in the family.

In a later session, Bob mentioned that there had been an incident at home when Patrick told Max to get off the computer and go to bed. Max turned around, grabbed a knife, and threatened Patrick with this if he didn't leave him alone. Patrick told Max to put the knife down. Ann expressed anger towards Bob for not managing these incidents and said that he dealt with violent outbursts from the children with his own threatening rage and that she was sick of this.

We commented that there was a violent reaction from Max to the unwelcome intrusion of Patrick (who had sexually penetrated Max) and there was anger from Ann that Bob had not done his duty. (Ann's father had been shielded from her sexual abuse by her mother and he had not intervened.) Bob's own aggression related to his own deprivation and neglect and meant there was little containment possible for managing destructive impulses from the boys.

As the parents talked more about the violent incident, which had enormous affect associated with it, the focus moved to Ann's increasing hostility with her husband and her wish to separate. When we began to talk *to each other* in the session about our observation of how much anger the family seemed to be holding about us at times, Ann exploded at us for talking to each other in a "smug way". It seemed that she could not tolerate our relating to each other as a couple.

Fundamental to the working through phase of therapy was managing the experience of persecution that was powerfully projected into us, which made it hard to think and speak about what had gone wrong in the family. We also had to process the raw and uncontained affect in the family. We had to tolerate these projections and used our countertransference to make sense of the family's experience. We also interpreted their feelings of love and hate towards us.

At times we were made to feel inadequate and bad. Often the sessions would be characterized by feelings of lifelessness and a lack of spontaneity and we would be left feeling drained.

Discussion

Looking across the two years of the therapeutic process, it can be seen that the family was initially plunged into a crisis with the disclosure that the sons had been sexually abusing each other. The family had "known" about the sexual behaviour between the boys prior to the disclosure by one of the boys. This was indicative that the family had no other way of dealing with its difficulties other than by acting them out. The "un-thought known" (the unconscious awareness of unresolved trauma) that was behind the acting out was impossible for the family to think about. They were unconsciously prone to re-enactments of sexual abuse because of the pressure of repetition compulsion.

The failure on the part of the parental couple to have internalized adequate parenting and secure attachment experiences led to them having difficulties with providing the necessary child protection capacity. Their rage about being failed themselves by parents came to life in the transference relationship with us, its origin slowly and painfully recognized as the therapy progressed. The children in the family, because of the trauma they had experienced and because of the lack of emotional containment emanating from a mother with borderline psychopathology, exhibited clear signs of disorganized attachment. This was linked to the overall borderline features of the family's functioning and the attention the family attracted from a variety of agencies.

As therapy proceeded we were able to achieve a greater level of emotional containment and to reduce the level of enactment. There was a developmental "progression" to more paranoid–schizoid psychopathology, with associated powerful splitting. Use of countertransference and a deeper understanding of their unconscious phantasies about us as parents was invaluable in working with these processes. Ultimately, the family was also able to begin to see the therapists as a helpful couple who could hold them in mind and provide a model of thinking.

Attachment issues

Aspects of the family's disorganized attachment began to moderate during the course of the therapy, with growing evidence of embryonic features of secure attachment as they became able to internalize more of their good experience of us. Conceptualizing the family by reference to attachment theory provided an important means of evaluating our progress with them. The features of the disorganized attachment that moderated included the fact that their discomfort concerning closeness seemed to diminish, along with a strengthening of a sense of trust with us in the transference. There was, however, a continued sense of wariness about getting hurt if they allowed themselves to show too much closeness to us or to others in the family, a characteristic of those with disorganized (child)/fearful (adult) attachment. In terms of Bartholomew's (1990) dimensions of fearful attachment, there was also a decrease in the reliance on self and the beginnings of a more positive view of others.

Borderline pathology and therapeutic style

As with individual borderline psychopathology, this family's internal experience was unlabelled and chaotic. Along with uncontained affect, this further perpetuated affect dysregulation and maintenance of an unstable sense of self and other object representations. As progress was made, some moderation of the severity of the central features of the borderline psychopathology was noted. In particular, there was a positive shift in their impulsivity, emotional instability, irritability, and extensive use of projective identification and splitting.

The identification and containment of the affect in the family was achieved largely by a focus on the relational (r^{ph}) aspects of the therapy, through the lens of the countertransference and with reference to what we knew about their attachment style. Next came the careful labelling of affect in the family. This was the first step in facing the biggest challenge with borderline pathology: dealing with the externalization of unbearable states of mind. In terms of therapeutic style with this family, the maintenance of a frame that at times required elasticity (especially in terms of extra-mural communication) was essential. The model of mind provided by the co-therapist couple was also essential in assisting the family to internalize the capacity to reflect on their experience and providing the necessary "third" to facilitate an increased capacity to separate and individuate.

Conclusions

The use of attachment theory as a means of understanding and evaluating the level of functioning and the dynamics in families, in a similar way to that which has been applied to couple dyads, appears helpful in delineating family psychopathology. In turn, matching therapeutic style with family psychopathology and attachment type, in the way Blatt & Shahar (2004) have described, also seems to be indicated.

Specifically, it is suggested that a therapeutic style that emphasizes the relational (i.e., moment to moment countertransference) aspects of family psychotherapy, an r^{ph} approach, is indicated in families, who are dominated by borderline psychopathology that has its roots in disorganized attachment.

While the current case findings need substantiation, they appear to represent a vindication of the value of a combined attachment theory–object relations approach to working with severely disturbed families.

The findings appear to provide evidence that attachment theory is not only a useful evaluation tool for the family therapist wishing to monitor progress with families, but assists in conceptualizing family psychopathology and dynamics. When used in conjunction with the richness of object relations theory as the primary framework guiding intervention and understanding, it appears to have significant clinical relevance when working with families who traditionally may have been considered too disturbed or unsuitable for such therapy.

References

Ainsworth, M. D. S., Blehar, M. C., Waters, E., & Wall, S. (1978). *Patterns of Attachment: A Psychological Study of the Strange Situation.* Hillsdale, NJ: Lawrence Erlbaum.

Bartholomew, K. (1990). Avoidance of intimacy: an attachment perspective. *Journal of Social and Personal Relationships, 7*: 147–178.

Blatt, S. J., & Shahar, G. (2004). Psychoanalysis—with whom, for what, and how? Comparison with psychotherapy. *Journal of the American Psychoanalytic Association, 52*(2): 1–55.

Bowlby, J. (1969). *Attachment and Loss: Volume 1.* London: Hogarth.

Britton, R. (1989). The missing link: parental sexuality in the Oedipus complex. In: J. Steiner (Ed.), *The Oedipus Complex Today: Clinical Implications* (pp. 83–101). London: Karnac.

Clulow, C. (2001a). *Adult Attachment and Couple Pychotherapy.* London: Brunner-Routledge.

Dicks, H. V. (1967). *Marital Tensions, Clinical Studies towards a Psychological Theory of Interaction.* London: Karnac, reprinted 1993.

Fairbairn, W. R. D. (1944). Endospychic structure considered in terms of object relationship. In: *Psychoanalytical Studies of the Personality* (pp. 82–136). London: Routledge and Kegan Paul. 1952

Fonagy, P. (2001). *Attachment Theory and Psychoanalysis.* New York: Other Press.

Frank, G. (1998). On the relational school of psychoanalysis. *Psychoanalytic Psychology, 15*: 141–153.

Freud, S. (1917e). Mourning and melancholia. *S.E., 14*: 239–258. London: Hogarth.

Keogh, T. (2002). Juvenile recidivism: new and surprising possibilities for mental health promotion and prevention. In: L. Rowling, G. Martin, & L. Walker (Eds.), *Mental Health Promotion and Young People: Concepts and Practice* (pp. 230–244). Sydney: McGraw Hill.

Klein, M. (1946). Notes on some schizoid mechanisms. *International Journal of Psychoanalysis, 27*(III): 99–110.

Main, M., Kaplan, N., & Cassidy, J. (1985). Security in infancy, childhood and adulthood: a move to the level of representation. In: I. Bretherton & E. Waters (Eds.), *Growing Points of Attachment Theory and Research* (pp. 66–104). Chicago, IL: University of Chicago Press.

Murphy, S. E. (2004). *Soft Percussion. Proof of Silhouettes.* Exeter: Stride Publications.

Sperling, M. B., & Berman, W. H. (Eds.) (1994). *Attachment in Adults: Clinical and Developmental Perspectives.* New York: Guilford.

INDEX